PEDIATRIC LABORATORY EXERCISE TESTING

Clinical Guidelines

Thomas W. Rowland, MD
Baystate Medical Center
Springfield, MA

Editor

Human Kinetics Publishers

Library of Congress Cataloging-in-Publication Data

Pediatric laboratory exercise testing : clinical guidelines / Thomas
    W. Rowland, editor.
        p.   cm.
    Includes index.
    ISBN 0-87322-380-2
    1. Exercise tests--Congresses.   2. Children--Medical examinations-
-Congresses.   3. Exercise--Physiological aspects--Congresses.
I. Rowland, Thomas W.
    [DNLM: 1. Exercise Test--in infancy & childhood--congresses.
2. Exercise Test--methods--congresses.   WG 141.5.F9 P371]
RJ51.E95P43   1993
618.92'0075--dc20
DNLM/DLC
for Library of Congress   92-1575
                                                                        CIP

ISBN: 0-87322-380-2   #2596716 1

Copyright © 1993 by Human Kinetics Publishers, Inc.

Campbell Taggart, the nation's second largest baker and the parent company of Rainbo,
Colonial, and Kilpatrick's Baking Companies, is a noted leader in working to improve
fitness for children through its national IronKids Bread Health and Fitness Program. The
company sponsored the Standards for Pediatric Exercise Testing Conference held in
October 1991 in Scottsdale, Arizona.

Acquisitions Editor: Rick Frey, PhD
Developmental Editor: Mary E. Fowler
Assistant Editors: Laura Bofinger,
    Moyra Knight, and John Wentworth
Copyeditor: Jane Bowers
Proofreader: Stefani Day
Indexer: Barbara E. Cohen
Production Director: Ernie Noa

Typesetter and Text Layout: Sandra Meier
Text Design: Keith Blomberg
Illustrations: Denise Lowry and
    Gretchen Walters
Cover Design: Jack Davis
Interior Photos: Kent Spiry
Printer: Braun-Brumfield

Printed in the United States of America

10 9 8 7 6 5 4 3 2 1

Human Kinetics Publishers
Box 5076, Champaign, IL 61825-5076
1-800-747-4457

Canada Office:
Human Kinetics Publishers
P.O. Box 2503, Windsor, ON N8Y 4S2
1-800-465-7301 (in Canada only)

Europe Office:
Human Kinetics Publishers (Europe) Ltd.
P.O. Box IW14
Leeds LS16 6TR
England
0532-781708

Australia Office:
Human Kinetics Publishers
P.O. Box 80
Kingswood 5062
South Australia
374-0433

Contents

Pediatric Exercise Electrocardiography   43

J. Timothy Bricker, MD

Blood Pressure Response to Dynamic Exercise   67

Bruce S. Alpert, MD
Mary E. Fox, MS

Measurement of Oxygen Consumption   91

Patty S. Freedson, PhD
Terri L. Goodman, MS

Preface

Pediatric Laboratory Exercise Testing: Clinical Guidelines provides professionals in sports medicine, exercise science, and pediatrics with valuable insight into the broader uses and interpretations of current pediatric exercise testing techniques. Whether you're involved in laboratory research, clinical diagnosis and treatment, or the evaluation or training of young athletes, the information on exercise testing presented in this text is relevant to your work.

This book is a compilation of presentations made at the Standards for Pediatric Exercise Testing Workshop held in October 1991 in Scottsdale, AZ. The meeting's purpose was to create a state-of-the-art document to serve as a resource for clinical laboratory exercise testing throughout the pediatric age range. The contributors are knowledgeable and prominent leaders in the field, individuals who are developing innovative approaches to exercise testing in children.

As editor, I believe that you will find *Pediatric Laboratory Exercise Testing: Clinical Guidelines* practical, informative, and stimulating as you conduct exercise testing in your unique environment. I also hope that identifying future research areas will allow exercise scientists not only to learn more about exercise response in children but to discover even better ways to measure it.

Thomas W. Rowland, MD

Acknowledgment

Gratitude is expressed to Campbell Taggart, Inc. for its generous support in the creation of this book. Its recognition of the importance of accurate laboratory measurement in assessing exercise capacities of children is greatly appreciated.

Introduction

The basic procedure for clinical exercise testing is straightforward: Place body systems under physical stress, evaluate their functional limits, and uncover deficiencies or abnormalities not evident in the resting state. It's a commonsense approach because most people do not typically spend much of their time lying supine on an examination table. Physicians are taught to assess wellness and disease in just this static state, with the human machine on idle. Exercise testing puts that machine on the test track, evaluating its performance characteristics in conditions that more closely mimic daily activities.

Most experience in exercise testing has involved evaluating adults with cardiovascular disorders—most particularly coronary artery disease. Standard methodologies for treadmill and cycle testing are well recognized. These are based mainly on electrocardiographic expressions of myocardial ischemia and dysrhythmias, important considerations in detecting and quantifying coronary vascular insufficiency. Exercise testing in children and adolescents is an outgrowth of this larger experience in adults; in many laboratories, equipment and testing protocols designed for older patients have been used to test pediatric subjects.

Clearly, however, several important considerations call for different testing approaches in evaluating children. The indications for exercise testing of pediatric patients are broader than in adults, and discrepancies of age, size, and fitness levels are much larger. The pediatric age group encompasses subjects ranging from elite endurance athletes to those who have difficulty walking or running on a moving treadmill belt or pedaling a cycle with a regular rhythm. Consider, for example, the different approaches needed to evaluate ventricular rate response in a 4-year-old with complete heart block and a 15-year-old cross country runner who complains of increasing shortness of breath during competitive events.

Laboratory personnel need special sensitivity to encourage children to exert a satisfactory exercise effort, and laboratory equipment must be appropriate for younger ages. A maximal exercise response is important in most testing situations; such a task is not difficult for the high school endurance athlete but requires considerable staff encouragement in the very young, unfit, or obese subject. Nevertheless, satisfactory maximal efforts can be achieved in patients as young as 3 to 5 years (4).

No component of pediatric exercise testing is more pivotal to success than that of a warm, enthusiastic, encouraging staff experienced in working with young subjects. Children are often intimidated by and fearful of the overwhelming array of equipment in the testing situation (which is hardly conducive to a high level of exercise motivation). Still, given a relaxed, reassuring approach by sensitive staff, even the most reticent child often can be convinced to work hard on the exercise test.

Usually, exercise testing of children carries very little risk. Special care needs to be taken with young subjects, however, to avoid physical injury (e.g., slipping and falling on the treadmill). Many children do not communicate well verbally during exercise testing, and staff must give constant attention to make sure that the young subject is experiencing no difficulties (cramps, light-headedness, discomfort from monitoring, etc.).

Indications for Pediatric Exercise Testing

The use of exercise testing to identify functional limits and to detect disease states of children is rapidly expanding. Newer applications (e.g., blood pressure responses as predictors of hypertension risk, assessment of surgery in patients with muscular dystrophy) continue to be added to more traditional indications (elicitation of exercise-induced asthma, provocation of ventricular dysrhythmias, etc.). Clearly, the value of exercise testing extends beyond that of cardiovascular function; testing may play an important role in evaluating patients with a wide range of endocrine, musculoskeletal, metabolic, and pulmonary disorders. The following list provides examples of the more common current indications for exercise testing of children.

1. *Evaluating cardiac and pulmonary functional capacity.* By exercise duration, direct or indirect measurement of maximal oxygen uptake, or determination of cardiac output, cardiac reserve can be established to help guide clinicians in treating patients with cardiac disease or in assessing results of surgery. Similarly, tests of pulmonary function during exercise help clinicians assess patient status and determine therapy in those with chronic lung diseases such as cystic fibrosis.

2. *Detecting myocardial ischemia.* In contrast to the adult population, diseases provoking myocardial ischemia are unusual in children. Still, exercise testing is useful in diagnosis of ischemia in pediatric patients, especially in assessing severity of aortic stenosis, congenital coronary artery anomalies, and Kawasaki disease.

3. *Evaluating cardiac rhythm and rate.* Exercise testing is useful in detecting and managing tachyarrhythmias (particularly ventricular), as well as in assessing sinus node function and response to exercise in those who have complete heart block.

4. *Determining blood pressure response.* Uncertainty surrounds the interpretation of exaggerated blood pressure levels with exercise. Excessive blood pressure rise during exercise in hypertensive patients, particularly competitive athletes, may indicate the need for medical therapy.

5. *Assessing symptoms with exercise.* It is not uncommon for a patient to complain of chest pain, dizziness, or shortness of breath during exercise or sports participation. While these symptoms do not always indicate significant disease, their evaluation is important. Such complaints are best assessed by placing the patient in monitored exercise conditions that mimic the conditions that elicit symptoms.

6. *Detecting and managing exercise-induced asthma.* Asthma provoked by exercise is probably the most common cause of chest pain, breathlessness, or cough during or immediately after physical activity in children. Although formal exercise testing is not always needed for a physician to make this diagnosis, treadmill or cycle testing can be used to assess effects of therapy, establish etiology in questionable cases, and separate exercise-induced asthma and competitive breathlessness in athletes.

7. *Assessing physical fitness.* Testing is used to verify a patient's complaint of fatigue during physical activity. This includes examining specific fitness components (i.e., determining whether daily performance in a patient with musculoskeletal disease is limited by endurance and strength or by aerobic fitness).

8. *Charting the course of a progressive disease and evaluating therapy.* Physical performance depends upon the complex contributions from muscular, hematologic, metabolic, cardiopulmonary, and psychological factors. The natural course of a disease such as muscular dystrophy and responses to therapy for any of these factors may be accurately reflected in exercise capacity.

9. *Assessing the success of rehabilitation programs.* This includes determining pre- and postexercise capacities of patients in cardiac and pulmonary programs as well as those in programs for youngsters with chronic musculoskeletal and metabolic disease.

Clearly, information gained from exercise testing is often essential in guiding diagnosis and treatment of young patients with a wide variety of clinical problems. These and newer applications of pediatric exercise testing are discussed in detail in this book.

Exercise Testing Guidelines

The amount of literature addressing the special needs of the pediatric exercise testing laboratory is small, and there is little uniformity in the way that tests on pediatric subjects are conducted. Godfrey addressed many of these issues in his 1974 book, *Exercise Testing in Children* (3), and the American Heart Association published pediatric exercise standards in 1982 (1). Bar-Or also has discussed testing methodologies in children (2). These sources provide some guidelines, but as is apparent from the disparate approaches to pediatric testing, more uniformity in testing techniques is needed.

This book was developed to provide source materials for clinical testing methodologies in the pediatric age group. In a field that is evolving at such a rapid rate, this information cannot justly be interpreted as a standard; rather the section authors have attempted to describe the state of the art in pediatric exercise testing techniques. Much of the material reviews traditional aspects of testing in children (e.g., evaluation of tachyarrhythmias); other discussions provide insight into the broader uses and interpretation of pediatric testing, particularly those measuring muscle strength and endurance. The usefulness of the latter clearly holds great promise, and the role for clinical exercise testing in children can be expected to grow in the future.

Throughout this text emphasis is placed on the clinical testing of children (e.g., testing of those with recognized or suspected disease). Many of the discussions are equally applicable to pediatric testing in other settings, such as the research laboratory or in the evaluation and training of young athletes. Indeed, the increased evaluation of young athletes and expanded clinical research efforts in children will undoubtedly lead to several forms of evaluation being performed in a given pediatric exercise testing laboratory.

Differences do exist in these approaches, however, and need to be recognized. For instance, research protocols examining steady state physiologic variables during cycle testing of children require longer than two-minute stages. These kinds of research tests in healthy children can be performed with one rather than 10-lead electrocardiographic monitoring.

It will become readily apparent to the reader of this book that a great many gaps exist in our knowledge of exercise responses in children and how to best measure them. This book thus serves the additional function of identifying those areas where future research efforts need to be focused. Only in building this base of information can the results of exercise testing be confidently applied to the pediatric patient.

Thomas W. Rowland, MD

References

1. American Heart Association Council on Cardiovascular Disease in the Young. Standards for exercise testing in the pediatric age group. *Circulation* 66:1377A-1397A, 1982.
2. Bar-Or, O. *Pediatric Sports Medicine for the Practitioner.* New York: Springer-Verlag, 1983, pp. 67-87.
3. Godfrey S. *Exercise Testing in Children.* London: Saunders, 1974.
4. Shuleva, K.M., G.R. Hunter, D.J. Hester, and D.L. Dunaway. Exercise oxygen uptake in 3- through 6-year-old children. *Pediatr. Exerc. Sci.* 2:130-139, 1990.

Contributors

Thomas W. Rowland, MD
Editor

Thomas W. Rowland, MD, is a pediatric cardiologist. He directs the pediatric exercise testing laboratory at Baystate Medical Center in Springfield, Massachusetts, where he is involved in exercise evaluation of both normal children and those with chronic cardiac and pulmonary disease. He is the editor of *Pediatric Exercise Science*, a quarterly journal, and author of the book, *Exercise and Children's Health*. Dr. Rowland is a member of the North American Society for Pediatric Exercise Medicine and past president of the New England Chapter of the American College of Sports Medicine. He received that organization's Honor Award in 1991.

Bruce S. Alpert, MD

Bruce S. Alpert, MD, is the Plough Foundation Professor of Pediatrics and chief of the Division of Pediatric Cardiology at the University of Tennessee, Memphis. Dr. Alpert is a founding member of the North American Society for Pediatric Exercise Medicine, and serves as the program director for that organization. His research interests include cardiovascular response to exercise, hypertension prevention, and aortic root growth in Marfan's syndrome. Prior to joining the faculty at UT, Memphis, Dr. Alpert taught at the Medical College of Georgia, where he received the Outstanding Young Faculty Award.

Oded Bar-Or, MD

Oded Bar-Or, MD, is professor of pediatrics and director of the Children's Exercise and Nutrition Center, McMaster University, Hamilton, Ontario. In his previous position at the Wingate Institute, Israel, he founded and directed for 12 years the Department of Research and Sport Medicine. His research on the effects of exertion on children in health and disease has spanned 22 years. Dr. Bar-Or has written more than 150 scientific papers and a textbook on pediatric sport medicine, and  has edited several books. He is past president of the International Council for Physical Fitness Research and of the Canadian Association of Sports Sciences. Dr. Bar-Or is a board member of the American College of Sports Medicine.

J. Timothy Bricker, MD

J. Timothy Bricker, MD, is chief of the Lillie Frank Abercrombie Section of Cardiology at Texas Children's Hospital and Baylor College of Medicine in Houston. He directs the exercise laboratory at Texas Children's Hospital. His research interests include exercise testing in patients with arrhythmias, preventive cardiology, and cardiac transplantation. Dr. Bricker has edited two cardiology texts and has contributed a number of papers to the literature on pediatric exercise testing.

Mary E. Fox, MS

Mary E. Fox, MS, is a senior research assistant in pediatrics at the University of Tennessee, Memphis. She works under the direction of Bruce S. Alpert, MD, assisting him in the research of cardiovascular response to exercise, aortic root growth in Marfan's syndrome, and hypertension prevention. Ms. Fox received her MS in wellness and fitness from Middle Tennessee State University in 1986. After graduation, she worked at Vanderbilt University for James O. Hill, PhD, conducting nutrition and metabolism research.

Patty S. Freedson, PhD

Patty S. Freedson, PhD, is an associate professor in the Department of Exercise Science at the University of Massachusetts at Amherst, where she teaches undergraduate and graduate courses in exercise physiology. She has published more than 50 papers in scientific journals; her primary research interests focus on children and exercise and measurement of physical activity. Dr. Freedson recently completed a project funded by the Ronald McDonald Children's Charities in which she developed a walking test to predict aerobic capacity for children. She also coordinated the development of a health and fitness curriculum for children. She is coauthor of *Dictionary of the Sport and Exercise Sciences* and is a fellow of the American College of Sports Medicine and the Research Consortium.

Terri L. Goodman, MS

Terri L. Goodman, MS, received her master's degree in exercise science from the University of Massachusetts at Amherst under the direction of Patty Freedson, PhD. Her research focused on the development of a one-mile walk test equation to predict aerobic capacity in 10- to 13-year-old boys. She is a member of the American College of Sports Medicine. Ms. Goodman is employed at The Jimmie Heuga Center in Vail, CO, where she is involved in exercise testing and designing exercise programs for people with multiple sclerosis.

David M. Orenstein, MD

David M. Orenstein, MD, is associate professor of pediatrics and associate professor of Exercise Physiology at the University of Pittsburgh; he is also director of the Cystic Fibrosis Center, the Pulmonary Department, and the Pulmonary Exercise Laboratory at Children's Hospital of Pittsburgh. During the past 20 years, his research has focused on exercise, particularly in children with pulmonary disorders. The areas he has explored include cardiopulmonary responses to exercise in patients with cystic fibrosis and asthma, gas exchange during exercise, the effects of oxygen supplementation during exercise, and the role of exercise programs for children with lung diseases. Dr. Orenstein has published more than 100 articles, chapters, and abstracts. He is the recipient of awards from the National Institutes of Health to explore aspects of exercise and pulmonary function.

Teresa L. Tomassoni, PhD

Teresa L. Tomassoni, PhD, is an assistant professor in the Department of Pediatrics and scientific director of the Pediatric Exercise Physiology Laboratory at Georgetown University Children's Medical Center in Washington, D.C. She is an exercise physiologist with extensive clinical and many years of research experience in pediatric exercise testing and cardiac rehabilitation. She has investigated the cardiopulmonary responses to exercise testing and the effects of exercise training in numerous pediatric populations. Dr. Tomassoni is a member of the American College of Sports Medicine, the North American Society for Pediatric Exercise Medicine, and the American Association for Cardiovascular and Pulmonary Rehabilitation.

Reginald L. Washington, MD, FAAP, FACC

Reginald L. Washington, MD, is a pediatric cardiologist with a special interest in preventive cardiology and exercise medicine in children. He is a founder and past president of the North American Society of Pediatric Exercise Medicine. He is a member of the executive committee of the American Academy of Pediatrics Sports Medicine Committee and has written several position papers for that organization. Dr. Washington also is a member of the executive committee of the Council of Cardiovascular Diseases of the Young, the American Heart Association, and the Subcommittee on Atherosclerosis and Hypertension and Exercise. He wrote the American Heart Association's updated standards for exercise testing in the pediatric age group. He is a member of the National Board of Directors for the American Academy of Pediatrics.

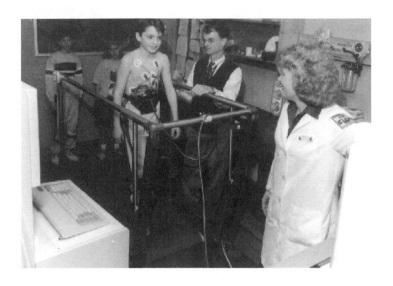

Conducting the Pediatric Exercise Test

Teresa L. Tomassoni, PhD
Georgetown University Children's Medical Center

Pediatric exercise testing is a valuable, noninvasive procedure used in the medical evaluation of children, preschool age through adolescence. In some ways, pediatric and adult exercise testing procedures are similar, but there are also important differences. Children, by their nature, require a special approach. Physically and emotionally, the child cannot simply be thought of as a "small adult." The approach of pediatric staff members should correspond to the developmental level and age of the child. Testers can obtain good results with children as young as 3 provided they pay special attention to the physical, cognitive, and psychosocial characteristics of the very young child.

The author wishes to thank Lisa Ashton for her secretarial assistance.

1

Testers must adhere to guidelines for exercise test administration to obtain safe and effective results, and a pleasant experience for the child should be an utmost concern. This section includes a step-by-step account of the actual pediatric exercise testing procedure and examples of practices that have proved useful with children, adolescents, and parents during testing.

Indications for Exercise Testing in Children

General indications for performing pediatric exercise tests should govern whether a child needs a test (see Table 1 for guidelines as specified by Bar-Or [5] and elaborated on by Zwiren [24]). Detailed information on the rationale for pediatric assessment in specific diagnoses can be found in numerous references (5, 10, 14, 18, 21, 24).

With changing technology and recent medical advances, new uses of pediatric exercise testing emerge continually; additional applications are addressed in subsequent sections of this book.

Table 1   Indications for Pediatric Exercise Testing

Measurement of physical working capacity
1. Assess daily function—establish whether daily activities are within physiologic functioning level
2. Identify deficiency in specific fitness component (e.g., a muscular endurance and strength condition such as muscular dystrophy versus aerobic capacity)
3. Establish a baseline before beginning an intervention program
4. Assess the effectiveness of an exercise prescription
5. Chart the course of a progressive disease (e.g., cystic fibrosis, Duchenne muscular dystrophy)

Exercise as a provocation test
1. Amplify pathophysiologic changes
2. Trigger changes otherwise not seen in the resting child

Exercise as an adjunct diagnostic test
1. Screen with a noninvasive exercise test to determine the need for an invasive test
2. Assess the severity of dysrhythmias
3. Assess the functional success of surgical correction
4. Assess the adequacy of drug regimens at varying exercise intensities

Assessment and differentiation of symptoms: chest pains (asthma from myocardial ischemia), breathlessness (bronchoconstriction from low physical capacity, coughing, easy fatigability)

Note. From "Exercise in Pediatric Assessment and Diagnosis" by O. Bar-Or. *Scand. J. Sports Sci.* 7:35-39, 1985. Adapted by permission of the journal.

Contraindications and Special Considerations

Before a child or adolescent undergoes an exercise test, a medical history should be taken. If the child has a history of disease, additional clinical tests (e.g., electrocardiogram [ECG], echocardiogram, 24-hour Holter monitor, pulmonary function tests) may be needed to rule out any contraindications to testing. Table 2 lists contraindications for exercise testing published by the American Heart Association (AHA; 17). In addition, the AHA recommends giving special consideration to the risk-benefit ratio of performing exercise tests in the following diseases or conditions:

1. Severe aortic stenosis
2. Severe pulmonary stenosis
3. Serious ventricular dysrhythmia, especially when associated with significant cardiac disease
4. Coronary arterial diseases (anomalous left coronary artery, homozygous hypercholesterolemia, Kawasaki disease [acute phase])
5. Severe pulmonary vascular disease
6. Metabolic disorders (glycogenolysis Types I and V)
7. Hemorrhagic diseases
8. Orthostatic hypotension

Safety Issues

Testers must consider safety throughout the pediatric exercise test. Contraindications must be ruled out before a child begins testing. Often exercise

Table 2   Contraindications for Exercise Testing

1. Acute inflammatory cardiac disease (e.g., pericarditis, myocarditis, acute rheumatic heart disease)
2. Uncontrolled congestive heart failure
3. Acute myocardial infarction
4. Acute pulmonary disease (e.g., acute asthma, pneumonia)
5. Severe systemic hypertension (e.g., blood pressure greater than 240/120 mmHg)
6. Acute renal disease (e.g., acute glomerulonephritis)
7. Acute hepatitis (within 3 months after onset)
8. Drug overdose affecting cardiorespiratory response to exercise (e.g., digitalis toxicity, salicylism, quinidine toxicity)

Note. From *Standards for Exercise Testing in the Pediatric Age Group* (p. 1383A) by the American Heart Association, 1981. Copyright © 1981 by the American Heart Association, Dallas. Reproduced with permission.

equipment must be modified. Staff should know what indications signal that a test should be terminated and should be trained to handle emergencies. The laboratory must have well-maintained pediatric emergency equipment, supplies, and medication. These issues are discussed later in this section.

Physical Environment of the Laboratory

The pediatric exercise testing laboratory should be large enough to comfortably accommodate an ECG monitor, treadmill and bicycle ergometer, gas analysis instruments, patient examining bed, and emergency equipment, medicine, and supplies suitable for pediatric use. About 400 square feet is needed to house this equipment and to provide work space for one or two staff members. If thallium or radionuclide imaging tests are performed, the laboratory should be located near the nuclear medicine department.

The laboratory should be clean, well-lit, well-ventilated, and reasonably quiet. Room temperature should be between 20° C and 23° C (68° F to 75°F), and humidity should be less than 60% (11, 23). The laboratory should have a thermometer and hygrometer to record temperature and humidity during testing (4). A cool, nonhumid environment is especially important in a pediatric laboratory because a child's thermoregulatory efficiency is lower than an adult's (4).

The laboratory should be aesthetically appealing to children. For example, colorful wall posters brighten a room, stimulate a child's interest, and give a child a warm feeling of familiarity.

Laboratory Staffing

According to AHA guidelines (17), an exercise laboratory must have on staff at least one physician who is trained in pediatric exercise testing. The physician is responsible for ensuring that

1. laboratory personnel are adequately trained in testing and emergency procedures;
2. the equipment works properly;
3. acceptable testing procedures are used; and
4. reliable results are conveyed to the referring physician, the patient, and the patient's family.

The physician may delegate the actual testing to other health care professionals, such as an exercise physiologist or a registered nurse. It is best to have a test conducted by two staff members, each with specific tasks. For example, one tester takes blood pressure and observes the child; the other controls the ergometer and records and observes the ECG. A staff member may need to stand behind a young child on the treadmill to ensure the child's safety.

Staff members should understand the principles of pediatric exercise physiology. They should also know how to interpret patient responses and data, understand criteria for terminating a test, and be able to recognize and respond to a cardiopulmonary emergency. All laboratory personnel must have current certification in cardiopulmonary resuscitation (CPR). The AHA recommends that, in addition to Basic Cardiac Life Support, at least one staff member present during testing be certified in Advanced Cardiac Life Support. A physician and other medical personnel must be immediately available in an emergency.

If a pediatric cardiologist will not be present during testing, it is important for the child to undergo a thorough medical evaluation beforehand and, if necessary, one or more clinical tests such as an ECG or an echocardiogram. If the physician thinks the child is at low risk, then the physician need not be in the room during testing; an experienced exercise technologist or a nurse or both, may administer the test. However, if the child is being studied for potentially life-threatening arrhythmias, exercise-induced syncope, or other critical conditions, the physician should be present during testing.

Laboratory Equipment

The most commonly used exercise inducers in pediatric exercise laboratories are the cycle ergometer and the treadmill. The cycle ergometer is less expensive, makes less noise, and takes less space. The treadmill elicits a greater level of oxygen consumption and peak heart rate and does not require the child to maintain a specified pedaling rate. On the cycle ergometer, the child can choose to stop pedaling and therefore terminate the test prior to attaining maximal exercise. On a treadmill, the poorly motivated or less fit child may exercise longer. Both exercise inducers collect diagnostic and functional data; therefore, the selection depends on the physician's objectives and the preferences and capabilities of the child (4). If more involved investigations, such as exercise cardiac catheterization or exercise echocardiography, are performed, the cycle ergometer may be the best choice. Ideally, a laboratory should have both.

Sometimes the equipment must be modified to make it safe and suitable for children. The cycle ergometer seat height and size, handlebars, and pedal crank should be adjustable (5). The treadmill should have front and side handrails. It is important to adapt the height of the handrails of the treadmill to accommodate the child's size. Orthopaedic bars can be configured into an adjustable front bar for small children. Commercially available accessories (e.g., overhead mask suspension bar) can also be adapted for this use.

The laboratory needs an ECG monitoring and recording system and a mercury sphygmomanometer blood pressure measuring system. More sophisticated laboratories have respiratory gas analyzers, pulse oximeters, and ultrasonic Doppler flow detectors to assist in measuring blood pressure.

The staff should calibrate all laboratory equipment on a regular basis. An electrical safety check should be performed periodically by the hospital biomedical department or its equivalent.

The AHA's "Specifications for Exercise Testing Equipment" (15) lists desirable equipment features. One should read this report before setting up an exercise laboratory.

Emergency Equipment, Supplies, and Medication

According to the AHA, an exercise laboratory must be equipped with ventilation and circulatory management equipment, including a defibrillator (11). The testing facility should also have oxygen, medications necessary for pediatric and adult advanced cardiac life support, and a well-stocked emergency crash cart. If pulmonary patients are tested frequently, a nebulizer and asthma medications should be available.

The laboratory should have a written emergency plan and should conduct simulated cardiopulmonary arrests to ensure quality emergency response. Telephone numbers for the emergency response team should be clearly marked near each telephone. Ideally, the clinical exercise lab should have its own dedicated emergency line directly linked to the hospital operator. The defibrillator should be checked frequently, and expiration dates for emergency medications should be reviewed weekly. As previously mentioned, staff members should be trained in pediatric and adult CPR (2, 3).

Legal Aspects

The risks and overall incidence of complications of exercise testing in children are low (1, 8, 13). Nevertheless, testers should have a consent form signed by the parent or legal guardian, or by the patient if he or she is 18 or older. Testers must clearly explain the recognized risks and possible complications so that the parent or patient understands. The process of obtaining informed consent differs from obtaining a mere release form. McNiece provides a good description of the law as it applies to exercise testing (19).

Although obtaining consent is recommended, there is controversy about whether a consent form is necessary. Detrano and Froelicher (9) believe that signing a consent form may make the adult patient overly anxious or may discourage the patient from having the test done. They believe that a signed consent form does not protect the physician from legal action; so provided that the risks and complications of the exercise test are carefully explained, a signed consent form is not needed. Nevertheless, parents are usually accustomed to signing consent forms and are not intimidated. In fact, most parents ask for more information about the test when asked to sign the form; as a result, a valuable discussion about the child's care takes place. Figure 1 shows an example of a consent form.

Regardless of whether a laboratory uses consent forms, good physician-patient communication is important for legal reasons. The physician should have a complete discussion with the parent or patient before and after the exercise test, should promptly interpret and transmit results to the parent or patient, and should provide recommendations based on the results (9).

Pretest Procedures

At the time of scheduling, the parent is given instructions about the test: The child should wear comfortable clothing, such as shorts and a T-shirt or a sweat suit; athletic or rubber-soled shoes are required. The child should eat lightly and no less than 2 hours before arrival or if thallium-201 imaging is to be performed, the child should not eat for about 8 hours before testing. Providing the parent with written instructions improves compliance. An example of instructions is given in Figure 2.

During the first meeting with the child and parent, staff members should be pleasant and friendly. They should approach the child in as nonthreatening a manner as possible. The amount and manner of attention given to the child depends on the child's age, personality, and maturity. If the child is very young or apprehensive, the staff member may need to sit down for a few minutes and talk with the child and family until the child feels comfortable and relaxed.

The choice of whether to allow parents in the testing room depends on the parent-child relationship and the child's general disposition. In our laboratory, we encourage parents to be present during the testing, but we caution them not to overprotect the child. We ask the parent to sit at a reasonable distance behind the child, so as not to distract the child or interfere with the test. The parent's presence usually enhances the child's cooperation. Sometimes, however, the tester finds it best to work with the child on a one-to-one basis. Occasionally the presence of siblings helps calm anxieties and provides a more enjoyable atmosphere for the young child.

The tester thoroughly explains the entire procedure to the child and parents, and answers any questions in a complete and reassuring manner. If the child is apprehensive about the equipment or the procedure, the tester patiently

Consent Form for an Exercise Test

1. Explanation of the Graded Exercise Test

   I understand that my child will walk/run on a motor-driven treadmill or pedal on a cycle ergometer at progressively increasing work loads. During the performance of this physical activity, his/her electrocardiogram and blood pressure will be monitored and recorded. Collections of expired air may be obtained for determination of respiratory parameters. If my child becomes distressed in any way or develops any abnormal response the physician considers significant, the test will be stopped. The test will end when a maximal effort has been obtained (as observed from various physical signs and measurements) or by voluntary discontinuation by my child due to fatigue.

2. Risks and Discomforts

   Every effort will be made to conduct the exercise test in such a way as to minimize any discomfort or risks. However, I realize that there are potential risks associated with an exercise test that may include light-headedness, chest discomfort, leg cramps, and in the rarest of instances heart attacks. Trained personnel are available to deal with unusual situations. Also, the exercise laboratory is equipped for such situations and emergency medical care is available at all times.

3. Benefits to be Expected

   The benefit to my child includes acquisition of diagnostic information about his/her exercise cardiopulmonary function. Any pertinent data gathered by the hospital may be used for its research purposes with complete anonymity being assured.

4. Freedom of Consent

   My child and I have had an adequate chance to ask questions and understand that we may ask additional questions any time while the study is in progress.

   I certify that my child is participating in this activity of his/her own free will and that either I or my child may discontinue participation at any time.

Signature of Parent or Guardian _____

Date _____

Witness _____

Figure 1:   Informed consent form.

Exercise Testing Instructions

A physician has ordered an exercise test to assess your child's

- exercise capacity,
- blood pressure response to exercise,
- exercise electrocardiography (ECG), and
- ability to engage in athletic activities.

Procedures

On the day of the exercise test, your child may eat a *light meal* 2 to 3 hours before the test is scheduled. The patient should WEAR COMFORTABLE CLOTHING during the test, such as shorts or sweatpants, T-shirt or a loosely fitting shirt, sneakers or comfortable rubber-soled shoes. Plan on arriving at the hospital at least a half hour before the test to allow time for parking and registration. Report to the Pediatric Cardiology Clinic. An exercise technologist will escort you and your child to the exercise testing area.

After describing the testing procedure, the technologist will attach 10 electrodes and lead wires to your child's chest. A resting ECG and blood pressure will be obtained, and then the test will begin with your child walking briskly on the treadmill (occasionally the test is performed on a stationary bicycle). The speed and grade of the treadmill will increase every 2 or 3 minutes, the ECG will be continuously monitored, and blood pressure will be measured during each stage. Some tests also require the patient to breathe through a mouthpiece so that respiratory parameters can be assessed during exercise. The exercise test will end when your child has reached a maximal effort. The speed and grade of the treadmill will be decreased gradually, and your child will be instructed to walk slowly for a 5-minute recovery phase. The entire testing procedure should take approximately 45 minutes to one hour.

It is important that your child give a maximal effort during the test. Discussing the entire testing procedure with your child before arriving at the hospital usually enhances his or her cooperation.

Your appointment is on _____ at _____.
  (date)   (time)

If you are unable to keep your appointment, please call the department (*phone number*) as soon as possible and reschedule the exercise test.

Figure 2: Information for parents.

tries to help the child understand the procedure is a nonharmful, positive experience. The tester emphasizes the concept of a challenge and the importance of doing one's best. The tester explains that, at the end of the test, the child will feel tired, just as he or she feels tired after physical education class, athletics, or running outside with friends. The child should understand that he or she must tell the tester when he or she is unable to continue. With a very young or shy child who is reluctant to speak, the tester should reassure the child and parents that the exercise test can be stopped if a problem occurs. After explaining all of this, the tester should ask the parent or patient to sign a consent form.

The tester reviews the medical records with the child and parent, paying particular attention to any contraindications to exercise and to performance during prior graded exercise tests. Particular emphasis is placed on diagnosis, indication for the test, accustomed activity levels, and presence of exercise-induced symptoms. Throughout the conversation, the tester gathers information to assess the relative physical and psychological maturity of the child. If the test is to evaluate medical therapy, the tester should verify that the patient has followed the prescribed program.

Preparation of the Skin and Electrode Attachment

The tester should carefully prepare the child's skin for the attachment of the electrodes. Letting the child see the electrodes and, if necessary, touch them may help the child prepare mentally for testing. First the skin should be cleansed of oil with an alcohol swab. The young child should be told that alcohol is used to clean the skin (emphasizing that he or she will not be getting a needle or shot). It may be necessary to shave the chest of male adolescents. Next, to lower the resistance of the skin, the epidermis is abraded using skin prep paper (similar to very fine sand paper). Some pre-gelled electrodes have a small piece of this paper on the disposable surface. Pre-gelled disposable electrodes are most commonly used and are relatively inexpensive. For very small children, it may be necessary to trim the outer edges of the electrodes.

Ten electrodes are used with modifications in accordance with the Mason-Likar system (20). The arm electrodes are placed at the lateral and superior corners of the sternum, and the leg electrodes are placed near the right and left inferior rib margins between the midclavicular and anterior axillary lines. Lower positions increase signal artifact, especially in obese children. The precordial electrodes are placed in the standard ECG position.

The monitoring of a single lead or bipolar lead system without recording the precordial leads is not optimal. It is always best to monitor 12 leads so that each lead can be analyzed for ischemia or arrhythmia.

The exercise cable is attached to the child's waist, with the lead-wire box positioned near the child's lower back. The child wears a special mesh T-shirt to reduce lead-wire movement during testing. These preparations allow excellent baseline stability during exercise and the recording of clear, diagnostic tracings even when heart rate exceeds 200 beats per minute (bpm).

Using information obtained up to this time, the tester selects a protocol based on the observed physical and psychological readiness of the child and on the clinical data needed. More detailed information on protocol selection is given in the next section of this book, "Aerobic Exercise Testing Protocols."

Ratings of perceived exertion (RPE) scales are sometimes used to assess exercise intensity. A commonly used RPE scale is the Borg scale (7), which is shown in Figure 3. Using this scale, the subject rates his or her perception of exertion at various stages of the exercise test. The scale also can be used to estimate the intensity of leg work, chest pain, or breathing effort. The Borg scale has been used mainly with adults; however, it has been used with some success in pediatric labs (6). Bar-Or provides a good explanation of how to describe the Borg scale to a child (4).

Testing Procedures

Before beginning the stress test, the tester records a baseline supine ECG. Some laboratories also have the child perform hyperventilation for approximately 15 s. The tester assesses the ECG for heart rate, rhythm, and morphologic features.

6	
7	Very, very light
8	
9	Very light
10	
11	Fairly light
12	
13	Somewhat hard
14	
15	Hard
16	
17	Very hard
18	
19	Very, very hard
20	

Figure 3: The Borg category scale for rating of perceived exertion. *Note.* From "Perceived Exertion: A Note on History and Methods" by G.V. Borg. *Med. Sci. Sports* 5(2):90-93. Copyright © by the American College of Sports Medicine, 1973. Reprinted by permission.

The tester measures resting blood pressure before the child begins exercising. An appropriate cuff size should be used, and the same cuff size should be used throughout the test. Muscular adolescents may require a larger cuff. For some children (e.g., those with coarctation), the tester will need to measure blood pressure in the leg. This can be done immediately after exercise while the child is either standing or in a supine position.

If respiratory parameters are to be assessed, the patient is taught how to hold the mouthpiece tightly in the mouth or how to breathe while wearing an airtight mask. The tester explains to the patient that it is possible to swallow while wearing either type of device.

If a cycle ergometer is used, the seat height is adjusted so that the leg is almost completely extended when the pedal is at its lowest point (approximately 160°) (4). The pedaling rates should be 50 to 60 revolutions per minute (4). If a mechanically braked cycle is used, a metronome can provide audible guidance to the child to help him or her maintain the correct revolutions per minute.

If a treadmill is used, time is provided for the child to become comfortable walking on the belt. Initially the child either straddles the treadmill belt or puts one foot ahead of the other on one side of the belt. The treadmill is started at a slow speed, and the child is shown how to step on the treadmill, with one foot at first, to become accustomed to the speed. Then the child is encouraged to step on the treadmill with the second foot and start walking. The child is instructed to hold the handrails for balance while becoming acclimated to walking on the treadmill and to walk erect keeping the head up. An interesting poster placed on the wall in front of the treadmill promotes this preferred posture.

The handrails should be used only for balance. Tightly gripping or leaning on the bars is not allowed because this has been shown to significantly alter oxygen consumption and increase muscle artifact (12).

After the child learns how to use the treadmill, he or she is told that the treadmill will increase in speed and grade during the test. The child is told to work as hard as possible but to verbally signal when he or she cannot continue (or, if on the mouthpiece, to signal with a thumbs-down). At that point, the child should not jump off the treadmill; it will decrease gradually both in speed and grade. The child should walk on the treadmill for a few minutes to cool down before stopping exercise. After all of this is explained to the child, the test can begin.

If the test is performed on the cycle ergometer, the child is allowed to pedal for a brief time to become familiar with the cycling motion. Once again, the child is discouraged from tightly gripping the handlebars.

Throughout the test, all ECG data can be continuously recorded without too much paper, by setting the paper speed at 5 mm/s. Three leads are viewed on the oscilloscope, usually II, V2, and V5. A full 12-lead ECG using a paper speed of 25 mm/s and blood pressure measurements are recorded at the end of each exercise stage. Skin and lip color and alertness are observed. The tester should communicate with the child throughout the test. Additional measurements of arterial oxygen saturation, oxygen consumption, ventilatory anaerobic threshold, and cardiac output may be recorded. An example of a sample test form is found in Figure 4.

During each phase of exercise, the tester carefully watches the child and tells the child exactly when the next higher level of work will begin. The tester tells the child to report any unusual sensations if or when they occur but does not name specific symptoms. This prevents the child from giving a false-positive verbal response to having chest pain, dizziness, or any other discomfort. If the child reports such symptoms but there are no signs of ECG changes or blood pressure variability, the test may continue. It is important that staff members recognize the indications to terminate an exercise test; these indications as listed by the AHA are shown in Table 3 (17). The physician may elect, however, to delay termination of the exercise test, despite the appearance of one of these indications. If the physician believes that important clinical data can be obtained without increasing risk, the testing may continue under close supervision.

Anxious or small children who are not used to sustained exercise may complain of leg fatigue. The child should be encouraged to exercise through these levels of discomfort, as long as exercise measurements are stable.

Regardless of age, however, the tester should not ask the child if he or she is tired during exercise. Invariably the child will respond positively and ask to stop the test. Instead of reminding the patient of his or her fatigue, the technologist or cardiologist looks for signs of the patient's inability to exercise further.

The tester must encourage or gently prod the child to perform maximal exercise by verbal encouragement and distraction from fatigue. In our laboratory, we distract the child from premaximal fatigue by having the child concentrate on a picture of children exercising. The tester asks the child to find and point out the different types of activities the children are doing as portrayed in the poster. This activity helps keep the child's attention and prevents boredom and premature termination of the test.

Another motivational technique, which is similar to a video game, appeals to the child's sense of challenge. The tester points out the digital heart rate display and tells the child to try to obtain a specified heart rate (at least 85% of maximal predicted heart rate for that child). Although the true maximal heart rate may be somewhat higher or lower than the predicted level, each child is expected to exercise to a point at which he or she is barely able to continue.

Exercise testers should recognize that motivation is important in conducting tests, especially tests of young children. Some exercise laboratories use motivation-enhancing techniques such as giving the child a reward of play money to buy small trinkets or toys (16). Play must often be used to motivate, especially in the preschool years. Later, competition or other motivators may be needed to gain the child's complete cooperation (22).

Cardiology Graphics/Exercise Physiology Laboratory
Graded Exercise Test With Computerized Breathing Study

Patient name _____

Medical record number _____

Date of birth _____

Sex _____

Type: ☐ Treadmill ☐ Bicycle ergometer   Date: _____ / _____ / _____
(month)   (day)   (year)

Study # _____

Clinical diagnosis: _____

Attending physician: _____

Amount of physical activity: _____

Cardiac medications: _____

Height _____ Weight _____ lbs. BSA _____ M²

85%PMHR _____

Resting heart rate _____ Resting blood pressure _____ Baseline ECG: _____

Total time	MPH	% grade	KPM	Estimated met level	Heart rate	Blood pressure	ECG changes	Breath by breath					Rebreathing			
								$\dot{V}O_2$ L/min	$\dot{V}CO_2$ L/min	$\dot{V}_E$ L/min	RQ	$\dot{V}O_2$ ml/kg/min	D_L ml/min/mmHg	Q_{EP} L/min	SV ml
						/									
						/									
						/									
						/									
						/									

Post Exercise Data

Heart rate response: _____

Blood pressure response: _____

ECG response: _____

Normal   Abnormal   Comments:

Reason(s) for termination: _____

Interpretation: _____

Conducted by: _____ Interpreted by: _____

(Technologist)   (Physician)

Figure 4: Sample test form.

Table 3   Indications to Terminate an Exercise Test

1. Onset of serious dysrhythmias (e.g., ventricular tachycardia, supraventricular tachycardia)
2. Appearance of potential hazard to the patient
    a. Failure of electrocardiographic monitoring system
    b. Symptoms such as pain, headache, dizziness, syncope, excessive dyspnea, and fatigue precipitated by exercise
    c. ST-segment depression or elevation greater than 3 mm during exercise
    d. Dysrhythmia precipitated or aggravated by exercise (e.g., premature ventricular contractions with increasing frequency; supraventricular tachycardia)
    e. Ventricular tachycardia (three or more consecutive beats)
    f. Recognized types of intracardiac block that are precipitated by exercise
    g. Excessive rise in blood pressure (systolic pressures exceeding 240 mmHg and diastolic pressures exceeding 120 mmHg)
    h. Progressive fall in blood pressure
    i. Pallor, clamminess of the skin, inappropriate affect

Note. From *Standards for Exercise Testing in the Pediatric Age Group* (p. 1383A) by the American Heart Association, 1981. Copyright © 1981 by the American Heart Association, Dallas. Reproduced with permission.

When the tester determines that the child can do no more exercise, the tester terminates the exercise by gradually slowing the treadmill and decreasing the grade, or by decreasing the work load on the cycle ergometer. Exercise may be stopped suddenly if additional procedures need to be performed, such as an immediate postexercise echocardiogram or a leg blood pressure measurement. A recovery period of at least 5 min of slow walking or pedaling against no resistance is recommended before the patient is allowed to stop. This is done to avoid peripheral venous pooling and syncope. The tester measures blood pressure at 1- or 2-min intervals during the recovery period and monitors the ECG to detect signs of arrhythmia or ischemia. The child is not detached from any of the ECG or blood pressure apparatuses for at least 5 min, or until he or she has returned to within 20% of baseline levels of heart rate and blood pressure.

Following the study, the data are carefully analyzed and the results are compared to normative data from the laboratory and the child's prior exercise test results, if available. A report is prepared, and the physician interprets the results and the ECG tracings.

Our experience has been that, although children may be uncomfortable during maximal exercise, they recover rapidly immediately following exercise. They quickly forget any unpleasantness they may have experienced as they are congratulated on how well they performed. At the end of the test, the child is rewarded with a cool drink of juice and a choice of stickers. The child usually enjoys taking the net shirt home to show siblings or friends when telling them about his or her great exercise effort.

The graded exercise test is often the first time many patients with congenital cardiac conditions exercise maximally following surgical intervention. This test gives them an opportunity to learn that their physical abilities are not as limited as they may have believed.

Conclusion

In many ways the approach for administering a graded exercise test on a child differs from the approach for an adult. Often the conduct of a pediatric exercise test must be modified to answer a specific clinical question.

The tester needs patience and experience in dealing with children to make the test pleasant enough for the child so that, if necessary, he or she will eagerly perform it again in future years.

Occasionally a child may be reluctant to cooperate due to age or shyness. To help persuade a child, the tester may recommend that the parent take the child to a local department store and show him or her a treadmill. Using this approach, we have successfully collected data on a 2-1/2-year-old child.

The special requirements of pediatric exercise testing pose a significant challenge; meeting this challenge can be truly rewarding. A pleasant testing facility, patience, a sense of humor, and genuine affection for children provide an excellent environment that facilitates the collection of good clinical data—and a positive experience for the child.

References

1. Alpert B., D. Verill, N. Flood, J. Boineau, and W. Strong. Complications of ergometer exercise in children. *Pediatr. Cardiol.* 4:91-96, 1983.
2. American Heart Association. *Textbook of Advanced Cardiac Life Support.* Dallas: AHA, 1987.
3. American Heart Association. *Cardiopulmonary Resuscitation* (3rd ed.). Tulsa: CPR, 1990.
4. Bar-Or, O. *Pediatric Sports Medicine for the Practitioner: From Physiologic Principles to Clinical Application.* New York: Springer-Verlag, 1983, pp. 67-87.
5. Bar-Or, O. Exercise in pediatric assessment and diagnosis. *Scand. J. Sports Sci.* 7:35-39, 1985.
6. Bar-Or, O., and D. Ward. Rating of perceived exertion in children. In: *Advances in Pediatric Sport Sciences: Biological Issues*, O. Bar-Or (Ed.). Champaign: Human Kinetics, 1989, pp. 151-168.

7. Borg, G. Psychophysical bases of perceived exertion. *Med. Sci. Sports Exerc.* 14:377-381, 1982.
8. Cumming, G.R. Exercise studies in clinical pediatric cardiology. In: *Frontiers of Activity and Child Health*, H. Lavallee and R.J. Shephard (Eds.). Quebec, PQ: Pelican, 1977, pp. 17-45.
9. Detrano, R., and V. Froelicher. Exercise testing: Uses and limitations considering recent studies. *Prog. Cardiovasc. Dis.* 34:173-204, 1988.
10. Ellestad, M.H. *Stress Testing: Principles and Practice.* Philadelphia: Davis, 1986, pp. 393-411.
11. Ellestad, M.H., C.G. Blomqvist, and J.P. Naughton. Standards for adult exercise testing laboratories. *Circulation* 59:421A-430A, 1979.
12. Fletcher, G., V. Froelicher, H. Hartley, W. Haskell, and M. Pollack. Exercise standards: A statement for health professionals from the American Heart Association. *Circulation* 82(6):2286-2322, 1990.
13. Freed, M. Exercise testing in children: A survey of techniques and safety [abstract]. *Circulation* 64(Suppl. IV): IV-278, 1981.
14. Galioto, F.M. Exercise testing. In: *The Science and Practice of Pediatric Cardiology*, A. Garson, J.T. Bricker, and D. McNamara (Eds.). Philadelphia: Lea & Febiger, 1990, pp. 828-835.
15. Hellerstein, H.K. Specifications for exercise testing equipment. *Circulation* 59:849A-854A, 1979.
16. Hester, D., G. Hunter, K. Shuleva, and D. Dunaway. Conducting maximal treadmill tests with young children: procedures and strategies. *JOPERD*, pp. 23-26, August, 1990.
17. James, F.W., G. Blomqvist, M.D. Freed, W.W. Miller, J.H. Moller, E.W. Nugent, D.A. Riopel, W.B. Strong, and H.U. Wessel. Standards for exercise testing in the pediatric age group. *Circulation* 66:1378A-1397A, 1982.
18. Klein, A. Pediatric exercise testing. *Pediatr. Ann.* 16(7):546-558, 1987.
19. McNiece, H.F. Legal aspects of exercise testing. *N. Y. State J. Med.* 72:1822-1824, 1972.
20. Pina, I.L., and R.A. Chahine. Lead systems: Sensitivity and specificity. *Cardiol. Clin.* 2:329-335, 1984.
21. Ruttenberg, H., J. Moller, W. Strong, G. Fisher, and T. Adams. Recommended guidelines for graded exercise testing and prescription for children with heart disease. *J. Cardiac Rehabil.* 4:10-16, 1984.
22. Thoren, C. Exercise testing in children. *Pediatrician* 7:100-115, 1978.
23. Vogel, J., B. Jones, and P. Rock. Environmental considerations in exercise testing and training. In: *Resource Manual for Guidelines for Exercise Testing and Prescription*, S.N. Blair, P. Painter, R.R. Pate, L.K. Smith, and C.B. Taylor (Eds.). Philadelphia: Lea & Febiger, 1988, pp. 90-97.
24. Zwiren, L. Exercise prescription for children. In: *Resource Manual for Guidelines for Exercise Testing and Prescription.* S.N. Blair, P. Painter, R.R. Pate, L.K. Smith, and C.B. Taylor (Eds.). Philadelphia: Lea & Febiger, 1988, pp. 309-314.

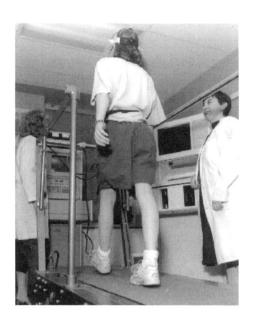

Aerobic Exercise Testing Protocols

Thomas W. Rowland, MD
Baystate Medical Center

The aerobic exercise stress test is conducted to tax the cardiovascular and pulmonary components of endurance fitness in a controlled and monitored laboratory setting. In this way clinicians can evaluate the functional limits of these systems and detect abnormalities that were not evident at rest. This process requires dynamic exercise of large muscle groups for at least several minutes at an intensity that pushes the cardiovascular and pulmonary systems to their functional limits.

It is important that exercise testing be performed in a standard, systematic manner, because performance on exercise tests depends largely on the type of exercise and the testing protocol used. Use of standardized protocols permits comparison of

- results of repeated testing of the same individual,
- tests performed in different laboratories, and
- test findings with established norms.

Moreover, if researchers use the same protocols, we can better understand the physiologic responses to exercise in well and ill children.

Numerous modes of exercise have been used for laboratory stress testing of children, including step climbing (33) and jumping (62), but most clinical testing is now performed with progressive work loads applied during either cycle ergometer or treadmill exercise (31). Protocols for cycle testing vary in pedaling cadence (revolutions per minute), work stage duration, and initial and subsequent increments of work rate (expressed either as watts or kilopond-meters per minute).

On the treadmill, work is intensified by increases in either slope (usually expressed as percent) or speed, or both, with varying duration of work stage. Percent slope indicates the number of feet in elevation for each 100 ft of distance traveled.

Historically, exercise testing was developed to evaluate adults with coronary artery disease and to elicit electrocardiographic and symptomatic evidence of myocardial ischemia. Certain protocols have gained popularity, particularly treadmill tests using the Bruce and Balke protocols and cycle tests with various work-load increments. The Bruce protocol (see Table 1) involves progressive increases in both treadmill slope and speed at 3-min intervals, beginning at 1.7 miles per hour (mph) and 10% grade (10). The work increments are not equal and have no physiologic basis; they were chosen simply to create light, moderate, and maximal exercise stress. Most adult subjects will walk during the first three stages and run during the fifth, with the fourth being intermediate.

Table 1   The Bruce Treadmill Protocol

Stage	Speed (mph)	Grade (%)	Time (min)
1	1.7	10	3
2	2.5	12	3
3	3.4	14	3
4	4.2	16	3
5	5.0	18	3
6	5.5	20	3
7	6.0	22	3

The Balke protocol provides a constant speed (3.3 mph) with a 2% increase in grade every minute (5). The short stages do not permit stabilization of physiologic measures at submaximal work (steady state), but the walking speed is particularly adaptable for elderly, obese, or ill subjects.

Selection of the Test Protocol

The approach to pediatric exercise testing has largely been an outgrowth of testing procedures for adults, particularly in medical centers in which children are tested in laboratories set up for adults. Certain important considerations, however, may affect protocol selection for children:

- Pediatric exercise testing laboratories must accommodate subjects of a wide variety of sizes. The protocol for evaluating a 6-year-old may need to be much different than that for a 15-year-old.
- Indications for exercise testing are broader in children than adults, who are being investigated primarily for evidence of myocardial ischemia. Pediatric laboratories must examine such wide-ranging problems as symptoms with exercise (chest pain, palpitations, syncope), blood pressure response in hypertensive athletes, sinus node function following surgery for congenital heart disease, and exercise-induced asthma.
- Differences in degrees of physical fitness are often greater among children. A different approach is necessary to test a high school cross-country runner with palpitations than a 10-year-old with cystic fibrosis and worsening lung function.

What is the best exercise testing protocol for children? The answer depends on the information required (blood pressure response, fitness level, estimation of anaerobic threshold); the age, fitness level, and health of the subject; and the familiarity of the testing laboratory with specific treadmill or cycle protocols. The ideal testing protocol for children would satisfy the following requirements:

1. The test should not be too long. Prolonged tests cause boredom, lack of concentration, decreased motivation, and failure to reach a maximal effort. Tests that are too short, on the other hand, are overly intense, which may prove intimidating to the unfit subject and may create risk to those with cardiovascular disease. The optimal test duration is about 8 to 12 min.

2. The test should provide for submaximal stages of uniform length and work increment. Treadmill protocols that increase only slope or speed, rather than both, minimize adaptive changes required of the small subject to increased exercise intensity.

3. On treadmill testing, protocols should avoid overly steep slopes, which may create insecurity; a need to hold on to handrails (thus prolonging the test); risk of falling; altered biomechanical factors; and augmented anaerobic work. Likewise, protocols should avoid high speeds, which might limit performance in children with a short stride length.

4. The test should assess the limits of cardiovascular and pulmonary capacities rather than peripheral muscle strength.

5. The test should be reproducible, safe, and adaptable to children in a wide range of age, size, and fitness levels.

6. The protocol should allow for accurate determination of physiologic measures (blood pressure, oximetry, cardiac output) at all exercise levels.

No single mode of exercise or testing protocol satisfies all of these requirements. This section examines the protocols used to test children and their applicability to pediatric subjects.

Current Practice

No comprehensive data are available on protocols used in pediatric testing, but an informal survey of 30 pediatric cardiac exercise testing laboratories found that the Bruce treadmill protocol is the most popular means of testing children in the clinical setting (Rowland, unpublished data). Fifteen (50%) of the laboratories contacted used this protocol or its modifications. Four used the Bruce protocol with 2-min rather than 3-min stages. Reasons cited for using this protocol included "The adult laboratory is used to it," "It's convenient because it's in our automated testing equipment," and "It provides some uniformity across laboratories, and we're able to compare it with published normal values."

Treadmill tests were used more than cycle protocols (17 vs. 13 laboratories, respectively). Two reported using a modified Balke protocol. Of the cycle protocols, the McMaster (four), James (four), and Godfrey (two) protocols were used most (see Table 2).

Protocols used for clinical testing differ considerably from those used in research laboratories. The literature indicates that pediatric research laboratories rarely use the Bruce protocol, and then mainly in clinical studies of pediatric cardiac patients. About half of the research protocols involve a modified Balke treadmill test; the other half use a variety of cycle protocols.

Cycle Versus Treadmill Tests

Cycle ergometer testing holds several practical advantages over treadmill testing (6, 31, 59, 69). The cycle is portable, cheaper, quieter, and less

Table 2   Cycle Ergometer Protocols

	Rate (rpm)	Body measure	Initial load	Increment	Stage duration (min)
McMaster	50	Height (cm)	(W)	(W)	
		< 120	12.5	12.5	2
		120-140	12.5	25	2
		140-160	25	25	2
		> 160	25	50 (male)	2
				25 (female)	
James	60-70	Surface area (m^2)	(kg · m/min)	(kg · m/min × 2)	
		< 1.0	200	100	3
		1.0-1.2	200	200	3
		> 1.2	200	300	3

If more than 3 levels of exercise are necessary, add 100-200 kg · m/min until exhaustion.

	Rate (rpm)	Body measure	Initial load	Increment	Stage duration (min)
Godfrey	60	Height (cm)	(W)	(W)	
		< 120	10	10	1
		120-150	15	15	1
		> 150	20	20	1

intimidating to exercising subjects. It poses essentially no risk of injury. Submaximal measurements of physiologic markers such as blood pressure and cardiac output are easier to obtain than on the treadmill, particularly with running protocols. In a research setting, it is easy to measure work rate on the cycle, whereas treadmill differences in running or walking economy confound determination of work performed. As I will outline later in this section, cycle endurance time may be a more valid indicator of cardiovascular functional reserve.

It has been contended, however, that treadmill exercise puts greater physiological stress on the cardiovascular system (9). Maximal oxygen uptake values are about 10% higher on the treadmill than on the cycle. Although this may be partly because cycle exercise uses less muscle mass, local muscle fatigue may significantly limit cycle exercise as well. The picture of a subject straining to pedal against high resistances at peak exercise with hands clenched to the handlebars supports this concept. Moreover, maximal respiratory exchange ratio (RER) and serum lactate levels (both markers of anaerobic work) are higher in subjects using cycle protocols. Bar-Or suggested that the limiting influence of muscle fatigue might be greater in small children because of their relatively undeveloped knee extensor muscle mass (6).

Treadmill exercise uses a natural form of locomotion, but it requires that the subject be able to walk or run. Cycle ergometer exercise, therefore, is sometimes more applicable for those with neuromuscular diseases. Even some healthy children have difficulty adapting to treadmill belt motion.

With mechanically braked cycle ergometers, proper work rate depends on the subject pedaling at a constant rate (usually 50 or 60 revolutions per minute, or rpm). Young, obese, or poorly fit subjects may have difficulty sustaining a constant pedal rate or maintaining pedaling for the test duration. On the treadmill, pace is controlled by the tester rather than the subject, allowing constant pace and maximal exercise to be achieved.

Boileau et al. compared physiologic responses and reproducibility during treadmill walking (modified Balke) and progressive cycle protocols in 21 healthy boys ages 11 to 14 (9). Greater mean values for maximal oxygen uptake (2.45 vs. 2.27 L · min^{-1}, $p<.01$) and maximal heart rate (194 vs. 186 beats per minute [bpm], $p<.01$) were observed on the treadmill, whereas the average maximal RER was higher during cycle testing (1.11 vs. 1.04). These values are comparable to those previously reported in adult subjects (42). Coefficients of variation for the test-retest $\dot{V}O_2$max data were 4.4% and 5.3% for the treadmill and cycle, respectively. Boileau et al. concluded that both modes of exercise testing are suitable for assessing maximal aerobic capacity, but the treadmill exhibited slightly better reproducibility. They suggested that this might be because children have difficulty maintaining the proper pedal rate during cycle testing. Macek et al. found a virtually identical magnitude of difference in maximal oxygen uptake between treadmill and cycle testing in 11- to 14-year-old boys (54.1 vs. 50.3 ml · kg^{-1} · min^{-1}, respectively) (38).

Treadmill Testing Protocols

A review of the literature reveals that pediatric testing has been performed with almost every conceivable combination of slope increments, speed increments, and stage duration. Indeed, with the exception of the Bruce protocol, it is difficult to find two reports that have used the same treadmill testing procedure.

Bruce Protocol

Cumming et al. provided physiologic data and endurance time norms for the Bruce protocol in 327 children ages 4 to 14 (15). Subjects were not allowed to hold on to the handrails, and no physiologic criteria were provided to define maximal effort. Treadmill endurance time ranged from about 8 to 16 min, with mean values of 10 to 14 min in the boys and 9 to 11 min in the girls. Most older subjects were running at 5 mph at a slope of 18% at the end of the test. Endurance times correlated closely to maximal oxygen uptake expressed relative to body weight ($r = .88$). Twenty children performed the test on two occasions 3 to 10 days apart, with a high degree of reproducibility of endurance time ($r = .94$).

These norms were reported with respect to age without consideration of body weight or composition. Linear regression analysis indicated that, as expected, a significant relationship existed between endurance time and the ratio of the subjects' weight to height (3). This supports the contention of Boileau et al. that "body weight appears to be the most influential factor in limiting the prediction of $\dot{V}O_2$max from performance time on the treadmill" (9).

Cumming et al. were impressed with the suitability of the Bruce protocol for children and outlined its advantages: The same protocol can be used for all ages, physiologic responses to submaximal work loads can be measured, maximal oxygen uptake can be estimated from endurance time, and longitudinal data can be obtained in a given subject by using the same protocol as he or she grows (15). The protocol starts slowly and gives the subject a chance to acclimate to treadmill exercise.

Others have been less impressed with the Bruce protocol for children. Houlsby noted several "practical difficulties" in using this protocol for subjects younger than 10 (28): The work increments between successive stages are too great, resulting in endurance times that are biased toward the first half of the current stage; 3-min stages are too long for young subjects, who become bored waiting for the next increment; and the increments are unequal, making it difficult to predict functional aerobic capacity from regression equations. Houlsby offered his modifications of the Bruce protocol, using 2-min stages and beginning with speeds of 3.0, 3.8, 4.3, and 4.7 mph (still unequal!) for the first four stages.

Additional concerns regarding the Bruce protocol for young subjects have included the following: It is inappropriate for testing highly fit individuals (such as high school runners), who must wait 12 min into the test before breaking into a slow run (and then at an 18% slope); it changes speed and slope at the same time, which may make adaptation to testing more difficult for unfit subjects; and most exercise is performed at relatively steep slopes, encouraging unfit subjects to hold on to the handrails.

Balke Protocol and Its Modifications

Balke and modified Balke protocols, which involve a constant treadmill speed with increasing slope, have been commonly used in pediatric research but less often in the clinical testing laboratory. Using a modified Balke protocol, Riopel et al. reported normal heart rate and blood pressure data in 288 healthy children (51). Treadmill walking speed ranged from 3.0 to 3.5 mph based on age, with a 2% increase in slope at 1-min intervals. Subjects were not allowed to hang on to the handrails, and the end point of exercise was "refusal by the child to exercise further, jumping off the treadmill, or falling back into the person standing behind him or her,'' or 15 min. Riopel et al. believed that during this fast walk "the measurement of physiologic data is facilitated" more than with running protocols. Mean endurance time values ranged from 9 to 13 min, depending on age and gender, and some subjects in the older age groups reached the 15-min limit. Fitter individuals were therefore presumably walking uphill at very steep grades (26% to 28%) at the end of the test.

Using this same protocol in a group of 27 children, Cumming and Langford (16) found 25% to 39% greater endurance times and significantly higher maximal heart rates than were reported by Riopel et al. Cumming and Langford stated that the differences "must be attributed to an inability to obtain a near maximal effort from many of [Riopel et al.'s] subjects." They concluded that it was "mandatory for all laboratories to establish and continuously update their own normal data."

Paterson et al. demonstrated a major disadvantage to the walking Balke protocol in active young subjects (47): The test duration is too long and the slope becomes too steep. The mean endurance time of their subjects walking at 3.4 mph, with a 2.5% increase every 2 min, was 18 min (at a 20% grade). This test can be shortened by beginning the protocol at a high initial grade (6% to 10%) (56, 58), but for fit subjects maximal exercise is still conducted at a high, uncomfortable treadmill slope.

For unfit, obese, or chronically ill subjects, however, the walking Balke protocol is well-suited. Rowland et al. assessed physiologic responses to exercise in obese adolescents walking at 3.25 mph, with a 2% increase in slope every 3 min beginning at 6% and treadmill endurance times of 6 to 9 min (8% to 10% maximal slope) (55).

Running Balke protocols have been used to shorten test times in fit individuals and increase maximal heart rate and oxygen uptake. Most active children older than 10 can be taught to run comfortably on a treadmill, and these protocols are particularly effective in assessing young athletes. Several authors have used protocols with constant speeds of about 5 mph and 2.5% slope increases every 2 min (2, 7, 47, 56). This usually results in a test duration of 8 to 12 min in the active 9- to 15-year-old child. Maximal effort is achieved at a comfortable pace and a slope typically not exceeding 10% to 12.5%. Others have simply identified a comfortable running speed without concern over rate, increasing slope in 2% increments with similar results (39, 68).

Paterson et al. examined physiologic responses in children and their reproducibility during Balke walking (3.4 mph) and running (4.9 mph) protocols, with a 2.5% slope increase every 2 min (47). With multiple testing, the walking protocol produced a lower mean maximal oxygen uptake (4 ml · kg^{-1} · min^{-1}) and higher intraindividual variability (8%).

Balke and modified Balke protocols have the advantage of uniform stages with changes in only one variable (slope). Speed can be adjusted to fit the subject's age and fitness level as a means of controlling test time. Treadmill speed should be kept constant because increasing speed at the same slope may lead to a nonlinear rise in the subject's energy expenditure (20).

Other Running Protocols

Running protocols other than the modified Balke have been adopted to obtain particular physiologic information. For instance, research protocols designed to assess both submaximal steady state and maximal values in the same test have been used by Cunningham (17) and others (24, 37, 52). Subjects run at three to four different speeds for 3-min stages before increasing the slope 2.5% per minute until the subject is exhausted.

Other running protocols have involved constant flat running at increasing speeds. Bailey et al. used 3 mph increments every 3 min and reported endurance times of 7.5 min (8-year-olds) to 9.6 min (15-year-olds) (4). King et al. started with horizontal running at 6 kilometers per hour (kph) and increased speed 0.5 kph every 30 s to exhaustion (35). These protocols can be expected to elicit lower $\dot{V}O_2$max than those using increasing slope. Moreover, the rapid stride frequency might intimidate young subjects who cannot maintain running skills at high speeds.

Treadmill exercise has been considered the most appropriate means of testing small children, who cannot (or will not) maintain pedaling cadence on the cycle ergometer to exhaustive levels. Shuleva et al. reported successful maximal treadmill testing to 3- to 6-year-old children using a protocol of 4 kph walking at a 10% slope (increasing 2.5% every 2 min up to 22.5%, when the speed was increased 1 kph) (57). Three approaches appeared to be important in encouraging these small subjects to a maximal effort: The subjects were carefully oriented to the treadmill, the subjects knew several individuals who were administering the test, and cash prizes were offered.

HOLDING ON TO HANDRAILS

There is a general consensus that, except in special circumstances (very young, disabled, or unfit subjects), subjects should not be allowed to grip handrails during the test. Holding on to handrails during exercise significantly depresses the rate of rise of heart rate and oxygen uptake and extends the test duration. Ragg et al. demonstrated in a small group of adults that mean treadmill time rose from 15 min during unassisted treadmill walking to 25 min when the same subjects held on to handrails (49). Maximal oxygen uptake and heart rate values were not affected, however. Likewise, Sheehan found no significant differences in maximal oxygen uptake or heart rate when the same boys performed a running Balke protocol both with and without holding on to handrails (56). Green and Foster demonstrated that the effect of diminishing oxygen cost of treadmill exercise depends on how tightly the subjects grasp the handrails (25).

Cycle Protocols

Most cycle protocols call for a cadence rate of 50 to 60 rpm and differ in stage length (from 1 to 3 min) and means of adjusting initial and increment work loads (Table 2). For some (1, 18, 23, 32, 67, 70), normative data have been published on a large number of pediatric subjects.

The James protocol divides subjects into three groups by body surface area (32). Exercise begins with three stages of 3 min apiece, with increments ranging from 100 to 300 (kg · m)/min. If maximal effort has not yet been achieved, 100 to 200 (kg · m)/min are added at 1-min intervals until subject exhaustion. Normative data have been provided by James et al. (32) and Washington et al. (67).

The Godfrey protocol is similar, but work-load increments are assigned to three groups identified by height, and work load is increased every minute (10 to 20 W). Godfrey et al. have published normal data for children with this protocol (23).

The McMaster protocol uses 2-min stages and applies work-load increments of 12.5, 25, or 50 W depending on body height and sex (6). Strong et al. have used a protocol with 3 min of incremental work rates designated for four groups defined by body weight (60).

There appears to be no major advantage to any of these protocols over the others, particularly when obtaining maximal values. When submaximal data are important, the McMaster protocol may be preferable, because work-load increments are linear, and submaximal stages are long enough to achieve steady state (discussed later in this section) and to measure physiologic variables (e.g., blood pressure).

Klimt and Voigt identified optimal cycle testing conditions for the most energy-efficient exercise in children ages 6 to 10 (36). At an intensity of 2 W/kg, the most efficient crank length is 13 cm in 6-year-olds and 15 cm in 8- to 10-year-olds. The optimal pedal rate is 50 rpm, and the saddle should be adjusted to create a knee angle of about 160° when the leg is extended. Elias et al. reported that a 17.5-cm crank arm could be used in pediatric subjects weighing 26 to 47 kg with no change in efficiency (19). Although optimal mechanical efficiency may not be critical in most clinical testing, I recommend that clinical laboratories use these settings to make it easier to compare physiologic data between laboratories.

Testing Protocols for Special Indications

As I noted previously, the cycle offers advantages over the treadmill (stability of torso, less noise, lower subject anxiety) that make this testing mode more useful in obtaining certain types of physiologic data. Most studies investigating blood pressure responses to exercise have used cycle protocols (43, 44, 66), although maximal blood pressure is difficult to determine regardless of testing modality. Likewise, exercise tests of children with chronic lung disease, who need submaximal assessment of data such as pulse oximetry, have usually been conducted on the cycle (13, 40, 46).

Most investigations of ventilatory anaerobic threshold (VAT) have employed cycle protocols with short (e.g., 1-min) work stages (8, 12, 26), although both walking Balke and Bruce protocols have been reported (50, 72). Running Balke protocols do not appear to be useful in identifying VAT because the oxygen uptake is too high at the initial stages.

Subjects with significant obesity are often best tested with cycle protocols, given the limited influence of body weight on cycle exercise (11). Nevertheless, treadmill protocols have been used successfully to evaluate exercise performance in overweight subjects. Zanconato used a speed of 6.5 kph with elevations of 2% every minute to test obese subjects (73). Rowland et al. reported maximal tests in obese high school students with a modified Balke walking protocol (3.25 mph beginning at 6% grade, increasing 2% every 3 min) that resulted in test times of 6 to 9 min (55).

Maximal testing of elite prepubertal athletes has been reported with a wide variety of protocols involving both cycle and treadmill, including McMaster (61), Bruce (45), and running and walking modified Balke (64, 65). Cunningham reported extensive experience using a treadmill protocol for investigating maximal and submaximal steady state data in high school runners (17). Subjects ran at 6, 7, 8, and 9 mph at 4-min intervals on a flat treadmill before slope was increased 1% per minute to exhaustion.

Stage Duration and Work Increment

The duration and work increment at each exercise stage are important considerations in the selection of testing protocols; they affect total test time as well as subject adaptability to increasing exercise stress.

Stage duration does not affect maximal heart rate and maximal oxygen uptake (74). Tanner et al. demonstrated similar values for these variables in a group of 6- to 16-year-olds exercising with both a James protocol and a ramp protocol (one that increases work at small or continuous rates) that caused work to rise 0.025 W/kg every 6 s (63). Stage duration is important, however, when one considers the need for steady state submaximal physiologic values, the time required to measure submaximal variables (e.g., blood pressure), and the potential for boredom with long submaximal stages.

Submaximal steady state refers to the leveling of physiologic values in response to an increased work load. In traditional exercise physiology studies, steady state values have been assessed with 6-min interrupted stages to assure that a true leveling occurs. In more recent progressive exercise tests, however, a 3-min stage has been considered sufficiently long to produce approximate steady state. Investigations in children have demonstrated that a reasonable steady state occurs even earlier, and several authors have contended that 2-min stages are sufficient to permit steady state values (22, 58).

Submaximal steady state is not required for most clinical exercise tests, but the boredom that may accompany long submaximal stages has stimulated the creation of protocols with 1- or 2-min stage duration. Ramp protocols (those that do not permit time for steady state) have generally involved 1-min stages. These allow a gradual increase in work load and avoid boredom; they permit little time for measuring submaximal variables, however, and the frequent changes in work load require constant attention from the testing staff.

The work increment at each stage is also important in governing test duration as well as the stress placed on the subject at each change in work load. All cycle protocols have accommodated the latter concern by allowing work increments to vary (watts or kilopond-meters per minute) according to body size (weight, height, or body surface area). Appropriate work increments relative to body weight can be estimated using the method suggested by Tanner et al. (63): The mean maximal work on the cycle ergometer is 3.5 W/kg for boys and 3.0 W/kg for girls across the pediatric years (14), and an optimal test duration is 10 min. For boys, work increments should be 0.35, 0.70, and 1.05 W/kg when stages of 1, 2, and 3 min are used, respectively. For girls, the values are 0.30, 0.60, and 0.90 W/kg for protocols of 1-, 2-, and 3-min stages, respectively.

On the treadmill, the oxygen requirement per kg body mass at a given grade decreases in children as they grow, but the rate of rise is similar at all ages. Skinner et al. demonstrated that a grade increase of 2.5% at 3.5 mph will cause oxygen uptake to increase 4 to 5 $ml \cdot kg^{-1} \cdot min^{-1}$ in children (58). This finding is consistent with the report of Kanaley et al. of a mean increase of 5 $ml \cdot kg^{-1} \cdot min^{-1}$ in 7- to 15-year-old subjects at the same treadmill conditions (34). As I noted previously, this load increment is appropriate for testing small or sedentary children but is too small for highly fit or athletic subjects. In contrast, Cumming et al. reported a mean rise in $\dot{V}O_2$ in children of 6 to 7 $ml \cdot kg^{-1} \cdot min^{-1}$ between Stages 1 and 2 of the Bruce protocol and 11 to 12 $ml \cdot kg^{-1} \cdot min^{-1}$ between Stages 2 and 3 (15).

Importance of Warm-Up

A short period (usually 3 min) of low-intensity exercise prior to the test familiarizes subjects with testing conditions, decreases anxiety, and optimizes motivation for an exhaustive effort, particularly in children. In adults, this warm-up also helps diminish risks for those with myocardial disease and lessens the chance of musculoskeletal injury (71). This has not been evaluated in children.

Limited data also suggested certain physiologic variables may be influenced by pretest exercise. Inbar and Bar-Or demonstrated that 7- to 9-year old boys performing a 4-min one-stage cycling task had about 8% greater oxygen uptake during the early minutes of exercise compared to cycling without warm-up (29). These differences might be important in the evaluation of submaximal physiologic measures. In certain testing situations, such as evaluation of exercise-induced asthma, a warm-up period is not indicated.

Endurance Time and Aerobic Fitness

Endurance time during exercise testing has been interpreted as a reflection of cardiovascular fitness. This assumes that endurance time is closely related to maximal oxygen uptake. Pediatric testing laboratories have used published norms for treadmill times with different protocols that demonstrate a high correlation between endurance time and $\dot{V}O_2$max per kilogram ($r = .88$ to .92) (15, 21, 48).

A critical analysis of the relationship between cardiac output, oxygen uptake, body composition, and test endurance time suggests caution, however, about the clinical use of endurance time as a marker of cardiovascular fitness. The most easily measured manifestation of cardiac functional reserve during exercise is absolute $\dot{V}O_2$max (liters per minute), which relates closely to maximal cardiac output. The difficulty arises in normalizing absolute $\dot{V}O_2$max for growth during the pediatric years. Customarily this has been done by relating $\dot{V}O_2$max to body weight ($\dot{V}O_2$max per kilogram), a maneuver that would probably be effective if all children were the same body composition and habitus. Unfortunately, $\dot{V}O_2$max per kilogram is also an indicator of the body's ability to move "baggage" (i.e., body fat) in weight-bearing activities such as treadmill exercise.

If $\dot{V}O_2$max is used to assess cardiovascular function, $\dot{V}O_2$max expressed per kilogram falsely elevates values for slender individuals and depresses values for those who are obese. In any heterogeneous population, absolute $\dot{V}O_2$max is a good measure of cardiovascular function, whereas $\dot{V}O_2$max per kilogram during weight-bearing exercise indicates performance capabilities. As emphasized by Astrand and Rodahl, "The ml/kg figure for maximal oxygen uptake is a good predictor of the subject's potential to move and lift his body, but it may not mirror cardiac performance" (3).

Treadmill endurance time is a good indicator of $\dot{V}O_2$max per kilogram (as long as the age span of the subjects studied is small) but not of absolute

$\dot{V}O_2$max. Boileau et al. reported a correlation of $r = .89$ between treadmill endurance time and $\dot{V}O_2$max per kilogram but only $r = .47$ with absolute $\dot{V}O_2$max (9). Endurance time during treadmill testing can be used only as a measure of aerobic fitness and cardiovascular function with body composition considered. Test time during treadmill exercise is as much a measure of body adiposity as of cardiovascular reserve (9).

Endurance time, or peak mechanical power (PMP), during cycle testing may be a better marker of cardiovascular fitness, because cycle exercise is not strongly affected by percent body fat. In contrast to the treadmill exercise, PMP on the cycle relates closely to absolute $\dot{V}O_2$max ($r = .95$ in the study by Boileau et al.), and presumably to maximal cardiac output.

Normalizing PMP (or absolute $\dot{V}O_2$max) during cycle testing by body weight is thought to be a more accurate means of normalizing cardiovascular function for the level of biologic maturation, because these values are less affected by body composition than those on the treadmill. (As I noted previously, however, critics have contended that local muscle fatigue rather than aerobic fitness may limit maximal exercise on the cycle ergometer.) Cumming presented data indicating that average PMP is 3.5 W/kg in males and 3.0 W/kg in females throughout childhood, with a wide range (14).

Defining a Maximal Exercise Effort

Because exercise testing is designed to place the cardiovascular system under stress, it is important that subjects exercise at a high intensity—they must exert a maximal effort. Questions about cardiovascular reserve, blood pressure response to exercise, and safety of sports participation cannot be appropriately answered unless subjects exercise to exhaustive levels. This is particularly true when comparisons are made between serial tests of the same subject or when test results are compared between different laboratories. For these reasons it is important to establish criteria for identifying an exercise effort as maximal.

Maximal effort in terms of performance (i.e., treadmill endurance time) is a poorly defined concept, which is ultimately determined by the degree of discomfort or fatigue that the subject is willing to withstand at high work intensities. As such, several factors (environmental, psychological, anthropometric, anatomic, metabolic, and physiologic) affect maximal performance.

On the other hand, maximal aerobic power ($\dot{V}O_2$max), the peak functional capacity of oxygen delivery systems, has traditionally been considered a finite, reproducible value identified by a plateau of oxygen uptake at high work intensities. According to this concept, a maximal treadmill test is best defined by a leveling of oxygen uptake in the final stages of the test (i.e., peak $\dot{V}O_2 = \dot{V}O_2max$). In this paradigm, failure to observe a $\dot{V}O_2$ plateau as exercise intensity increases implies that the observed peak $\dot{V}O_2$ is not indicative of a subject's true cardiovascular functional capacity.

Exercise tests in children indicate, however, that only 20% to 60% show a plateau in oxygen uptake during a progressive continuous treadmill test (53). Moreover, these tests imply that the achievement of a plateau is independent of subject effort, aerobic fitness level, or anaerobic capacity. A plateau of $\dot{V}O_2$ does not thus appear to be a useful criterion for defining a maximal exercise test in children. These observations also raise questions about the influence of aerobic capacity in limiting treadmill exercise performance.

Peak heart rate has traditionally been used as a marker of exercise effort during testing because heart rate is linearly related to work intensity. Target heart rates for defining a maximal test have been suggested, including $220 - age$, or $210 - (0.65 \times age)$. These formulas do not apply to children because maximal heart rate does not change during the growing years. Bar-Or stated that maximal heart rate (HRmax) in children varied from 195 to 215 bpm and that this value was stable across age groups (6). Cumming and Langford reported mean HRmax (*SD*) values for the Godfrey, James, Bruce, and Balke walking protocols in the same individuals as 195 (5), 197 (7), 204 (5), and 198 (5), respectively (16). Sheehan et al. reported a mean HRmax of 194 (12) bpm for the Balke walking protocol and 202 (9) for running (56). Sheehan also reviewed HRmax values for children in the literature and found mean values of 193 and 200 bpm, respectively. Washington et al. described average HRmax values of 191 to 196 bpm in their study of 151 7- to 12-year-old children, which used the James cycle protocol (67).

These data suggest that it would be reasonable to define a target HRmax of 200 bpm for treadmill running protocols and 195 bpm for treadmill walking or cycle protocols, but HRmax varies widely among individuals. For instance, in the study by Cumming and Langford, the standard deviation for all protocols ranged from 5 to 7 bpm (16). In Sheehan's study the standard deviation was 12 for the treadmill walking protocol and 9 for the run (56). These ranges do not simply reflect variations in effort; similar variability is observed in the testing of elite prepubertal athletes (41).

Because statistically 2 of 6 subjects will have values either above or below the standard deviation, the pitfall of the target HRmax criterion is obvious. In Sheehan's runners, for instance, 17% would be expected to have an HRmax below 191 despite an exhaustive effort, and an equal number would have an HRmax above 211. In any study in which a target HRmax of 200 ($\pm$ 5%) is used as a criterion for a maximal effort, the former group would be excluded, and many of the latter group, with high HRmax, would not approximate a maximal effort even at a heart rate of 200.

The RER, the ratio of carbon dioxide produced to oxygen consumed, rises during progressive exercise tests and has often been used as a measure of maximal effort. A value of approximately .70 is common at rest; RER typically increases to more than 1.0 in adults at maximal effort. Issekutz et al. suggested a value as high as 1.15 as a criterion for maximal effort in adults (30). Generally, a criterion of greater than 1.0 has been used in pediatric subjects.

The literature reveals, however, that RERmax is often less in prepubertal children than in adults and that mean RERmax is often less than 1.0 in pediatric subjects, particularly during treadmill exercise. In Sheehan's study, mean RERmax (SD) was .99 (.08) and .99 (.09) during the walking and running treadmill protocols (56). In that study, if RERmax exceeding 1.0 had been used as a criterion for maximal effort, 63% of the walking and 56% of the running tests would have been excluded. Rowland et al. found average RERmax of .99 (.09) and 1.06 (.10) in boys and young men, respectively, on a treadmill running protocol (52). Paterson described a mean RERmax of .98 (.07) during treadmill walking by children and .99 (.07) with running (47). Mean maximal values in prepubertal distance runners have ranged from .99 to 1.02.

Mimicking findings in adults, RERmax appears to be higher in children during cycling than on the treadmill. Hansen et al. reported mean RERmax in 9- to 11-year-old children of 1.02 (.06) to 1.06 (.06) during a progressive cycle test (27). Mean cycling RERmax was 1.06 (.06) in the 19 prepubertal boys reported by Rowland et al. (54). Tanner et al. described average RERmax of 1.09 on their ramp protocol and of 1.11 with the James protocol (63). The average RERmax of the 21 boys ages 11 to 14 reported by Boileau et al. was 1.04 (.04) during treadmill walking and 1.11 (.05) during cycle testing ($p<.01$) (9).

As with HRmax, defining maximal effort by a single RERmax criterion is confounded by the wide variability reported. RERmax values of .90 to .95 are not uncommon during treadmill testing in children, nor are values of 1.05 to 1.10. Based on reports in the literature, mean RERmax can be expected to reach .99 during treadmill exercise and 1.06 during cycling.

Another way to measure maximal effort is for the tester to observe the subject for signs of intense effort (hyperpnea, sweating, facial flushing, unsteady gait, facial grimacing). However, Riopel et al. (51) and Cumming and Langford (16) published data indicating a 25% to 39% difference in treadmill times in their separate laboratories using the same walking protocol and subjective end points of subject effort.

There is no clear answer to the question of defining the maximal test in children. Some subjects provide an exhaustive effort at a maximal heart rate of 185 bpm and RERmax of .95, whereas others are at no more than 75% of maximal effort with similar values. For practical guidelines, however, a peak effort resulting in a heart rate over 200 during treadmill running, or 195 with walking or cycling, usually indicates a maximal test. Peak exercise can be expected to reflect maximal effort with an RERmax over .99 during treadmill exercise and 1.06 with cycling. The subject should show evidence of maximal effort regardless of peak values if a maximal test is to be assumed.

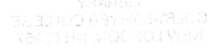

Conclusion

The major difficulty in the standardizing of exercise testing protocols for children is the wide disparity of ages, body sizes, and fitness levels in the pediatric age group. The need to accommodate these differences must be balanced against the advantages of using standardized testing methods. It is highly unlikely that any single protocol will be adopted for testing children, yet reducing the number of testing methods would make it easier to collect and compare information on exercise responses in young subjects. The data summarized in this review provide guidelines that may help in decisions about optimal pediatric protocols.

1. Many factors contribute to the success of exercise testing in children. Among the most prominent, however, is the comfort and experience of each laboratory staff in the testing methods used. The ease with which testing is conducted based on this experience may outweigh minor differences in protocols used. Thus, gaining experience with one or two particular protocols is a major key to success in exercise testing of children.

2. Each laboratory should develop its own normative data, particularly on criteria for defining maximal effort, rather than relying on published norms. As Cumming et al. have emphasized, differences between laboratories in equipment, personnel, and means of encouraging maximal effort can strongly influence results (15). In most cases, treadmill and cycle ergometer are equally effective in maximal testing of children; however, for obtaining certain data each has its advantages. Cycle testing is particularly advantageous for obtaining submaximal data (blood pressure, pulse oximetry, cardiac output) and in testing subjects for whom treadmill exercise is difficult (e.g., the obese child). For other subjects (young children, athletes), the treadmill is preferable. The pediatric exercise testing laboratory should develop staff expertise with both modalities.

3. Many different protocols are successful in achieving maximal testing of children. The following discussion examines the advantages of particular protocols and provides guidelines for selecting a satisfactory pediatric testing modality.

The optimal cycling protocol would provide for uniform submaximal stages of sufficient duration to obtain steady state data and physiologic measurements yet short enough to avoid subject boredom. Load increments need to be appropriate for body size, neither too great (causes excessive work stress) nor too small (prolongs the test). Of the standard cycle protocols, the McMaster protocol, with 2-min stages and loads related to body height, appears to best fit these needs.

Successful treadmill testing calls for a protocol that is neither too steep nor too long. Again, stages should be uniform and should allow time for measuring submaximal variables. The optimal protocol should alter slope rather than treadmill speed. Settings should be adaptable for subjects of a variety of fitness levels.

Despite its popularity, the Bruce protocol fails to satisfy many of these guidelines, particularly at the extremes of fitness and pediatric age range. The 2-min Balke protocol, with constant speed and increasing elevation, is preferable, but this protocol must be adjusted for subject age and fitness level. Walking protocols offer too little work for fit individuals without prolonged work time or very high treadmill slope, whereas running protocols cannot be achieved by small, obese, or poorly fit subjects. For treadmill testing of children, a Balke or modified Balke protocol should be selected relative to fitness level, not size or age (see guidelines in Table 3).

Table 3   Modified Balke Treadmill Protocol

Subject	Speed (mph)	Initial grade (%)	Increment (%)	Stage duration (min)
Poorly fit	3.0	6	2	2
Sedentary	3.25	6	2	2
Active	5.00	0	2-1/2	2
Athlete	5.25	0	2-1/2	2

References

1. Alpert, B.S., N.L. Flood, W.B. Strong, E.V. Dover, R.H. DuRant, A.M. Martin, and D.L. Booker. Responses to ergometer exercise in a healthy biracial population of children. *J. Pediatr.* 101:538-545, 1982.
2. Armstrong, N., J. Balding, P. Gentle, J. Williams, and B. Kirby. Peak oxygen uptake and physical capacity in 11- to 16-year olds. *Pediatr. Exerc. Sci.* 2:349-358, 1990.
3. Astrand, P.O., and K. Rodahl. *Textbook of Work Physiology* (2nd Ed.). New York: McGraw-Hill, 1977, p. 342.
4. Bailey, D.A., W.D. Ross, R.L. Mirwald, and C. Weese. Size dissociation of maximal aerobic power during growth in boys. *Med. Sport* 11:140-151, 1978.
5. Balke, B., and R.W. Ware. An experimental study of "physical fitness" of Air Force personnel. *U.S. Armed Forces Med. J.* 10:675-688, 1959.
6. Bar-Or, O. *Pediatric Sports Medicine for the Practitioner*. New York: Springer-Verlag, 1983, pp. 315-338.

7. Bar-Or, O., and L.D. Zwiren. Maximal oxygen consumption test during arm exercise: Reliability and validity. *J. Appl. Physiol.* 38:424-426, 1975.

8. Becker, D.M., and P. Vaccaro. Anaerobic threshold alterations caused by endurance training in young children. *J. Sports Med.* 23:445-449, 1983.

9. Boileau, R.A., A. Bonen, V.H. Heyward, and B.H. Massey. Maximal aerobic capacity on the treadmill and bicycle ergometer of boys 11-14 years of age. *J. Sports Med.* 17:153-162, 1977.

10. Bruce, R.A. Evaluation of functional capacity and exercise tolerance of cardiac patients. *Mod. Concepts Cardiovasc. Dis.* 25:321-329, 1956.

11. Cooper, D.M., J. Poage, T.J. Barstow, and C. Springer. Are obese children truly unfit? Minimizing the confounding effect of body size on the exercise response. *J. Pediatr.* 116:223-230, 1990.

12. Cooper, D.M., D. Weiler-Ravell, B.J. Whipp, and K. Wasserman. Aerobic parameters of exercise as a function of body size during growth in children. *J. Appl. Physiol.* 56:628-634, 1984.

13. Cropp, G.J., T.P. Pullano, F.J. Cerny, and I.T. Nathanson. Exercise tolerance and cardiorespiratory adjustments at peak work capacity in cystic fibrosis. *Am. Rev. Respir. Dis.* 126:211-216, 1982.

14. Cumming, G.R. Exercise studies in clinical pediatric cardiology. In: *Frontiers of Activity and Child Health*, H. Levalee and R.J. Shephard (Eds.). Quebec, PQ: Pelican, 1977, pp. 17-45.

15. Cumming, G.R., D. Everatt, and L. Hastman. Bruce treadmill test in children: Normal values in a clinic population. *Am. J. Cardiol.* 41:69-75. 1978.

16. Cumming, G.R., and S. Langford. Comparison of nine exercise tests used in pediatric cardiology. In: *Children and Exercise XI*, R.A. Binkhorst, H.C.G. Kemper, and W.H.M. Saris (Eds.). Champaign, IL: Human Kinetics, 1985, pp. 58-68.

17. Cunningham, L. Physiologic characteristics and team performance of female high school runners. *Pediatr. Exerc. Sci.* 1:73-79. 1989.

18. DuRant, R.H., E.V. Dover, and B.S. Alpert. An evaluation of five indices of physical working capacity in children. *Med. Sci. Sports Exerc.* 15:83-87, 1983.

19. Elias, B., T. Ryschon, K. Berg, and P. Hofschire. Body size and mechanical efficiency during cycling in children [abstract]. *Med. Sci. Sports Exerc.* 23(Suppl.):S32, 1991.

20. Freedson, P.S., V.L. Katch, T.B. Gilliam, and S. MacConnie. Energy expenditure in prepubescent children: Influence of sex and age. *Am. J. Clin. Nutr.* 34:1827-1830, 1981.

21. Froelicher, V.F., H. Brammell, G. Davis, I. Niguera, A. Stewart, and M.C. Lancaster. A comparison of three maximal treadmill exercise protocols. *J. Appl. Physiol.* 36:720-725, 1974.

22. Godfrey, S. *Exercise Testing in Children*. London: Saunders, 1974.

23. Godfrey, S., C.T.M. Davies, E. Wozniak, and C.A. Barnes. Cardiorespiratory response to exercise in normal children. *Clin. Sci.* 40:419-431, 1971.

24. Golden, J.C., K.F. Janz, W.R. Clarke, and L.T. Mahoney. New protocol for submaximal and peak exercise values for children and adolescents: The Muscatine study. *Pediatr. Exerc. Sci.* 3:129-140, 1991.

25. Green, M.A., and C. Foster. Effect of magnitude of handrail support on prediction of oxygen uptake during treadmill testing [abstract]. *Med. Sci. Sports Exerc.* 23(Suppl.):S166, 1991.

26. Haffor, A.A., and P.A.C. Kirk. Anaerobic threshold and relation of ventilation to CO_2 output during exercise in 11 year olds. *J. Sports Med. Phys. Fitness.* 28:74-78, 1988.

27. Hansen H.S., K. Froberg, J.R. Nielsen, and N. Hyldebrandt. A new approach to assessing maximal aerobic power in children: The Odense School Child Study. *Eur. J. Appl. Physiol.* 58:618-624, 1989.

28. Houlsby, W.T. Functional aerobic capacity and body size. *Arch. Dis. Child.* 61:388-393, 1986.

29. Inbar, O., and O. Bar-Or. The effects of intermittent warm-up on 7- to 9-year-old boys. *Eur. J. Appl. Physiol.* 34:81-89, 1975.

30. Issekutz, B., N.C. Birkhead, and K. Rodahl. Use of respiratory quotients in assessment of aerobic work capacity. *J. Appl. Physiol.* 17:47-50, 1962.

31. James, F.W., G. Blomqvist, M.D. Freed, W.W. Miller, J.H. Moller, E.W. Nugent, D.A. Riopel, W.B. Strong, and H.U. Wessel. Standards for exercise testing in the pediatric age group (American Heart Association Council on Cardiovascular Disease in the Young). *Circulation* 66:1377A-1397A, 1982.

32. James, F.W., S. Kaplan, C.J. Glueck, J.Y. Tsay, M.J.S. Knight, and C.J. Sarwar. Responses of normal children and young adults to controlled bicycle exercise. *Circulation* 61:902-912, 1980.

33. Jette, M., N.J. Ashton, and M.T. Sharratt. Development of a cardiorespiratory step-test of fitness for children 7-14 years of age. *Can. J. Public Health* 75:212-217, 1984.

34. Kanaley, J.A., R.A. Boileau, B.H. Massey, and J.E. Misner. Muscular efficiency during treadmill walking: The effects of age and workload. *Pediatr. Exerc. Sci.* 1:155-162, 1989.

35. King, M.J., T.D. Noakes, and E.G. Weimby. Physiological effect of a physical training program in children with exercise-induced asthma. *Pediatr. Exerc. Sci.* 1:137-144, 1989.

36. Klimt, F., and E.D. Voight. Investigations on the standardization of ergometry in children. *Acta Paediatr. Scand.* 217(Suppl.):35-36, 1971.

37. Krahenbuhl, G.S., R.P. Pangrazi, W.J. Stone, D.W. Morgan, and T. Williams. Fractional utilization of maximal aerobic capacity in children 6 to 8 years of age. *Pediatr. Exerc. Sci.* 1:271-277, 1989.

38. Macek, M., J. Vavra, and J. Novosadova. Prolonged exercise in prepubertal boys: I. Cardiovascular and metabolic adjustment. *Eur. J. Appl. Physiol.* 35:291-298, 1976.

39. Mahon, A.D., and P. Vaccaro. Ventilatory threshold and $\dot{V}O_2$max changes in children following endurance training. *Med. Sci. Sports Exerc.* 21:425-431, 1989.

40. Marcotte, J.E., R.K. Grisdale, H. Levison, A.L. Coates, and G.J. Canny. Multiple factors limit exercise capacity in cystic fibrosis. *Pediatr. Pulmonol.* 2:274-281, 1986.
41. Mayers, N., and B. Gutin. Physiologic characteristics of elite prepubertal cross country runners. *Med. Sci. Sports* 11:172-176, 1979.
42. Miles, D.S., J.B. Critz, and R.G. Knowlton. Cardiovascular, metabolic, and ventilatory responses of women to equivalent cycle ergometer and treadmill exercise. *Med. Sci. Sports Exerc.* 12:14-19, 1980.
43. Molineux, D., and A. Steptoe. Exaggerated blood pressure responses to submaximal exercise in normotensive adolescents with a family history of hypertension. *J. Hypertens.* 6:361-365, 1988.
44. Nudel, D.B., N. Gootman, S.C. Brunson, A. Stenzler, I.R. Shenker, and B.G. Gauthier. Exercise performance of hypertensive adolescents. *Pediatrics* 65:1073-1078, 1980.
45. Nudel, D.B., I. Hassett, A. Gurian, S. Diamant, E. Weinhouse, and N. Gootman. Young long distance runners: Physiological and psychological characteristics. *Clin. Pediatr.* (Phila.) 28:500-505, 1989.
46. Orenstein, D.M., M.E. Reed, F.T. Grogan, and L.V. Crawford. Exercise conditioning in children with asthma. *J. Pediatr.* 106:556-560, 1985.
47. Paterson, D.H., D.A. Cunningham, and A. Donner. The effect of different treadmill speeds on the variability of $\dot{V}O_2$max in children. *Eur. J. Appl. Physiol.* 47:113-122, 1981.
48. Pollock, M.L., R.L. Bohannon, K.H. Cooper, J.J. Ayres, A. Ward, S.R. White, and A.C. Linnerud. A comparative analysis of four protocols for maximal treadmill stress testing. *Am. Heart J.* 92:39-46, 1976.
49. Ragg, K.E., T.F. Murray, L.M. Karbonit, and D.A. Jump. Errors in predicting functional capacity from a treadmill exercise stress test. *Am. Heart J.* 100:581-583, 1980.
50. Reybrouck, T., M. Weymans, H. Stijns, and L.G. Van der Hauwaert. Ventilatory anaerobic threshold for evaluating exercise performance in children with congenital left-to-right intracardiac shunts. *Pediatr. Cardiol.* 7:19-24, 1986.
51. Riopel, D.A., A.B. Taylor, and A.R. Hohn. Blood pressure, heart rate, pressure-rate product, and electrocardiographic changes in healthy children during treadmill exercise. *Am. J. Cardiol.* 44:697-704.
52. Rowland, T.W., J.A. Auchinachie, T.J. Keenan, and G.M. Green. Physiologic responses to treadmill running in adult and prepubertal males. *Int. J. Sports Med.* 8:292-297, 1987.
53. Rowland, T.W., and L. Cunningham. Oxygen uptake plateau in children. *Chest* (in press).
54. Rowland, T.W., J.S. Staab, V.B. Unnithan, J.M. Rambusch, and S.F. Siconolfi. Mechanical efficiency during cycling in prepubertal and adult males. *Int. J. Sports Med.* 11:452-455, 1990.
55. Rowland, T.W., M.R. Varzeus, and C.A. Walsh. Aerobic responses to walking training in sedentary adolescents. *J. Adolesc. Health Care* 12:30-34, 1991.

56. Sheehan, J.M., T.W. Rowland, and E.J. Burke. A comparison of four treadmill protocols for determination of maximal oxygen uptake in 10- to 12-year-old boys. *Int. J. Sports Med.* 8:31-34, 1987.

57. Shuleva, K.M., G.R. Hunter, D.J. Hester, and D.L. Dunaway. Exercise oxygen uptake in 3- through 6-year-old children. *Pediatr. Exerc. Sci.* 2:130-139, 1990.

58. Skinner, J.S., O. Bar-Or, V. Bergsteinova, C.W. Bell, D. Royer, and E.R. Buskirk. Comparison of continuous and intermittent tests for determining maximal oxygen uptake in children. *Acta Paediatr. Scand.* 217(Suppl.): 24-28, 1971.

59. Smodlaka, V.N. Treadmill vs. bicycle ergometers. *Physician Sportsmed.* 10:75-80, 1982.

60. Strong, W.B., D. Spencer, M.D. Miller, and M. Salehbhai. The physical work capacity of healthy black children. *Am. J. Disc. Child.* 132:244-248, 1978.

61. Sundberg, S., and R. Elovainio. Cardiorespiratory function in competitive endurance runners aged 12-16 years compared with ordinary boys. *Acta Paediatr. Scand.* 71:987-992, 1982.

62. Tamura, T., K. Nakajima, T. Togawa, R. Wakabayashi, and M. Osano. Development of a new exercise test for children. *J. Med. Biol. Eng.* 23:482-486, 1985.

63. Tanner, C.S., C.T. Heise, and G. Barber. Correlation of the physiologic parameters of a continuous ramp versus an incremental James exercise protocol in normal children. *Am. J. Cardiol.* 67:309-312, 1991.

64. Vaccaro, P., and D.H. Clarke. Cardiorespiratory alterations in 9 to 11 year old children following a season of competitive swimming. *Med. Sci. Sports* 10:204-207, 1978.

65. Van Huss, W., S.A. Evans, T. Kurowski, D.J. Anderson, R. Allen, and K. Stephens. Physiological characteristics of male and female age group runners. In: *Competitive Sports for Children and Youth*, E.W. Brown and C.F. Branta (Eds.). Champaign, IL: Human Kinetics, 1988, pp. 143-158.

66. Wanne, O.P.S., and E. Haapoja. Blood pressure during exercise in healthy children. *Eur. J. Appl. Physiol.* 58:62-67, 1988.

67. Washington, R.L., J.C. van Gundy, C. Cohen, H.M. Sondheimer, and R.R. Wolfe. Normal aerobic and anaerobic exercise data for North American school-age children. *J. Pediatr.* 112:223-233, 1988.

68. Webber, L.M., W.C. Byrnes, T.W. Rowland, and V.L. Foster. Serum creatine kinase activity and delayed onset muscle soreness in prepubescent children: A preliminary study. *Pediatr. Exerc. Sci.* 1:351-359, 1989.

69. Wessel, H.U. Integrated cardiopulmonary approach to exercise testing in pediatrics. *Pediatrician* 13:26-33, 1986.

70. Wilmore, J.H., and P.O. Sigerseth. Physical work capacity of young girls 7-13 years of age. *J. Appl. Physiol.* 22:923-928, 1967.

71. Wilson, P.K., P.S. Fardy, and V.F. Froelicher. *Cardiac Rehabilitation, Adult Fitness, and Exercise Testing.* Philadephia: Lea & Febiger, 1981, p. 360.

72. Wolfe, R.R., R. Washington, E. Daberkow, J.R. Murphy, and H.L. Brammel. Anaerobic threshold as a predictor of athletic performance in prepubertal female runners. *Am. J. Dis. Child.* 140:922-924, 1986.
73. Zanconato, S., E. Baraldi, P. Santuz, F. Rigon, L. Vido, L. DaDalt, and F. Zacchello. Gas exchange during exercise in obese children. *Eur. J. Pediatr.* 148:614-617, 1989.
74. Zhang, Y.Y., M.C. Johnson, N. Chow, and K. Wasserman. Effects of exercise testing protocol on parameters of aerobic function. *Med. Sci. Sports Exerc.* 23:625-630, 1991.

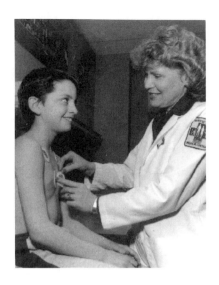

Pediatric Exercise Electrocardiography

J. Timothy Bricker, MD
Texas Children's Hospital
Baylor College of Medicine

Electrocardiographic monitoring of exercise provides a precise measurement of cardiac rate response to the exercise load, and heart rate monitoring provides one objective measure of the adequacy of effort and a test of maximal performance. Exercise electrocardiography is also useful for assessing arrhythmias that occur during exercise and for identifying stress-related ischemia. Moreover, electrocardiographic monitoring of rhythm and ST-segment changes during testing makes the exercise study safer for children who might be prone to exertional arrhythmias or ischemia. Recording the electrocardiogram (ECG) while exercise-related symptoms develop during testing may help confirm or exclude various diagnoses (see Table 1 for a list of ECG uses).

This section reviews methodology for pediatric exercise electrocardiography as well as normal and abnormal electrocardiographic responses to exercise.

Data Acquisition Techniques

An important aspect of pediatric exercise electrocardiography is optimal data acquisition. In most respects, equipment for adult testing is suitable, but some modifications in technique or equipment may be needed.

Electrocardiography Recording Equipment

Some laboratories acquire old equipment as it is retired from diagnostic work in an ECG department. Although this may be adequate in some circumstances, there are potential limitations. Early direct writing devices had distortions (attenuated peak deflections and blunted small deflections), and the need for frequent maintenance was often ignored. Pressurized ink physiologic recorders had less inertia and were used in some electrocardiographic research applications. The amplifier output could also be attached to a cathode-ray oscilloscope, which was virtually without distortion. The low-input impedance transistorized amplifiers of the early 1960s made the machines more compact and reliable, but they also were prone to considerable signal distortion. High-input impedance transistorized amplifiers in current machines have eliminated that distortion. Contemporary state-of-the-art electrocardiography units digitize the amplified and filtered analog electrical signal (each 1/250th

Table 1   Uses for the Pediatric Exercise Electrocardiogram

Precise measurement of heart rate during exercise testing

Evaluation of possible or suspected ischemia

Evaluation of severity of aortic stenosis

Evaluation of symptoms that suggest a possible exercise-induced arrhythmia

Evaluation of patients who have had surgery for cardiac malformations that are known to be related to late occurrence of arrhythmias

Evaluation of the response to drug therapy in the setting of a known exercise-induced arrhythmia

Assessment of pacemaker function

of a second). The analog tracing, which is printed out by the direct-writer free of distortion, is then reconstructed from that digitized information.

Electrocardiography instruments have been available over the years that were variable with regard to dynamic range, high-amplitude response accuracy, levels of sensitivity on the chart recorder, frequency response of the amplifier, amplitude resolution, recording speed and speed error, input impedance, current leakage and grounding, damping, and filtering. Specifics of the minimal performance requirements for electrocardiographic equipment have been published by the American Heart Association's Committee on Electrocardiography (52), and more detailed discussions are available in cardiology textbooks (25). The hospital biomedical engineering department should be able to confirm that an electrocardiographic recording apparatus conforms to these current minimal standards.

In addition to these equipment requirements for diagnostic pediatric electrocardiography, the exercise laboratory requires an oscilloscope screen for continuous observation of the rhythm and the ST segments (usually leads II, aVF, and V5). This can be done with either continuous hard copy recording or continuous digital or magnetic tape recording of the ECG. Or, the data sent to the ECG recorder can be delayed a few seconds so that when the tester sees an arrhythmia on the oscilloscope screen and pushes the print button, the ECG recorder begins printing before the arrhythmia is transmitted. The recording at the onset or termination of a tachycardia is the most valuable portion of the exercise ECG for determining the mechanism of the arrhythmia.

Some laboratories have used commercially available heart rate telemetry systems (e.g., Sport Tester) to monitor only the heart rate increase with exercise during testing rather than to record a complete ECG.

Electrodes and Skin Preparation

Although the search for the perfect lead continues, considerable progress has been made in developing leads appropriate for pediatric exercise electrocardiography. If two electrodes of a pair are not identical, they will generate a voltage difference that produces an artifact. This artifact can be minimized by limiting the frequency range of the amplifier response because artifact voltages change slowly in comparison to ECG voltages.

Movement artifacts occur when the electrode-electrolyte interface is mechanically disturbed, resulting in a voltage change. Electrodes for exercise testing avoid metal-to-skin contact; the electrode "floats" on an electrolyte-gel mixture to minimize artifact from muscle movement. A large contracting muscle mass between two electrodes will cause an artifact that cannot be filtered. Occasionally electrodes must be moved to avoid large muscle groups, even though leads are placed on the torso (as is discussed later in this section).

Although this may require some repositioning of electrodes for optimal recordings when testing a heavily muscled adolescent, it is usually not a major problem in testing smaller children.

Silver–silver chloride electrodes have very low impedance for optimal recording of low-frequency electrical phenomena and perform better than the less expensive metals that have been used to make electrodes. Electrodes that are too small have an excessively high impedance; the large electrodes used on adults do not provide good contact on a small child and do not stay on as well. Electrode adhesion, which is essential for quality recordings in children, varies among brands. The use of a stretch net shirt or elastic bandage wrap helps limit potential motion artifact but should not be so tight as to restrict motion or thoracic excursion during ventilation.

Skin preparation can be done without causing pain or frightening the child. The epidermis possesses a layer of dead skin cells (stratum corneum) with a high electrical resistance; the dermis itself has low electrical resistance. First, the skin is cleansed with alcohol or acetone; then gentle abrasion removes the stratum corneum prior to electrode placement. This can be done gently by briskly rubbing with rough cloth, fine sandpaper, emery board, skin cleaning gel containing a mild abrasive, dental drill, or commercially available electrode placement guns. Attention to skin preparation technique is the most crucial aspect of obtaining excellent electrocardiographic recordings on exercising children.

Lead Placement

The right and left arm electrodes are placed in the right and left infraclavicular fossae. The left leg electrode is placed on the lower abdomen above the left anterior superior iliac crest. The right leg lead may or may not be used on the lower abdomen. Some laboratories use a higher placement on the torso for the lower limb leads, which is of particular value in testing obese children. Precordial leads V1 through V6 are placed in the same locations as for a routine resting ECG. Some investigators have used additional electrodes to record Frank orthogonal leads X, Y, and Z (4, 37), but this practice is not widely used in current clinical applications. When a single lead recording is used for noncardiac exercise testing, the bipolar CM5 lead is the one most likely to demonstrate ST abnormalities in adults with ischemic exercise changes.

Interpretation of the Resting ECG

Supine and upright resting ECGs are obtained prior to exercise. Certain findings on the resting ECG (e.g., the presence of a rhythm other than sinus rhythm at rest, a long QT interval, resting ST segment abnormalities, or unexpected severe ventricular hypertrophy) should concern the exercise test physicians and affect the testing procedure. The resting ECG must be interpreted before exercise testing begins. Only the electrocardiographic tracing obtained from the supine position should be interpreted. The norms used for hypertrophy and for axis measurements have been determined from ECGs obtained on supine children and are not applicable to the upright ECG.

Computer Processing

Current equipment uses analog-to-digital conversion of the electrical signal and subsequent generation of an analog ECG tracing to eliminate pen inertia. Smoothing of baseline drift and beat-to-beat averaging to reduce motion artifact are valuable features. Measurement programs, arrhythmia recognition programs, and ST-change recognition based on the digitized data are also available. (See Table 2 for a listing of measurements made from the pediatric exercise ECG.) Interpretation software and systems for on-line comparative analysis of ST segments developed for use in adults have little current application to testing of children (57).

Table 2   Measurements Made From the Pediatric Exercise Electrocardiogram

Routine	Measurements in selected situations
Heart rate	Electrocardiographic intervals
ST segments	QRS voltage
Arrhythmias	QRS axis

Normal Electrocardiographic Responses to Exercise

Assumptions upon which classical electrocardiography were based include

1. the body is a homogeneous resistance medium,
2. the net electrical dipole is at the center of this medium, and
3. the dipole undergoes no change in location during the cardiac cycle (25).

Although useful for approximating reality in the clinic, none of these assumptions are completely true and they become even less valid during intense exercise. The exercise ECG records the surface electrical potential changes from a bouncing, rapidly ventilating child; these readings should reflect the changes in variation of the electrical vector at the heart's surface during the cardiac cycle. Electrocardiographic changes observed in a healthy child during exercise probably include changes due to the heart becoming shifted in its position and orientation within the thorax, an increase in lung volumes with hyperventilation, and alteration in the cardiac chamber volumes.

Changes in the Heart Rate

An increase in heart rate is expected with exercise, but the formula for heart rate at maximal exercise is not applicable to pediatric testing because, in general, the peak heart rate in children is similar regardless of age. Although there have been reports of extreme sinus tachycardia above 230 in conditions such as thyrotoxicosis, sepsis, or aminophylline toxicity (23), sinus tachycardia with maximal exertion does not reach this level. Maximal heart rates of 190 to 210 are expected at all ages with pediatric exercise testing, whereas the heart rate at a given submaximal work rate is higher for younger children than for these who are older. A slightly higher maximal heart rate and faster heart rate rise at work rates below maximum is found in females than in males (even before puberty).

Heart rate can be measured with analog measurement devices or digitized data from the electrocardiography recording cart. The analog output may be sent to the computer and, by means of an analog-to-digital converter, heart rate is entered directly into the exercise report. Assuring the accuracy of heart rate measurement in pediatric exercise testing has been addressed (38). Although heart rate measurement from current electrocardiographic carts is highly accurate, manual calculation of the heart rate from measurement of the (R-to-R) interval at each stage of exercise can be done quickly and is recommended to assure test report accuracy.

Peak heart rate with exercise testing is discussed in the section ''Aerobic Exercise Testing Protocols'' by Rowland. When a child achieves a heart rate above 190 beats per minutes (bpm) this is one indication that maximal performance has been achieved. An uncooperative child may stop exercising before becoming fatigued and have a low peak exercise heart rate. Peripheral muscle fatigue may occur before maximal cardiac adaptation. Early peripheral muscle fatigue with testing may be caused by poor conditioning, peripheral musculoskeletal disease, an artifact of the testing protocol (e.g., arm ergometry), or the child's inexperience or inefficiency with the testing procedure. Therapy with beta-adrenergic blocking agents will elicit a low heart rate at a given work load and a low peak exercise heart rate. Chronotropic incompetence has been noted in testing of individuals with cardiac disease (19). In adult exercise testing, poor chronotropic response (heart rate below 5th percentile for age and gender) has been found to be a predictor of subsequent ischemia with or without ST depression (19).

Changes in Electrocardiographic Intervals

The RR interval shortens with an increase in heart rate, the PR interval decreases during exercise, and the QRS duration decreases slightly or remains the same (55). The QT interval also shortens with exercise (55). The corrected QT interval (calculated by the Bazette formula: measured QT divided by the square root of the RR interval) changes little with exercise, but measurement is difficult. Although peak exercise QT interval observations in children are reported in the literature (64), confident measurement of the QT interval is limited when the end of the T wave and the beginning of the P wave merge into each other (42). The QX interval, extrapolation of the downslope of the T wave to the isoelectric baseline (30), has been attempted to improve the accuracy of the estimated QT interval change during exercise in pediatric patients (42). A high interobserver variability is still found with this approach (42). At low-intensity exercise, where the heart rate is still low enough to measure the QT interval reliably, the RR interval shortens more rapidly with an increase in work load than the QT interval does. This relative inertia in the shortening of the QT interval with exercise compared to the RR interval results in a transient lengthening of the corrected QT interval until steady state is achieved at a given work load. Following exercise, the RR interval returns to baseline more quickly than the QT interval.

Changes in P-Wave Voltage

It has long been noted that the surface P-wave voltage in adults increases in amplitude with exertion; this is also seen in children (13). Despite the increased voltage on the ECG, the endocardial or epicardial voltage measured on the atrium usually decreases with exercise. This phenomenon may be explained by some degree of atrial dilation and thinning of atrial muscle that occurs with exercise. It also may be related to some of the problems with atrial undersensing observed during exercise in the early experience with dual-chambered pacing in pediatrics (8, 13), but otherwise it is not of great clinical significance.

Changes in QRS Axis and Voltage

Studies of healthy adults show that the R-wave voltage tends to decrease with exercise in 70% to 100% of subjects, whereas the R-wave voltage tends to remain the same or to increase in populations with clinical or angiographic evidence of myocardial ischemia (5, 16, 30, 32, 54, 58). Quantitative analysis studies of QRS voltage and axis change during pediatric exercise testing (20, 21, 48, 61, 69) have found that the QRS-voltage response to exercise in adolescents is similar to the response in adults. Some investigators have proposed that voltage changes be used for diagnostic purposes. However, 72% of healthy boys under age 11 were found to have an increase or no change in QRS voltage with exercise (48).

The frontal plane QRS vector does not change with exercise in children, whereas there is a slight posterior shift in the horizontal QRS vector. QRS voltage and axis changes in exercise testing of children have low specificity, and no practical application has been found for them. The explanations for voltage changes with exercise are speculative and probably include dilation of abnormal hearts in some cases and changes of heart position within the thorax with lung expansion from hyperventilation.

Changes in T-Wave Height, Axis, and ST Segments

The ST segment and T wave reflect repolarization of the ventricles. The U wave is thought to reflect repolarization of the His-Purkinje system, which repolarizes last. The amplitude of the T wave initially decreases with exercise but returns to normal at maximal exercise (61). A peaked T wave may be noted immediately after exercise.

Changes in the electrocardiographic findings during ventricular repolarization are especially relevant for diagnosis of a mismatch of myocardial blood flow supply and demand. One must understand the normal changes with exercise to interpret ischemic ST- and T-wave changes.

The electrocardiographic criteria for ischemia in children with heart disease have been extrapolated from ST changes recognized in adults. Traditionally, this ischemic response has been characterized by a horizontal or downward ST-segment depression of 0.1 mV or more for greater than 80 ms. How accurately these criteria can be applied to pediatric patients remains uncertain. Clearly, however, when normal children exercise, the ST segment rapidly returns to baseline (within 80 ms) and is not flat or downward (see Figure 1).

Two methods have been described to measure ST-segment changes: The isoelectric line may be drawn from the PQ to PQ junction or from the beginning of the P wave to the beginning of the QRS (PR isoelectric line method) (2, 15) (see Figure 2). Thapar et al. compared the two methods (61). They noted normal physiologic J point depression in 9% of boys and 18% of girls when measuring with the PQ-PQ isoelectric line method and in 2.3% of boys or girls with the PR isoelectric line. Similarly, using the PQ-PQ isoelectric line method, James found 7% of healthy boys and 14% of healthy girls had physiologic ST depression (37).

One advantage of the PR isoelectric line is its higher specificity. The PQ-PQ isoelectric line method seems more vulnerable to a wandering electrical baseline with a poor quality recording during exercise. When using this method, one should establish a PQ isoelectric line with at least three consecutive complexes to be certain that the isoelectric baseline is stable.

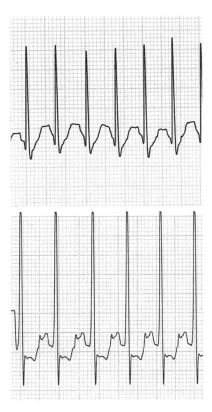

Figure 1: Physiologic ST-segment depression is shown in the upper panel. Ischemic changes showing flat or downward ST depression are illustrated in the lower panel.

Healthy individuals may show ST-T wave changes with increased ventilation. A prospective study of maximum voluntary hyperventilation in 161 consecutive children referred to an exercise laboratory for diagnostic testing showed repolarization changes in 22%. T-wave flattening was the most common change, but 6% had T-wave inversion and 3% showed ST-segment depression of 1 mm or more (63).

ST- or T-wave changes that occur with voluntary hyperventilation at rest may or may not be seen during the increased ventilation that occurs at peak exercise; such alterations can cause a false-positive test for myocardial ischemia. In some laboratories, subjects perform 30 s of maximal voluntary ventilation with continuous ECG recording prior to exercise testing. This helps identify ST-T wave changes caused by increased ventilation that might confound identification of electrocardiographic evidence of myocardial ischemia during exercise.

Healthy individuals may show changes in atrial repolarization with exercise in addition to the changes due to ventricular depolarization (56). Augmentation of the Ta (atrial repolarization wave or the ''T wave of the P wave'') is

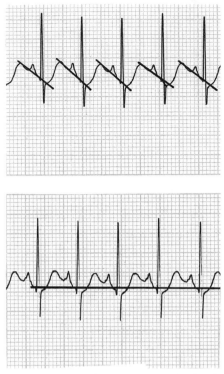

Figure 2: Two methods of determining the isoelectric line for measurement of ST-segment depression are illustrated above. In the PR isoelectric method (top panel), a line is drawn from the onset of the P wave to the onset of the QRS complex. This method is felt to be less affected by artifact. The PQ-PQ isoelectric line (lower panel) is drawn from the beginning of one QRS complex to the beginning of the next. This is the more conventional method. A flat baseline of the electrocardiogram provides for an acceptable ST-segment measurement (61).

characteristic with exercise. Atrial repolarization is usually a very low voltage phenomenon and is lost in the QRS. This Ta wave augmentation is unlikely to confound interpretation of ST segments but is considered a cause of false-positive ST changes in healthy individuals (56). A tester is unlikely to recognize a Ta wave during exercise testing with certainty unless the subject's P waves show no relationship to the QRS (such as happens with third-degree atrioventricular block and a slow junctional rate or with a ventricular demand pacemaker set on a low rate in a patient without atrioventricular conduction).

Stress Electrocardiography for Ischemia

Identification of ischemic electrocardiographic changes is the major use of exercise testing in adult patients and has great applicability in pediatric testing.

Causes of False-Positive Tests

Numerous factors may cause false-positive exercise tests. Two possible causes, normal changes from ventilation or atrial repolarization, were discussed previously. Digoxin may cause ST-segment depression with exercise in individuals without structural heart disease. This is more common among older adults and is not likely to cause a false-positive test for a child on digoxin (59). Left ventricular hypertrophy will result in positive ST changes that may be unrelated to coronary artery disease but may be due to subendocardial ischemia and mismatch of demand and supply (47).

Abnormalities of repolarization (i.e., ST-segment and T-wave changes) cannot be interpreted if depolarization is abnormal. Bundle branch block, a common finding among children with heart disease or postoperative heart disease, makes the ST segments uninterpretable with exercise testing. The ST segments with exercise are also uninterpretable in patients with ventricular pacemakers. Wolff-Parkinson-White syndrome, a condition with abnormal depolarization in which repolarization appears abnormal, can simulate an ischemic finding on the exercise test. This is particularly confusing in the exercise laboratory if Wolff-Parkinson-White has not been recognized on the resting ECG. False-positive tests also have been reported among individuals with hypokalemia, mitral valve prolapse, pectus excavatum, or autonomic abnormalities; among persons taking estrogen or anti-depressant drug therapy; and among healthy individuals without explanation (17).

The interpretation of ST-segment changes in early phases of sudden strenuous exercise (e.g., sudden sprinting at high speed on the treadmill) might be confusing. Transient subendocardial ischemia is found with sudden strenuous exertion in animal models; a momentary decrease in function in healthy adults upon sudden strenuous exertion without warm-up may reflect a brief demand/supply mismatch (24).

Causes of False-Negative Tests

There is little quantitative information on how frequently children with ischemic cardiac disease have normal treadmill tests, although false-negative tests may occur (51, 66). Prematurely terminating testing with inadequate exercise or with a submaximal protocol is a major source of false-negative tests in adult exercise laboratories. Propranolol and nitroglycerin therapy also cause false-negative tests in patients with coronary disease, and single vessel coronary artery disease with abundant collateral supply is another potential cause of false-negative tests (17).

Abnormalities That Result in Ischemic Changes

The most common cause of "ischemic" ST changes in pediatric exercise testing occurs in patients with aortic stenosis. The ischemic changes are due to a relative inadequacy of perfusion of the subendocardium to which ventricular hypertrophy, high diastolic intraventricular pressures, and suboptimal cardiac output may all contribute (40).

Exercise testing in patients with aortic stenosis may show ischemic ST- and T-wave changes (14, 40) and development of ventricular arrhythmias with exercise (65). Although exercise-induced ST-segment changes have been correlated with severity of obstruction, the resting gradient is not the sole determinant of these ST-segment changes. The major hemodynamic determinant of ST depression during exercise in patients with aortic stenosis seems to be the left ventricular O_2 demand/supply ratio (40). The abnormal exercise test results may improve after successful surgical treatment of aortic stenosis (65). The predictive value of exercise testing in postoperative aortic stenosis for identifying residual obstruction is poor (3).

The interpretation of ST-segment changes to identify severity of aortic regurgitation is also unreliable (29). Left ventricular dilation is seen with both dynamic and isometric exercise in patients with aortic insufficiency; this dilation causes ST-segment changes that are unrelated to the aortic peak-systolic transvalvular gradient. No criteria for reoperation based on the results of exercise testing alone can be recommended.

Myocardial ischemia in adults is almost always due to atherosclerotic coronary artery disease. Anomalous origin of the left coronary artery from the pulmonary trunk (Bland-Garland-White syndrome) is the leading congenital cause of myocardial infarction in children, and Kawasaki disease in the most common cause of acquired coronary disease in pediatric patients. Our review of 100,000 resting electrocardiographic tracings from 54,000 pediatric patients at Texas Children's Hospital revealed 85 with electrocardiographic evidence of infarction (62). Anomalous origin of the coronary artery from the pulmonary trunk was found in 20% of these infarctions, and Kawasaki disease was the reason for infarction in 14% (62).

Although some patients with anomalous origin of the coronary artery from the pulmonary trunk may be minimally symptomatic by the time they are old enough for exercise testing, surgery is usually done early in childhood. Exercise testing is more likely to be used for postoperative evaluation. Impaired chronotropic response, ventricular arrhythmias, and ST depression have been observed in patients who have been successfully treated for this malformation (49). Wiles et al. noted that positive exercise tests (ischemic ST and T changes) could be found in some postoperative patients with a good repair who had angiographic demonstration of a two-coronary system. Negative tests for ischemia were found among patients who had been treated with surgical ligation of the anomalous coronary artery years ago when that was an accepted treatment (66). Paridon et al. found chronotropic incompetence to be the exercise finding most correlated with perfusion defects by thallium scintigraphy (49). Although no center has numbers adequate for Bayesian analysis, one should be cautious about using exercise ST changes alone to evaluate the adequacy of repair when following up on surgical treatment of anomalous origin of the coronary artery from the pulmonary trunk.

Angina with ischemic ST depression can result from severe coronary stenosis with Kawasaki disease (18). Patients with Kawasaki disease and residual coronary artery disease including abnormal nuclear exercise testing may fail to demonstrate exercise-induced ST changes (51). Exercise electrocardiography has been used to evaluate surgical outcome of aortocoronary bypass treatment of coronary insufficiency resulting from Kawasaki disease (60). The odds of finding a false-positive or a false-negative test in a Kawasaki disease patient or in a child who is postoperative coronary bypass for Kawasaki disease cannot be confidently assessed because of an insufficient number of patients.

Exercise testing may show ischemic findings in a patient with an anomalous course of a coronary artery running between the aorta and pulmonary artery (origin of the left coronary artery from the right coronary artery or left coronary artery from the anterior sinus of Valsalva) or an anomalous intramyocardial course (myocardial bridging). A positive stress test may also indicate congenital coronary stenosis or "hooded" coronary arteries. Premature atherosclerotic coronary disease severe enough to cause ischemic changes with exercise in children might occur with some of the hyperlipidemias (such as a homozygote for Type II hyperlipoproteinemia); with premature aging syndromes (such as progeria, Werner syndrome, or Cockayne syndrome), following cardiac transplantation, and with atherosclerosis associated with coronary vasculitis (such as systemic lupus erythematosus). Ischemic changes may be seen with exercise in patients with hypertensive cardiac disease and with hypertrophic cardiomyopathy. Although the ST changes seen with severe hypertrophy have been considered false positives by some, there is good evidence that hypertrophy may be associated with regional perfusion deficits in exercise thallium studies (41) and with pathologic evidence of myocardial infarction (62). Thromboembolic disease, myocarditis, surgical or traumatic coronary lesions, inherited disorders of connective tissue, and mucopolysaccharidoses are among the potential causes of ischemic findings in pediatric exercise testing (62).

ST-segment depression and T-wave changes are often seen in the right chest leads (V1 and V2) during and immediately after exercise testing of asymptomatic patients who have had the Mustard operation for transposition of the great arteries. This is easily overlooked because usually not as much attention is paid to right precordial leads during exercise testing. Healthy postoperative Mustard patients with a high physical working capacity seem to be the most likely to demonstrate this phenomenon, which is related to the high work intensity they achieve during testing. The ST changes do not seem to be related to angina or disability and have not been considered an indication for further investigation. These ST changes could reflect some demand-to-supply perfusion mismatch in this setting in which the right ventricle serves as the systemic ventricle. These ST changes might be an exaggeration of a right ventricular strain pattern. It is not known whether ventricular strain patterns seen on the resting ECG are due to subendocardial ischemia or to a difference in endocardial and epicardial conduction times found with hypertrophy.

Children who have undergone the arterial switch operation for transposition of the great arteries may develop coronary abnormalities or stenosis at the site of either aortic or pulmonary anastomosis. Exercise electrocardiography will probably be found to be useful in the long-term follow-up of these children who have had this procedure as they enter adolescence.

Bundle Branch Block

Bundle branch block on the resting ECG is common in patients with repair of tetralogy of Fallot and is often seen in other postoperative patients. The presence of bundle branch block makes the interpretation of ST segments invalid. Bundle branch block that develops during exercise testing is usually related to coronary artery disease in adults (22). Exercise-induced bundle branch block in pediatric testing has been found to be associated with various cardiac defects including aortic stenosis and surgically treated congenital heart defects (10). Although exercise-precipitated bundle branch block does occur in ostensibly healthy children and adults, further investigation is warranted. The abrupt onset of bundle branch block during exercise can be confused with ventricular tachycardia. Differentiating between these two findings generally requires recording the onset or the termination of the wide QRS rhythm. The identification of atrioventricular dissociation confirms the ventricular tachycardia diagnosis.

Stress Electrocardiography for Arrhythmias

Exercise testing may result in arrhythmias that are not present at rest. Following the test, residual elevation of catecholamines from the exercise bout is accompanied by an increase in vagal tone, which increases arrhythmias. Exercise testing has been used to evaluate pharmacologic suppression of arrhythmias in patients with exercise-induced arrhythmias and to provide information about the adequacy of pharmacologic beta blockade.

Premature Ventricular Contractions

Premature ventricular contractions (PVCs) are found in many healthy children at rest and are usually suppressed during exercise (36). During treadmill exercise testing using the modified Bruce protocol PVCs disappeared in 89% (72 out of 82) of children who had an anatomically normal heart but who had PVCs on the resting ECG. The mean heart rate at PVC disappearance was 146 bpm and ranged from 116 to 190 bpm. For a researcher to determine with confidence that PVCs persist with exercise, a subject may need to achieve a heart rate of more than 200 bpm in the laboratory. However, this is seldom necessary in evaluating a patient with PVCs. Development of couplets or multiform PVCs with exercise is considered abnormal and should be investigated further (12).

Premature Atrial Contractions

Premature atrial contractions are common among healthy children and are usually benign. Premature atrial contractions were noted in 105 of 2,761 (3.8%) patients referred for exercise testing from a pediatric cardiology clinic. Premature atrial contractions were observed in the postexercise period but were not present at rest in 27% of these patients. Of those who had premature atrial contractions at rest or during early stages of exercise, the premature atrial contractions continued until peak exercise in 40% and disappeared in 60%. Premature atrial contractions that appear during exercise testing or persist at advanced stages of exercise do not require additional investigation (12).

Cardiomyopathy

Patients with either a dilated cardiomyopathy or a hypertrophic cardiomyopathy may have arrhythmias (26, 34, 43). Exercise testing has been recommended in the evaluation of these patients (67). Arrhythmogenic right ventricular dysplasia is particularly likely to be associated with exercise-related ventricular arrhythmias (27, 31, 53).

Tetralogy of Fallot

A correlation between poor hemodynamic result, exertional ventricular arrhythmias, and sudden death after repair of tetralogy of Fallot has been demonstrated (28). Exercise-related arrhythmias may develop long after repair, and exercise testing is recommended every 3 to 4 years. The correlation between exercise-related ventricular arrhythmias and ventricular arrhythmias induced by programmed stimulation during electrophysiologic testing is poor (67). Pharmacologic treatment (or surgical treatment of residual hemodynamic abnormalities) of ventricular arrhythmias, especially ventricular tachycardia or couplets, that develop during exercise is generally recommended in patients with tetralogy of Fallot (28, 67).

Postoperative Surgery for Transposition

Exercise testing can be used to identify rhythm disorders in patients who have undergone the Mustard or Senning operation for transposition (44). Dysrhythmias with exercise are common among these patients. Matthews found arrhythmias with stress testing in 11 of 21 subjects who were asymptomatic 3 years or more after their Mustard operation (41). All had histories of normal exercise tolerance, participated regularly in noncompetitive physical activity, and seemed healthy. Exercise electrocardiography of 29 patients who were postoperative Mustard operation for transposition of the great arteries demonstrated subnormal chronotropic response with high reproducibility that was unrelated to digoxin treatment or to measured exercise tolerance (33). This was attributed to possible sinus node dysfunction. Subsequent prospective studies have not shown a relationship between exercise test evidence of chronotropic incompetence and either the sinoatrial conduction time or the sinus node recovery time measured by endocavitary electrophysiologic testing (7). Chronotropic incompetence in the postoperative Mustard patients is correlated with right ventricular dilation but does not seem to be the cause of the low peak-exercise O_2 uptake (50).

Hereditary Prolongation of the QT Interval

Because patients with syndromes of hereditary QT-interval prolongation are at risk for sudden cardiac death due to arrhythmia during exertion, they are likely to be referred to the stress laboratory for exercise electrocardiography. Findings may include ventricular arrhythmias with exercise and bradycardia at rest or in the postexercise period (6, 39). Failure of the corrected QT interval to shorten with exercise has been reported in patients with long QT-interval syndromes (64). Measuring the corrected QT-interval response during exercise has been advocated as a way to identify borderline cases or to confirm uncertain diagnoses (64). It's difficult to obtain a confident measurement of T-wave duration during exercise, the measurement's reproducibility is low (42), and some have found the change in the corrected QT interval with exercise testing to be of limited value in discriminating between healthy individuals and patients with the long QT-interval syndrome (46). T-wave alternans is a rare but specific finding with exercise electrocardiography in the long QT-interval syndrome. T-wave alternans is generally seen in cases with impressive QT prolongation on the resting ECG; it is not likely to be the finding that confirms the diagnosis in the obscure or borderline case.

T-wave alternans with exercise may indicate a poor prognosis for patients with hereditary prolongation of the QT interval (64).

Congenital Complete Heart Block

The change in ventricular rate with exercise electrocardiography can be examined in congenital complete heart block. Exercise-related ventricular arrhythmias with complete atrioventricular block have been reported in relation to sudden cardiac death (68), although this risk is generally associated with serious congenital malformation. Single chamber pacing does not reliably prevent exercise-related ventricular arrhythmias (12). There are no current exercise test criteria for pacemaker implantation in patients with congenital complete atrioventricular block.

Wolff-Parkinson-White Syndrome

Wolff-Parkinson-White syndrome may be a source of difficulty in the interpretation of ST segments. Exercise-induced supraventricular tachycardia may be more frequent in children with this syndrome than in adults, but it is still uncommon. Exercise testing has been used to identify children with a long antegrade effective refractory period of the accessory connection (9). The antegrade effective refractory period during exercise has limited value in predicting the shortest RR in atrial flutter, however, and cannot be used as the sole criterion for decisions about therapy for patients with Wolff-Parkinson-White syndrome (44).

Supraventricular Tachycardia

Most children with paroxysmal supraventricular tachycardia (SVT) do not have exercise-induced tachycardia. Therefore, clinicians are not reassured when exercise testing fails to produce tachycardia in a child whose history suggests SVT. However, exercise testing may be a useful adjunct in the evaluation or follow-up of some children suspected to have SVT. A study of 23 children with SVT, identified from exercise testing, found that 8 of the children had no previous record of tachycardia (11). Exercise testing of 56 patients referred with palpitations in a one-year period identified SVT in only 2 patients. The efficiency and cost-effectiveness of exercise testing in evaluating patients with suspected SVT have not been prospectively compared to other noninvasive diagnostic approaches such as transtelephonic telemetry. In only one third of the patients in which exercise testing identifies SVT does the tachycardia develop during exercise; in two thirds the tachycardia begins in the postexercise period. The substrates for exercise-induced SVT are diverse. Half of the children with exercise-induced SVT have an accessory connection (either Wolff-Parkinson-White syndrome or a unidirectional retrograde accessory pathway). Atrial ectopic tachycardia, atrial muscle reentry, and atrioventricular node reentry tachycardia may be induced with exercise (12). Exercise may change the rate of atrioventricular conduction in the setting of atrial flutter or atrial fibrillation.

Ventricular Tachycardia

Alpert et al. reported ventricular tachycardia with exercise in 3 children who did not show ventricular tachycardia on a 24-hr ambulatory electrocardiography (1). Ventricular tachycardia with exercise resolved on subsequent testing in 2 of the children who were treated with propranolol. Exercise testing may be of value in diagnosing ventricular tachycardia and is useful in testing the efficacy of treatment.

Exercise testing is more likely to precipitate ventricular tachycardia in patients with chronic recurrent ventricular tachycardia and a structurally normal heart than in patients with ventricular tachycardia who have an underlying cardiac disease (35). In a review of 18 children with ventricular tachycardia and a structurally normal heart, Noh et al. found ventricular tachycardia with exercise in 7 of the 14 children in whom testing could be performed (45).

Conclusion

As with adults, electrocardiographic monitoring is an essential component of the pediatric exercise test. Heart rate responses provide information regarding sinus node function and serve as a marker of exercise effort. Maximal heart rate does not change with age during the childhood years, but the rate at a given work load falls progressively with increasing age. Ischemic ST changes during exercise can provide valuable information regarding severity of aortic outflow obstruction and coronary artery anomalies, but criteria for ischemia and the clinical interpretation of ST changes in children have not been clearly established. Changes in the electrocardiographic intervals, QRS voltage, and QRS axis can be assessed during exercise testing of children, but these measures have little diagnostic value. Exercise testing can be useful in the provocation of tachyarrhythmias, particularly those that are ventricular in origin. Testing may serve as an effective diagnostic tool in patients with palpitations, dizziness, or syncope during exercise and is a useful means of assessing response of exercise-induced arrhythmias to drug therapy.

References

1. Alpert, B.S., J. Boineau, and W.B. Strong. Exercise-induced ventricular tachycardia. *Pediatr. Cardiol.* 2:51-55, 1982.
2. Alpert, B.S., P.A. Gilman, W.B. Strong, M.F. Ellison, M.D. Miller, J. McFarlane, and T. Hayashidera. Hemodynamic and ECG responses to exercise in children with sickle cell anemia. *Am. J. Dis. Child.* 135:362-366, 1981.
3. Barton, C.W., B. Katz, M.A. Schork, and A. Rosenthal. Value of treadmill exercise test in pre- and postoperative children with valvular aortic stenosis. *Clin. Cardiol.* 6:473-477, 1983.
4. Blomqvist, G.C. The Frank lead exercise electrocardiogram: Quantitative study based on averaging technical and digital computer analysis. *Acta Med. Scand.* 178(Suppl. 440):1-110, 1975.
5. Bonoris, P.E., P.S. Greenberg, M.J. Castellanet, and M.H. Ellestad. Significance of changes in R wave amplitude during treadmill stress testing: Angiographic correlation. *Am. J. Cardiol.* 41:846-851, 1978.
6. Bricker J.T., A. Garson, Jr., and P.C. Gillette. A family history of seizures associated with sudden cardiac deaths. *Am. J. Dis. Child.* 138:866-868, 1984.
7. Bricker, J.T., A. Garson, Jr., S.M. Paridon, and T.A. Vargo. Exercise correlates of electrophysiologic assessment of sinus node function in young individuals. *Pediatr. Exerc. Sci.* 2:163-168, 1990.
8. Bricker, J.T., A. Garson, Jr., M.S. Traweek, R.T. Smith, K.A. Ward, T.A. Vargo, and P.C. Gillette. The use of exercise testing in children to evaluate abnormalities of pacemaker function not apparent at rest. *PACE* 8:656-660, 1985.
9. Bricker, J.T., C.J. Porter, A. Garson, Jr., P.C. Gillette, P. McVey, M. Traweek, and D.G. McNamara. Exercise testing in children with the Wolff-Parkinson-White syndrome. *Am. J. Cardiol.* 55:1001-1004, 1985.
10. Bricker, J.T., M.S. Traweek, D.A. Danford, T.A. Vargo, and A. Garson, Jr. Exercise related bundle branch block in children. *Am. J. Cardiol.* 56:796-797, 1985.
11. Bricker, J.T., M.S. Traweek, R.T. Smith, K.A. Ward, T.A. Vargo, and A. Garson, Jr. SVT during exercise testing in children. In: *Abstracts of the 2nd World Congress of Pediatric Cardiology*, June 1985. New York: Springer-Verlag, 1985, p. 107.
12. Bricker, J.T., and T.A. Vargo. Advances in exercise testing. In: *Pediatric Cardiology: Its Current Practice*, J.T. Bricker and D.G. McNamara (Eds.). London: Edward Arnold, 1988, pp. 99-111.
13. Bricker, J.T., K.A. Ward, A. Zinner, and P.C. Gillette. Decrease in canine endocardial and epicardial electrogram voltages with exercise: Implications for pacemaker sensing. *PACE* 11:460-464, 1988.

14. Chandramouli, B., D.A. Ehmke, and R.M. Lauer. Exercise-induced electrocardiographic changes in children with congenital aortic stenosis. *J. Pediatr.* 87:725-730, 1975.
15. Christiansen, J.L., and W.B. Strong. Exercise testing (Part 4. Noninvasive diagnostic methods, Chapter 4). In: *Heart Disease in Infants, Children, and Adolescents* (4th Ed.), F.H. Adams, G.C. Emmanouilides, and T.A. Riemenschneider (Eds). Baltimore: Williams & Wilkens, 1989, pp. 93-106.
16. Christison, G.W., P.E. Bonoris, P.S. Greenberg, M.J. Castellanet, and M.H. Ellestad. Predicting coronary artery disease with treadmill stress testing: Changes in R-wave amplitude compared with ST segment depression. *J. Electrocardiol.* 12:179-185, 1979.
17. Chung, E.K. Interpretation of the exercise ECG test. In: *Exercise Electrocardiography: A Practical Approach* (2nd Ed.), E.K. Chung (Ed.). Baltimore: Williams & Wilkens, 1983, pp. 164-226.
18. Condo, C., M. Hiroe, T. Nakanishi, and A. Takao. Detection of coronary artery stenosis in children with Kawasaki disease: Usefulness of pharmacologic stress 201T1 myocardial tomography. *Circulation* 80:615-624, 1989.
19. Ellestad, M.H. *Stress Testing: Principles and Practice.* Philadelphia: Davis, 1975.
20. Falkner, B., D.T. Fowenthal, M.B. Affrime, and F. Harriston. Changes in R wave amplitude during aerobic exercise stress testing in hypertensive adolescents. *Am. J. Cardiol.* 50:152-156, 1982.
21. Fernhall, B., L.N. Burkett, and S.C. Walters. The effect of training on exercise-induced R-wave amplitude changes in young females. *Med. Sci. Sports.* 18:128-140, 1986.
22. Fisch, C., D.P. Zipes, and P.L. McHenry. Rate dependent aberrancy. *Circulation* 48:714-724, 1973.
23. Fisher, D.J., D.M. Gross, and A. Garson, Jr. Rapid sinus tachycardia: Differentiation from supraventricular tachycardia. *Am. J. Dis. Child.* 137:164-166, 1983.
24. Foster, C., J.D. Anholm, C.K. Hellman, J. Carpenter, M.L. Pollock, and D.H. Schmidt. Left ventricular function during sudden strenuous exercise. *Circulation* 63:592-596, 1981.
25. Fournier, A. Basic science aspects of the electrocardiogram. In: *The Science and Practice of Pediatric Cardiology*, A. Garson, Jr., J.T. Bricker, and D.G. McNamara (Eds.). Philadelphia: Lea & Febiger, 1990, pp. 500-523.
26. Friedman, R.A., J.P. Moak, and A. Garson, Jr. Clinical course of idiopathic dilated cardiomyopathy in children. *J. Am. Coll. Cardiol.* 18:152-156, 1991.
27. Furlanello, F., R. Bettini, A. Bertoldi, G. Vergara, L. Visona, G.B. Durante, G. Inama, L. Frisano, R. Antolini, and D. Zanuttini. Arrhythmia

patterns in athletes with arrhythmogenic right ventricular dysplasia. *Eur. Heart J.* 10(Suppl. D):16-19, 1989.

28. Garson, A., Jr., P.C. Gillette, and H.P. Gutgesell. Stress-induced ventricular arrhythmia after repair of tetralogy of Fallot. *Am. J. Cardiol.* 46:1006-1012, 1980.

29. Goforth, D., F.W. James, S. Kaplan, R. Donner, and W. Mays. Maximal exercise in children with aortic regurgitation: An adjunct to noninvasive assessment of disease severity. *Am. Heart J.* 108:1306-1311, 1984.

30. Greenberg, P.S., D.A. Friscia, and M.H. Ellestad. Predictive accuracy of QX/QT ratio, Q-Tc interval, ST depression and R wave amplitude during stress testing. *Am. J. Cardiol.* 44:18-23, 1979.

31. Haissaguerre, M., P. Le Metayer, C. D'Ivernois, J.L. Barat, P. Montserrat, and J.F. Warin. Distinctive response of arrhythmogenic right ventricular disease to high dose isoproterenol. *PACE* 13:2119-2126, 1990.

32. Hakki, A., A.S. Iskandrian, S. Kutalek, T.W. Hare, and N.M. Sokoloff. R wave amplitude: A new determinant of failure of patients with coronary heart disease to manifest ST segment depression during exercise. *J. Am. Coll. Cardiol.* 3:1155-1160, 1984.

33. Hesslein, P.S., H.P. Gutgesell, P.C. Gillette, and D.G. McNamara. Exercise assessment of sinoatrial node function following the Mustard operation. *Am. Heart J.* 103:351-357, 1982.

34. Hofmann, T., T. Meinertz, W. Kasper, A. Geibel, M. Zehander, S. Hohnloser, U. Steinen, N. Treese, and H. Just. Mode of death in idiopathic dilated cardiomyopathy: A multivariate analysis of prognostic determinants. *Am. Heart J.* 116:1455-1463, 1988.

35. Ino, T. Clinical characteristics of chronic recurrent ventricular tachycardia. *Nippon Ika Diagaku Zasshi* 56:267-280, 1989.

36. Jacobsen, J.R., A. Garson, Jr., P.C. Gillette, and D.G. McNamara. Premature ventricular contractions in normal children. *J. Pediatr.* 92:36-38, 1978.

37. James, F.W. Exercise ECG test in children. In: *Exercise Electrocardiography: A Practical Approach* (2nd Ed.), E.K. Chung (Ed.). Baltimore: Williams & Wilkens, 1983, pp. 132-154.

38. James, F.W., G. Blomqvist, M.D. Freed, W.W. Miller, J.H. Moller, E.W. Nugent, D.A. Riopel, W.B. Strong, and H.U. Wessel. Standards for exercise testing in the pediatric age group. *Circulation* 66:1378A-1397A, 1982.

39. Kugler, J.D. Sinus nodal dysfunction in young patients with long QT syndrome. *Am. Heart J.* 121:1132-1136, 1991.

40. Kveselis, D.A., A.P. Rocchini, A. Rosenthal, D.C. Crowley, M. Dick, A.R. Snider, and C. Moorehead. Hemodynamic determinants of exercise-induced ST-segment depression in children with valvar aortic stenosis. *Am. J. Cardiol.* 55:1133-1139, 1985.

41. Matthews, R.A., F.J. Fricker, L.B. Beerman, R.J. Stephenson, D.R. Fischer, W.H. Neches, S.C. Park, C.C. Lenox, and J.R. Zuberbuhler.

Exercise studies after the Mustard operation in transposition of the great arteries. *Am. J. Cardiol.* 51:1526-1529, 1983.

42. McArthur, P.D., B.A. Ross, J.T. Bricker, P.C. Gillette, and A. Garson, Jr. Exercise-induced changes in QTc in diagnosing long QT syndrome. *Pediatr. Res.* 23:222A, 1988.

43. McKenna, W.J., S. Chetty, C.M. Oakley, and J.M. Goodwin. Arrhythmia in hypertrophic cardiomyopathy: Exercise and 48 hour ambulatory electrocardiographic assessment with and without beta adrenergic blocking therapy. *Am. J. Cardiol.* 45:1-5, 1980.

44. Neish, S.R., R.A. Friedman, and J.T. Bricker. Exercise evaluation of patients with arrhythmias. *Pediatr. Exerc. Sci.* 3:230-284, 1990.

45. Noh, C.I., P.C. Gillette, C.L. Case, and V.L. Zeigler. Clinical and electrophysiologic characteristics of ventricular tachycardia in children with normal hearts. *Am. Heart J.* 120:1326-1333, 1990.

46. O'Brien, J.J., G. Barber, C.T. Heise, C.S. Tanner, and V.L. Vetter. Effects of position and exercise on the QT interval in children. *J. Am. Coll. Cardiol.* 13:171A, 1989.

47. O'Gara, P.T., R.O. Bonow, B.J. Maron, and S.E. Epstein. Myocardial perfusion abnormalities in patients with hypertrophic cardiomyopathy: Assessment with thallium-201 emission computed tomography. *Circulation* 76:1214-1223, 1987.

48. Paridon, S.M., and J.T. Bricker. Quantitative QRS changes with exercise in children and adolescents. *Med. Sci. Sports Exerc.* 22:159-164, 1990.

49. Paridon, S.M., Z.Q. Farooki, L.R. Kuhns, E. Arciniegas, and W.W. Pinsky. Exercise performance after repair of anomalous origin of the left coronary artery from the pulmonary artery. *Circulation* 81:1287-1292, 1990.

50. Paridon, S.M., R.A. Humes, and W.W. Pinsky. The role of chronotropic impairment during exercise after the Mustard operation. *J. Am. Coll. Cardiol.* 17:729-732, 1991.

51. Paridon, S.M., R.D. Ross, L.R. Kuhns, and W.W. Pinsky. Myocardial performance and perfusion during exercise in patients with coronary artery disease caused by Kawasaki disease. *J. Pediatr.* 116:52-56, 1990.

52. Pipberger, H.V., R.C. Arzbaecher, A.S. Berson, S.A. Briller, D.A. Brody, N.C. Flowers, D.B. Geselowitz, E. Lepeschkin, G.C. Oliver, O.H. Schmitt, and M. Spach. Recommendations for standardization of leads and of specifications for instruments in electrocardiography and vectorcardiography (Report of the Committee on Electrocardiography, American Heart Association; News from the American Heart Association). *Circulation* 52:11-31, 1975.

53. Rossi, P.A. Arrhythmogenic right ventricular dysplasia: Clinical features. *Eur. Heart J.* 10(Suppl. D):7-9, 1989.

54. Rowe, D.W., A. Alonzo, C.M. deCastro, E. Garcia, and R.J. Hall. The value of electrocardiographic R-wave changes in exercise testing: Preexercise versus postexercise measurement. *Bull. Tex. Heart Inst.* 8:333-343, 1981.

55. Sandberg, L. Studies on electrocardiographic changes during exercise tests. *Acta Med. Scand.* 170(Suppl. 365):1-113, 1961.
56. Sapin, P.M., G. Koch, M.B. Blauwet, J.J. McCarthy, S.W. Hinds, and L.S. Gettes. Identification of false positive exercise tests with use of electrocardiographic criteria: A possible role for atrial repolarization waves. *J. Am. Coll. Cardiol.* 18:127-135, 1991.
57. Sheffield, L.T. Computer-aided electrocardiography. *J. Am. Coll. Cardiol.* 10:448-455, 1987.
58. Simoons, M.L., and P.G. Hugenholz. Gradual changes of ECG waveform during and after exercise in normal subjects. *Circulation* 52:570-577, 1975.
59. Sketch, M.H., A.N. Mooss, M.L. Butler, C.K. Nair, and S.M. Mohiuddin. Digoxin-induced positive exercise tests: Their clinical and prognostic significance. *Am. J. Cardiol.* 48:655-659, 1981.
60. Suzuki, A., T. Kamiya, Y. Ono, M. Okuno, and T. Yagahara. Aortocoronary bypass surgery for coronary arterial lesions resulting from Kawasaki disease. *J. Pediatr.* 116:567-573, 1990.
61. Thapar, M.K., W.B. Strong, M.D. Miller, L. Leatherbury, and M. Salehbhai. Exercise electrocardiography of healthy black children. *Am. J. Dis. Child.* 132:592-595, 1978.
62. Towbin, J.A. Myocardial infarction in childhood. In: *The Science and Practice of Pediatric Cardiology*, A. Garson, Jr., J.T. Bricker, and D.G. McNarara (Eds.). Philadelphia: Lea & Febiger, 1990, pp. 1684-1722.
63. Traweek, M.S., J.T. Bricker, P. McVey, C.J. Porter, T.A. Vargo, K. Ward, and G.H. Hartung. Electrocardiographic changes with hyperventilation in children [abstract]. *Med. Sci. Sports Excer.* 16:158, 1984.
64. Weintraub, R.G., R.B. Gow, and J.L. Wilkinson. The congenital long QT syndromes in childhood. *J. Am. Coll. Cardiol.* 16:674-680, 1990.
65. Whitmer, J.T., F.W. James, S. Kaplan, D.C. Schwartz, and M.J.S. Knight. Exercise testing in children before and after treatment of aortic stenosis. *Circulation* 63:254-263, 1981.
66. Wiles, H.B., J.T. Bricker, and D.G. McNamara. Treadmill exercise testing in patients with anomalous left coronary artery from the pulmonary artery. In: *Abstracts of the 2nd World Congress of Pediatric Cardiology*. New York: Springer-Verlag, 1985, p. 117.
67. Wiles, H.B., D.S. Buckles, and V.L. Zeigler. *Noninvasive Diagnostic Techniques In Pediatric Arrhythmias: Electrophysiology and Pacing*, P.C. Gillette and A. Garson, Jr. (Eds.). Philadelphia: Saunders, 1990, pp. 205-215.
68. Winkler, R.B., M.D. Freed, and A.S. Nadas. Exercise-induced ventricular ectopy in children and young adults with complete heart block. *Am. Heart J.* 99:87-92, 1980.
69. Wright, S.A., A. Rosenthal, J. Bronberg, and A. Schork. R-wave amplitude changes during exercise in adolescents with left ventricular pressure and volume overload. *Am. J. Cardiol.* 52:841-846, 1983.

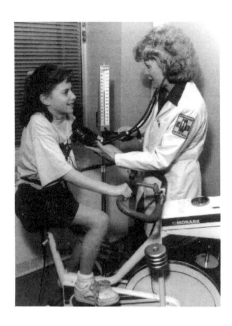

Blood Pressure Response to Dynamic Exercise

Bruce S. Alpert, MD
Mary E. Fox, MS
University of Tennessee, Memphis

Dynamic exercise causes increases in cardiac output and heart rate with simultaneous dilation of the systemic vascular bed. Because blood pressure is the product of cardiac output and resistance, the rise or fall of blood pressure may help to assess the integrity of myocardial contractility, chronotropic competence, and dilation of peripheral arterioles. For this reason, blood

The authors wish to thank Judy Adams for her editorial and secretarial assistance. We also thank the authors and publishers who consented to have portions of published material included in the figures and tables contained here.

pressure is measured routinely as a part of any dynamic stress test on either a cycle ergometer or a treadmill. The aims of this section are the following:

1. Review blood pressure data from published studies of healthy children with no disabilities
2. Note racial differences in maximal exercise blood pressure
3. Discuss the blood pressure response for patients with cardiac, pulmonary, or systemic diseases

Several issues will not be addressed: blood pressure response to submaximal exercise, blood pressure during isometric exercise, and prediction of future resting blood pressure from maximal exercise blood pressure values.

Technical Aspects
of Measurement of Blood Pressure

The technical aspects of exercise blood pressure measurement are critical. When blood pressure is measured, every effort must be made to ensure that the arm is stable and not involved in an isometric contraction. It is also essential for accurate measurement that the individual doing the assessment be experienced performing manual auscultation in children. Environmental noise from equipment (treadmills, monitors, fans, air conditioners, etc.) as well as the subject's respiration make auscultation of Korotkoff sounds very difficult. If a treadmill is used as the exercise stimulus, arm motion becomes a major variable as well, because on the cycle no pendulum-like reciprocal motion is used. Whether using a treadmill or cycle ergometer, the blood pressure cuff must be wrapped and usually taped in place to avoid slippage.

Arm motion can be reduced in various ways. If the child is undergoing testing on a treadmill, the arm can be steadied by the person measuring the blood pressure. (By lightly taping the stethoscope head over the brachial artery before the study begins, the tester will have a hand free to reduce arm motion.)

The use of a cycle ergometer makes the measurement of blood pressure significantly easier: The observer does not have to "chase" the child up and down the treadmill to obtain blood pressure, and the arm may be supported by a cradle or the tester during blood pressure measurement. A device developed at the Medical College of Georgia by William Strong, MD, has proved to be very useful in this regard. A U-shaped metal trough is attached to an intravenous pole so that it can be set at variable heights. When it is time for a blood pressure reading, the child places the arm into the support, allowing the tester the use of both hands to perform each reading.

Several automated systems have been commercially available for measuring exercise blood pressure. In one study (2), Alpert et al. compared an automated system (Critikon 1165; no longer manufactured) to a single observer (a 2nd-year fellow in pediatric cardiology). There were excellent correlations between the automated system and the observer for systolic blood pressure and acceptable values for the comparisons of diastolic blood pressure. Some laboratories prefer to use an automated system because it has no terminal digit preference and is consistent from day to day. The amount of change from one observer to another during serial testing of the same subject probably exceeds the inaccuracies of the automated system. Algorithms for measuring Korotkoff sounds that involve the differential subtraction of sounds recorded by the microphone on the artery rather than an external microphone may be more accurate than the human ear. Because some frequency components of the Korotkoff sounds are at the lower end of the human ear frequency response, the automated system may have another inherent advantage.

In short, if the measurement of exercise blood pressure is a critical variable, such as in the long-term follow-up of patients with coarctation, a cycle ergometer protocol allows measurements to be taken with more technical ease. If the observer is likely to change from year to year, then an automated system has advantages as well.

Physiology of Blood Pressure Response

The circulatory changes from rest to exercise are complex and are not within the realm of this section. Several features, however, are of importance. The heart rate elevation that occurs with exercise, as well as the increase in ejection fraction, leads to an augmentation of cardiac output and stroke volume. From rest to maximal exercise, cardiac output increases three- to fivefold. This increase is needed to deliver oxygen to the exercising muscle mass. Because blood pressure is the product of cardiac output and peripheral resistance, the response of the peripheral vascular bed is also of importance. During exercise, there is a dramatic dilation of the peripheral vascular bed, which results in a reduction of resistance. The increase in cardiac output leads to an increase in systolic pressure, whereas the vasodilation allows the diastolic pressure to remain largely unchanged. Increasing exercise intensity calls for increased O_2 consumption and cardiac output, so blood pressure rises with each progressive stage of an exercise protocol.

It is widely held (9) that "a lack of increase or a decrease in systolic pressure below the normal resting level indicates serious impairment of cardiac performance" and that a fall in blood pressure during progressively increasing work loads is also a significant sign of myocardial failure or severe aortic stenosis. In a review of 1,730 maximal cycle ergometer tests performed in one laboratory, Alpert et al. (8) reported 6 patients in whom systolic blood pressure decreased at least 10 mmHg during progressive exercise stages. Of these 6 patients, 4 were asymptomatic. The diagnoses of the 2 symptomatic adolescents were mitral and aortic regurgitation in a 12-year-old who became dizzy immediately following exercise and a similar phenomenon in a 20-year-old with an atrial septal defect and small ventricular septal defect. The electrocardiogram on each failed to show ischemia or a dysrhythmia. The only patient to show ischemia on an exercise electrocardiogram was an 11-year-old with atrial tachycardia and mitral valve prolapse who remained asymptomatic and in sinus rhythm. Thus, none of the 6 patients whose exercise systolic blood pressure showed a decrease had an important complication. Therefore, decreases in systolic blood pressure during exercise progression are not uniformly indicative of severe dysfunction and may be seen in patients who are not in danger. A decrease in systolic blood pressure, however, is not necessarily benign, and a decline below resting levels is clearly significant. If cardiac output falls or remains the same, oxygen delivery may not be able to rise, and the child's ability to exercise will be impaired.

Healthy Control Subjects

Several studies have included the measurement of exercise blood pressure. It is of interest that Godfrey, in his classic monograph from 1974 (21), did not mention blood pressure response to exercise in any study of healthy subjects or of patients with either pulmonary or cardiac disease.

Riopel et al. were the first to report systolic and diastolic blood pressure data from large groups of healthy children (31). They studied 279 healthy 4- to 21-year-olds (119 white males, 50 black males, 66 white females, and 44 black females) during treadmill stress testing. The children were divided into four groups by body surface area. Results were reported separately for male, female, black, and white, and several black-white, male-female differences were noted. The study found that the largest increase in systolic blood pressure occurred during the first minute of exercise, with a more gradual increase occurring with each subsequent minute. (See Figure 1 and Tables 1 and 2.) There was a progressively higher systolic blood pressure value with increasing body surface area, whereas diastolic blood pressure remained unchanged or decreased slightly. Pulse pressure was greater in larger subjects at maximal exercise.

James et al. (24) studied 149 healthy subjects (95% white), 5 to 33 years of age. Ninety males and 59 females underwent maximal cycle ergometer stress testing. The subjects were stratified by body surface area divisions (less than 1 m^2, 1 to 1.19 m^2, and greater than 1.2 m^2). Maximal systolic blood pressure was positively correlated with body size and age. Maximal diastolic blood pressure increased up to 14% above the value obtained preexercise while sitting. These results are in contrast to the data obtained by Riopel (31), discussed earlier in this section.

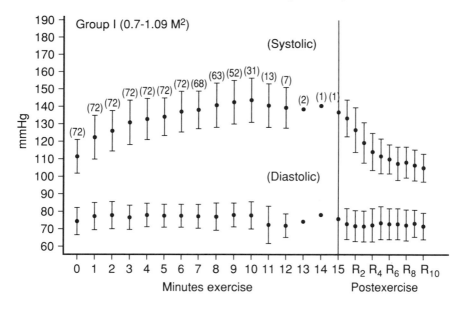

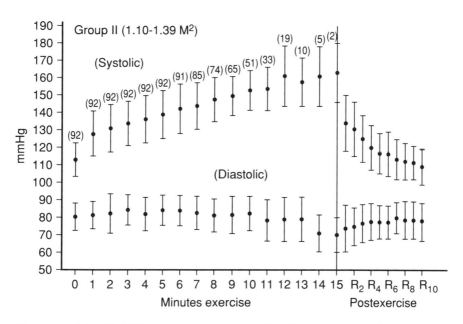

Figure 1: Mean (± 1 *SD*) systolic (top data) and diastolic (bottom data) blood pressures at each minute during and after exercise in the four groups. Numbers in parentheses indicate the number of subjects exercising at that minute. R_2 through R_{10} indicate values obtained during the 10-min postexercise period. *Note.* From D.A. Riopel, A.B. Taylor, and R.A. Hohen, 1979, p. 700 (31). Copyright 1979 by The Yorke Medical Group. Reprinted by permission.

(Cont.)

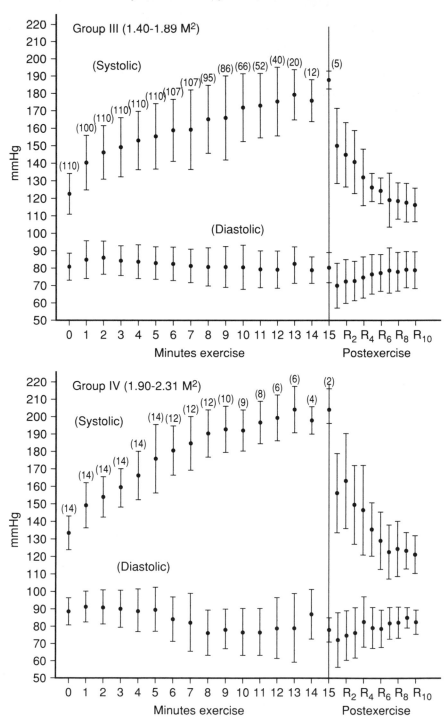

Figure 1: (Continued)

Table 1   Systolic Blood Pressure (mmHg ± 1 Standard Deviation)

	Group I		Group II		Group III		Group IV	
	W	B	W	B	W	B	W	B
Boys								
No.	(28)	(15)	(41)	(19)	(44)	(19)	(6)	(6)
Pre ex	107± 9	121±12	108±12	113± 8	118±13	124±11	128± 5	119±10
1 min ex	121±12	129±16	121±14	131± 9	137±17	139±11	150±10	146±14
Peak ex	142±16	145±16	145±15	154±17	171±22	181±16	206± 9	200±22
Girls								
No.	(19)	(10)	(21)	(11)	(25)	(22)	(1)	(1)
Pre ex	110± 9	113±13	106±12	112±11	112±10	118± 7	124	100
1 min ex	123±11	123±13	122±14	128±15	126±14	141±17	150	122
Peak ex	147±12	145±14	145±13	154±24	155±14	161±20	184	140

$*p < 0.05$. $†p < 0.02$. $‡p < 0.01$. $§p < 0.005$. B = black. No. = number of subjects. 1 min ex = 1 minute of exercise. Peak ex = peak exercise. Pre ex = before exercise. W = white.

Note. From "Blood pressure, heart rate, pressure-rate product and electrocardiographic changes in healthy children during treadmill exercise" by D.A. Riopel, B.A. Taylor, and R.A. Hohen. *Am. J. Cardiol.* 44:701, 1979. Copyright 1979 by The Yorke Medical Group. Reprinted by permission.

The maximal systolic blood pressure for the upper 2.5% of James's total population ranged from 234 to 254 mmHg. No stated complications occurred in these subjects, whose systolic blood pressure exceeded 230 mmHg. The maximal systolic blood pressure value was related to both power output and resting systolic blood pressure. James et al. speculated that there may have been differences in stroke volume, systemic vascular resistance, and duration of left ventricular ejection that interacted to produce high levels of exercise systolic blood pressure.

Alpert et al. tested 405 healthy children (221 whites and 184 blacks) ages 6 to 15 (3). The protocol was performed on a mechanically braked cycle ergometer, with 3-min stages, to maximal voluntary effort. Statistical analyses yielded regression lines with confidence bands for the 5th, 25th, 50th, 75th, and 95th percentiles of systolic blood pressure (see Figure 2). Alpert et al. did not report diastolic blood pressure values because of technical problems with measuring diastolic blood pressure during exercise on a mechanical ergometer in a noisy environment and because the authors lacked confidence in the accuracy of the measurements of the fourth and fifth Korotkoff sounds (muffling and disappearance, respectively).

These nomogram plots allow the estimation of the maximal systolic blood pressure value (which occurs either during exercise or immediately post-exercise) in relation to the other exercise variables, such as heart rate, maximal

Table 2   Diastolic Blood Pressure (mmHg ± 1 Standard Deviation)

	Group I		Group II		Group III		Group IV	
	W	B	W	B	W	B	W	B
Boys								
No.	(28)	(15)	(41)	(19)	(44)	(19)	(6)	(6)
Pre ex	74±7	79±9	75±11	79±11	79± 9	85±10	85±9	80± 9
1 min ex	76±6	82±9	77± 9	81± 8	83±12	80± 4	86±9	85±10
Peak ex	85±7	85±7	84± 9	87± 9	77±12	84±11	95±8	87±11
Girls								
No.	(19)	(10)	(21)	(11)	(25)	(22)	(1)	(1)
Pre ex	71±9	77±5	76± 7	74± 8	78± 6	84± 7	92	96
1 min ex	74±9	82±4	79± 7	83±12	81± 9	89±11	96	92
Peak ex	79±7	83±4	84± 6	85±11	79±10	84±12	110	100

$*p < 0.05.$ $†p < 0.02.$ $‡p < 0.01.$ $§p < 0.005.$ B = black. No. = number of subjects. 1 min ex = 1 minute of exercise. Peak ex = peak exercise. Pre ex = before exercise. W = white.

Note. From "Hemodynamic responses to ergometer exercise in children and young adults with left ventricle pressure or volume overload" by B.S. Alpert, D.M. Moes, M.A. DuRant, W.B. Strong, and N.L. Flood. *Am. J. Cardiol.* 52:564. Copyright 1983 by The Yorke Medical Group. Reprinted by permission.

work rate, and peak working capacity index (work load per kilogram of body weight). The effort that the subject or patient puts forth is often judged by variables such as heart rate, work rate, or oxygen consumption. If a patient with aortic stenosis achieves a 25th percentile systolic blood pressure response with 75th percentile heart rate and working capacity, this may imply, for example, that the patient has a gradient severe enough to limit exercise blood pressure significantly. If a patient postoperative for coarctation of the aorta has a systolic blood pressure response in excess of the 95th percentile but only a 5th percentile working capacity, the clinician may consider recatheterization and possible balloon angioplasty or reoperation. Previous investigators (25, 34) expressed their data as mean and standard deviation, making prediction of expected individual responses cumbersome.

Another measure of data expression, such as $\dot{V}O_2$ divided by heart rate (oxygen pulse) or $\dot{V}O_2$ divided by systolic blood pressure, may allow detection of truly abnormal systolic blood pressure responses in clinical patients or research subjects. We await the publication of such investigations.

Figure 2 shows that systolic blood pressure response varies directly with body size (m^2 of surface area). (The findings on racial differences will be discussed later in this next section.) The nomograms demonstrate that maximal systolic blood pressure values greater than 220 mmHg are above the normal range for subjects with body surface area less than 2 m^2, confirming the

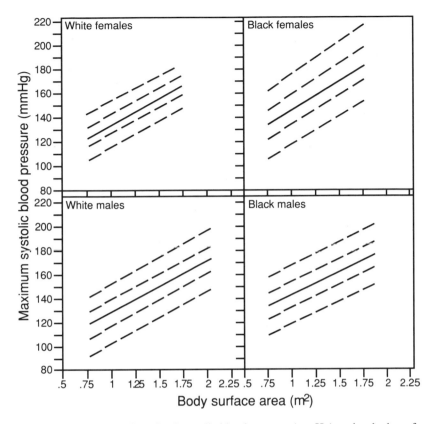

Figure 2: Nomograms of maximal systolic blood pressure (mmHg) against body surface area. Solid line represents 50th percentile of systolic blood pressure. Top line represents 95th percentile confidence band with dashed lines below representing 75th, 25th, and 5th percentile confidence bands. *Note*. From ''Responses to ergometry exercise in a healthy biracial population of children'' by B.S. Alpert, N.L. Flood, W.B. Strong, E.V. Dover, R.H. DuRant, A.M. Martin, and D.L. Booker, 1982, *J. Pediatr.*, 101:538. Copyright by Mosby-Year Book, Inc. Reprinted by permission.

treadmill data reported by Riopel et al. (31). James et al. (24) used a cycle ergometer and reported systolic blood pressure values that were higher than those of Alpert et al. (3). No explanation for this difference could be found. Alpert speculated that methodologic differences, the use of mechanically braked versus electronically braked ergometers, might explain this.

Washington et al. (35) reported data from cycle ergometer exercise using the protocol of James et al. (24) on 151 white children (70 girls and 81 boys) from ages 7-1/2 to 12-3/4. They used an automated apparatus to measure blood pressure, a technique previously validated by Alpert et al. (2) in a study of 121 children. They used the divisions of body surface area that had been described by James et al. (24). The data show a trend of increasing mean maximal systolic blood pressure from smaller to larger—122 to 130 to 139 mmHg in males and 126 to 131 to 142 mmHg in females—but no statistical significance of this trend was found. Maximal systolic blood pressure values did not exceed 183 mmHg in any child. The studies were performed at intermediate altitude (1,600 m) in Denver, CO; some of the values, such as $\dot{V}O_2$max, may have been limited because of this. The effect of altitude on exercise blood pressure could be tested either by having children at altitude (such as in Denver) breathe 21% oxygen at one atmospheric (760 mmHg) pressure through a face mask or by having children at sea level breathe 18% oxygen during exercise.

The values of maximal diastolic blood pressure obtained by Washington and his co-workers were invariably higher than the values obtained at rest for each child. This is in contrast to the report by Riopel et al. (31) that a majority of children decreased their diastolic blood pressure values. Washington considered a decrease in diastolic blood pressure during exercise "an abnormal response." This finding may relate to differences between treadmill and cycle ergometer exercise physiology or to technical differences in measurement of diastolic blood pressure. In addition, Riopel's study was performed at sea level, and Washington's at 1,600 m. The degree of hypoxia reached in Washington's subjects may have led to a difference in vasodilation during maximal exercise from that which occurs at sea level. These Denver children may have undergone a relative vasoconstriction, or a failure to vasodilate maximally, leading to the difference observed.

Wanne and Haapoja (34) performed maximal cycle ergometer studies on 497 healthy 9- to 18-year-old children. They reported data for systolic blood pressure at various submaximal heart rates, up to 170, and into recovery. Boys consistently demonstrated higher systolic blood pressure values than girls, and postpubertal boys had the highest systolic blood pressure values of any group. Diastolic blood pressure decreased significantly in every group tested, in sharp contrast to the findings of James et al. (24) and Washington et al. (35). Maximal systolic blood pressure values in excess of 200 mmHg were found in 22 subjects. Only 2 of these subjects had demonstrated elevated resting systolic blood pressure. Three of the 15-year-old males had maximal systolic blood pressure values of 240 mmHg at submaximal exercise. No complications were noted in these subjects.

In a review of studies of normotensive and hypertensive youths, Dlin (17) summarized data on children who had been trained by either dynamic or static exercise. He noted that highly trained adolescents had higher systolic blood pressure response values than untrained youths. Because training produces lower heart rates both at rest and during exercise, Dlin hypothesized that the higher blood pressures occurred because athletes can achieve higher work rates at equivalent heart rate values compared to untrained individuals and that these higher work rates lead to high systolic blood pressure.

Data are available for healthy children and adolescents for both systolic and diastolic blood pressure. Every study has shown that systolic blood pressure tends to increase with progressive work loads. The height of the systolic blood pressure response has been tabulated. No investigator has found absolute systolic blood pressure to be predictive of complications. We do not recommend that an exercise test be stopped because an arbitrary value of systolic blood pressure has been reached. There is no definite evidence of an intrinsic danger of a systolic blood pressure value of 230, 240, or 250 mmHg. We do, however, believe that systolic blood pressure must remain within a range that the tester can measure. If systolic blood pressure exceeds a measurable value, then there is adequate justification to stop the test.

The normal diastolic blood pressure response to exercise in children is not widely agreed upon. The investigations described previously in this section found varying and conflicting trends. It is highly unusual for children exercising on a treadmill to have significant increases in diastolic blood pressure. Diastolic blood pressure response during a cycle ergometer study or a treadmill protocol may be too difficult to determine and impossible to interpret.

Racial Differences in Systolic Blood Pressure Response

A series of studies from the Medical College of Georgia investigated differences between blacks and whites in responses to dynamic exercise testing. In the initial study, Alpert et al. (1) described racial differences among the 405 children discussed previously. They found no significant systolic blood pressure differences at rest between blacks and whites, but when the groups were compared by body surface area, blacks had significantly higher maximal systolic blood pressure values. These differences remained significant when the data for changes in systolic blood pressure from rest to exercise, or percent of this change, were compared. No published data, to our knowledge, have determined whether exercise blood pressure responses of black patients with cardiac disease differ from those of their white counterparts.

Treiber et al. (33) replicated the finding by Alpert et al. Black children ages 4 to 6 had higher exercise systolic blood pressures than did whites. Treiber et al. discussed these findings with respect to prediction of essential hypertension. It seems important that clinicians testing children with diseases should be able to compare the data to those of healthy children of the same race (as well as possibly gender, stage of development, altitude, etc.). We are unaware of data for large populations of Hispanics, Orientals, and other groups for use in clinical pediatrics.

Arensman et al. (11) found that, in a population of 10-year-old boys, whites demonstrated higher cardiac output responses to exercise (supine) and blacks had greater systemic vascular resistance. The height of exercise systolic blood presure has been shown in adults to be highly predictive as a marker for later-onset essential hypertension. Mechanisms of exercise response in a biracial population of children must be considered.

Because sickle cell anemia occurs primarily in blacks, we will discuss the limited data available for children with sickle cell anemia next. Alpert et al. compared data from 47 children ages 5 to 18 with data from 170 healthy, black, age-matched controls (4). All patients with sickle cell anemia had lower values of systolic blood pressure and work rate than did the control subjects. Patients who demonstrated ischemia on the exercise electrocardiogram, and males in general, had the lowest exercise systolic blood pressure responses. The degree of impairment was directly correlated to the hemoglobin value.

In a similar, more recent study, McConnell et al. reported systolic blood pressure responses from 43 patients with sickle cell anemia (29). Systolic blood pressure responses in sickle cell anemia patients who showed ST-segment depression to cycle ergometer exercise were higher than that in sickle cell anemia patients who did not. No comparisons with healthy subjects were performed. Only patients with hemoglobin values below 8.5 g/dl had ST-segment depression. The mechanism of the comparatively higher systolic blood pressure in the presence of myocardial ischemia is unknown.

Congenital Heart Disease

Virtually all data on exercise blood pressure in children have been collected on patients with congenital heart disease. The types of congenital heart disease may be categorized as obstructive (pressure overload), left-to-right shunt, cyanotic, and volume overload. Most data available relate either to coarctation of the aorta or to the Fontan procedure.

Left Ventricular Pressure or Volume Overload

It is widely believed that as aortic valve (or subvalve or supravalve) stenosis becomes more severe, the systolic blood pressure response to exercise reduces significantly. Alpert et al. (5) published data from 29 patients (19 males and 10 females) with aortic stenosis who were 11.8 ± 3.9 (SD) years of age. The maximal systolic blood pressure values in these patients in response to treadmill exercise were compared to data from 116 control subjects of comparable age (12.2 ± 3.6) and sex distribution (68 males, 48 females). Only 1 patient's exercise test was terminated prior to maximal voluntary effort because of ischemia. The increase from resting to maximal exercise (δ) was 30.3 mmHg in the patients with aortic stenosis, compared to the δ value in the controls of 43.1 mmHg ($p<.001$). A δ value of exercise systolic blood pressure greater than 35 mmHg was of excellent predictive value in patients with aortic stenosis. If a patient's systolic blood pressure rose by more than

35 mmHg during exercise, then the patient had only a 10% chance of having a catheterization gradient that exceeded 50 mmHg (i.e., the patient had a 10% chance of having moderate or severe aortic stenosis). Thus, the exercise responses of the patients with aortic stenosis were lower than the responses of the control subjects; the authors speculated that "blood pressure measurement during exercise may increase the clinician's ability to select for catheterization only those patients with aortic stenosis who are likely to require surgery."

Two reports from Cincinnati, Whitmer et al. (37) and James et al. (25), also addressed the patient with aortic stenosis, both pre- and postoperatively. Whitmer et al. reported results from cycle ergometer testing in 23 patients (19 males, 4 females) within 6 months before and 3 to 30 months after surgical intervention for valvar or discreet subvalvar aortic stenosis. The patients were 5 to 19 years of age (mean age was 10.7). In 16 patients with both pre- and postoperative systolic blood pressure responses to exercise, a significant increase ($p<.025$) was noted from a mean ($\pm$ SD) of 121 $\pm$ 22 mmHg to 143 $\pm$ 33 mmHg.

James et al. (25) studied only preoperative patients with valvular aortic stenosis or subvalvular aortic stenosis of varying severities. Sixty-five patients (52 males, 13 females) from 4 to 24 years of age (mean age was 12)—56 with valvular and 9 with subvalvular aortic stenosis—underwent cycle ergometer testing. For patients with the most severe aortic or subaortic stenosis, peak-exercise systolic blood pressure was lower than that of the control subjects ($p<.03$) and tended to be lowest in patients with the highest resting left ventricular-to-aortic pressure gradients. Systolic blood pressure decreased during exercise to levels below resting values in 32% of patients whose resting gradient was greater than 70 mmHg. These data are comparable to those published by Riopel et al. (30) in abstract form, in which severity of aortic stenosis was the prime determinant of exercise systolic blood pressure.

Alpert et al. (6) studied exercise responses in 137 patients with either left ventricular pressure or volume overload. There were 70 patients with aortic stenosis, 25 with coarctation, 20 with aortic regurgitation, and 22 with mitral regurgitation. Alpert et al. compared these patients to the 405 healthy control children discussed earlier in this section (3). The patients were 8 to 23 years old, with a mean age of 14 $\pm$ 4 years. (See Table 3 and Figure 3.)

For the aortic stenosis patients, maximal systolic blood pressure did not differ from the control subjects' values, despite reductions in both heart rate and work load achieved. In the 25 patients with coarctation, systolic blood pressure exceeded that in the control subjects; heart rate and work-load values were comparable.

The patients with aortic regurgitation also had maximal systolic blood pressure that exceeded the value predicted from control data. These patients' values were very close to those obtained in the patients with coarctation; the values exceeded those for both patients with aortic stenosis and patients with mitral regurgitation.

Table 3   Hemodynamic Indexes of Exercise

Diagnosis	Systolic blood pressure (mmHg)
Pressure overload	
Aortic stenosis	144 ± 26
White males	145 ± 27
White females	137 ± 20
Black males	176 ± 28
Black females	140 ± 14
Coarctation	188 ± 47†
White males	180 ± 48
White females	159 ± 55
Black males	216 ± 37
Volume overload	
Aortic regurgitation	189 ± 36†
White males	207 ± 15
Black males	200 ± 30
Black females	172 ± 41
Mitral regurgitation	154 ± 39
White males	165 ± 21
White females	119 ± 9
Black males	166 ± 46
Black females	141 ± 12

Note. All values are expressed as mean ± standard deviation.

†Significant difference from values in normal subjects, groups with aortic stenosis, and groups with myocardial infarction.

The physiology of the patients with coarctation and aortic regurgitation differed greatly, but their systolic blood pressure responses exceeded the normal response significantly. In the small number of subjects with mitral regurgitation, blood pressure responses did not differ from those of the control subjects.

Numerous manuscripts have noted that right arm systolic blood pressure response to exercise (in the absence of an anomalous right subclavian artery) is elevated in patients with coarctation of the aorta. Arm pressure is considered a direct reflection of central aortic pressure, a concept addressed as early as 1970 by Cumming and Mir (16). These authors studied the mechanical and possible hormonal variables that lead to both the arm (upper compartment) hypertension at rest and the exaggerated systolic blood pressure response to exercise. Propranolol was administered intravenously to patients and led to a reduction in systolic blood pressure by changes in cardiac output, heart rate, systolic ejection period, and increased systemic vascular resistance. Plasma renin was not measured in this study.

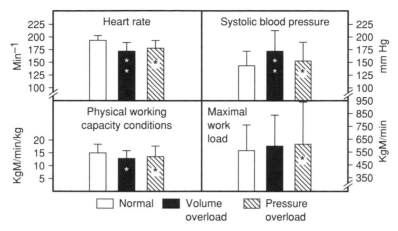

Figure 3: Plots of the 4 variables tested, showing the mean (± standard deviation) values (*$p < .05$ compared with control subjects; **$p < .05$ compared with control subjects and pressure overload groups). *Note.* From B.S. Alpert, D.M. Moes, M.A. DuRant, W.B. Strong, and N.L. Flood, 1983, p. 566 (6). Copyright 1983 by The Yorke Medical Group. Reprinted by permission.

Although James and Kaplan (23) performed only submaximal exercise tests, several of their patients with coarctation developed substantially elevated systolic blood pressure values. They studied 14 patients from 9 to 22 years of age who had undergone surgical repair of coarctation during childhood. Nine patients had maximal systolic blood pressures ranging from 212 to 270 mmHg. In 1 patient, diastolic blood pressure was elevated to 100 mmHg. The patients frequently had preexercise signs of significant recoarctation or residual coarctation. James and Kaplan stressed that preexisting vascular changes were responsible for the excessive systolic blood pressure response. These changes include those occurring in essential hypertension in peripheral arteries and a "minor obstruction" at the anastomotic site that may be "greatly aggravated during exercise." In two articles of critical importance in incorporating exercise blood pressure in the routine evaluation of patients with coarctation, Connor (14) and Connor and Baker (15) described the use of the arm-leg systolic blood pressure gradient as a measure of significant coarctation or residual (recurrent) coarctation. In the first article (14), Connor noted that an arm-leg gradient immediately following exercise that exceeded 35 mmHg suggested that recatheterization was indicated. The exercise study, by increasing cardiac output and reducing systemic vascular resistance, was able to unmask a fixed obstruction at the level of the coarctation or coarctation repair.

The concept of unmasking an obstruction is important. When an angiogram does not suggest that a significant coarctation is present, a patient may exhibit an exaggerated systolic blood pressure response to dynamic maximal exercise. The clinician may judge that a particular systolic blood pressure value (e.g.,

230 mmHg, 250 mmHg, 270 mmHg) may be too high for the patient and that additional intervention, either balloon angioplasty or surgery, may be warranted. The physician also may consider whether studies to define the presence or absence of cerebral aneurysms (Berry aneurysms) are indicated. We do not routinely perform these studies. To date, no data in healthy individuals exist (to the best of our knowledge) that could help determine whether any arbitrary systolic blood pressure level is of danger to any specific patient. In addition, the vascular changes of essential hypertension may already be significant and may progress relentlessly, despite adequate resection of the coarctation. The landmark study by Maron et al. (27) demonstrated without a doubt that hypertension in coarctation can have devastating consequences.

In the follow-up paper, Connor and Baker (15) compared the arm-leg systolic blood pressure gradient postexercise for a group of patients whose coarctation had been repaired using a Dacron patch angioplasty with that of 18 patients treated with end-to-end anastomosis (before the era of absorbable suture). The arm-leg gradient postexercise was 6.8 mmHg in the former group and 36.1 in the latter, despite very small blood pressure differences between the groups at rest. The technique of subclavian flap angioplasty was in use during this era, but too few patients were old enough to exercise to allow comparison of surgical data. In assessing series such as this, the clinician should be careful to define whether age at operation, age at exercise testing, and time since surgery are known so he or she can compare the results fully.

The Connor articles (14, 15) evaluated the utility of arm-leg gradients pre- to postexercise and found them to be of great use in the evaluation of patients for functional adequacy of repair.

At the same time as Connor's papers appeared, Freed et al. (20) reported data on exercise-induced systolic hypertension in 30 patients postrepair of coarctation who were then 6 to 30 years of age. The study used a Bruce treadmill protocol to voluntary exhaustion as the end point. Twenty patients with mild cardiac disease served as the control population. As expected, the patients with coarctation had higher postexercise systolic blood pressure than did the control patients ($p<.001$). The arm-leg difference in the coarctation patients increased from 10 mmHg at rest to 69 mmHg after exercise ($p<.001$). The arm systolic blood pressure value correlated highly ($r = .91$) with the arm-leg gradient; the authors suggested that the residual obstruction at the coarctation resection site formed a mechanical impediment to flow and thus caused the postexercise systolic blood pressure elevations in the arm. The authors recommended routine exercise testing in all patients after coarctation repair. In the patients whose arm systolic blood pressure exceeded 200 mmHg, catheterization was recommended to measure central aortic exercise systolic blood pressure. Freed and his colleagues recommended these studies to indicate whether further therapy such as reoperation, antihypertensive medications, or restriction of ''severe physical effort may be necessary'' (20).

Markel et al. (26) studied the effects of both arm and leg exercise in 28 children who had undergone repair of coarctation, 14 by end-to-end anastomosis and 14 by patch angioplasty. The patients were from 8 to 20 years of age (mean age was 13.8 ± 2.8), and surgery had been performed 4.1 ± 3.7 years (range was from 1 to 12) previously. The patients were divided by arm-leg gradients both at rest and immediately following exercise. Maximal systolic blood pressure after exercise was equivalent to control for the patients with no arm-leg gradient either pre- or postexercise. Systolic blood pressure was greatly increased, with mean values of 194 ± 28 and 196 ± 19 mmHg for the two groups with arm-leg gradients following exercise and those with resting gradients, respectively. Diastolic blood pressure values did not differ among the four groups. Market et al. concluded that patients with no arm-leg gradient at rest and systolic hypertension were very unlikely to have an operable recoarctation and should receive antihypertensive therapy or be limited from strenuous physical activity.

Smith and his co-workers at the Medical University of South Carolina (32) compared blood pressure at rest and during exercise in 50 patients who were postcoarctectomy. In 26 patients end-to-end anastomosis was used and in 24, synthetic patch aortoplasty. The patients and 20 control subjects underwent treadmill testing as described earlier in this section (31). Blood pressure was measured in the right arm. The systolic blood pressure mean was higher in the patients with end-to-end anastomosis than in those with patch aortoplasty. The arm-leg pressure difference was also greater in the former group. These data suggest that the patch aortoplasty was superior to end-to-end anastomosis in that institution's experience. Again, no exercise testing was available for patients with subclavian flap angioplasty. The long-term significance of higher systolic blood pressure responses to exercise is still undetermined.

The investigation by Earley et al. (19) contained data and implications that are contrary to the conclusions reached by all the authors whose work has been discussed in this section. Systolic blood pressure was measured at rest and during exercise in 43 children who had undergone coarctation surgery, 5 preoperative coarctation patients, and 22 control subjects. The patients' mean age was 7.6 years, with a range from 2 to 15 years. The exercise systolic blood pressure response tended to increase more in both the pre- and postoperative coarctation patients, but the wide range of variability noted made the trends nonsignificant. "Persistence of a gradient between upper and lower limb pressures did not affect the rise in blood pressure on exercise either, as the mean rise in blood pressure in the children with gradients was 21 mmHg," Earley et al. reported. Surprisingly, the increase in the preoperative group was only 25 mmHg, and in the postoperative group, 24 mmHg. The highest systolic blood pressure increases during exercise, 50 mmHg and 80 mmHg, were reported in 1 normotensive patient and 1 hypertensive patient (the paper does not state which was which). Earley et al. did not find the exercise test helpful in assessing the severity of the coarctation in this young population. There was, in addition, no relationship between the presence of resting systolic hypertension and age at operation. There was a significant difference ($p<.01$) for time since operation, 53 ± 30 months in the hypertensive children, compared to the normotensive ones, 80 ± 37 months. The authors queried whether there might be some value in detecting subjects who are, at most, mildly hypertensive at rest and have very high blood pressure values with exercise.

The utility of exercise blood pressure data in the clinical management of patients with coarctation was studied by Zellers and Driscoll (38). The investigators mailed questionnaires to 80 randomly selected pediatric cardiologists. Forty-nine questionnaires were returned. The clinicians were presented with four scenarios relating to level of arm exercise blood pressure and arm-leg gradient. A majority of the responding clinicians (60%) recommended intervention, either surgery or balloon angioplasty, if the arm-leg gradient was 60 mmHg, but only 2% recommended intervention if the arm-leg gradient was only 15 mmHg. Thirty percent recommended intervention for a maximal arm blood pressure of 280 mmHg and a 15-mmHg arm-leg gradient. Why these clinicians suspected significant recoarctation in the presence of a minimal gradient is unclear. What is more unclear, however, is why 6% of clinicians presented with a scenario of maximal systolic pressure of 280 mmHg and a 60-mmHg arm-leg gradient did not recommend intervention. No explanation is possible from the data gathered.

From the studies presented, it appears that the systolic blood pressure value, as well as the arm-leg gradient, is of use for clinicians seeking to define whether a residual or recoarctation is present. Insufficient long-term prospective data are available to determine the utility of exercise blood pressure measurement in predicting subsequent blood pressure, morbidity, or mortality. Because of the success of balloon angioplasty for the "nonoperative" relief of coarctation, the authors assume that exercise blood pressure measurement will be used more in the future.

Systemic Hypertension

Dlin (17) reviewed exercise data from hypertensive youth, reviewed the literature, and summarized blood pressure findings. Most reports suggest that hypertensive adolescents have higher exercise systolic blood pressure than their normotensive counterparts but no difference in the pre- to postexercise change value. No data suggest that exercise is of harm in hypertensive youth; several studies suggest that systolic blood pressure is reduced following aerobic training (17).

Exercise Blood Pressure Response
With Other Congenital Cardiac Defects

Barber et al. (12) studied 14 patients with Ebstein's anomaly who ranged in age from 7 to 23 years (mean age was 14). Blood pressure was measured with an automated system (Narco). The patients exercised on an electronically braked cycle ergometer using the James protocol. Data were compared to those obtained in 22 control subjects in Barber's laboratory and the data of James et al. (24). Systolic blood pressure and diastolic blood pressure at rest did not differ from control values. The systolic blood pressure at maximal exercise reached from 65% to 95% of predicted normal values. For a group, this was significantly less than normal ($p<.001$). The diastolic blood pressure values did not differ from the control subjects' values. The maximal heart rate values of the patients with Ebstein's anomaly were also substantially reduced, so the blood pressure response may be the result of either reduced stroke volume or systemic vascular resistance.

Barber and his co-workers (13) at the Mayo Clinic studied responses to cycle ergometer exercise using the James protocol in 35 tests on 34 patients with pulmonary atresia and ventricular septal defect (14 patients without any repair, 11 with right ventricular-pulmonary artery conduit and open ventricular septal defect, and 10 following complete repair [ventricular septal defect closure and right ventricular-pulmonary artery conduit]). Exercise systolic blood pressure was equivalent to control values in the first two groups but was significantly reduced in the last group (complete repair). The investigators speculated that the isolated right ventricle postrepair may not be able to generate sufficient stroke volume to produce enough cardiac output to allow normal systolic blood pressure. Prior to repair, the right ventricle and left ventricle act in parallel, and this may augment right ventricular output.

Matthews et al. (28) reported the results of treadmill exercise in 21 patients following repair of d-transposition of the great vessels. The children were 4 to 15 years of age, with a mean age of 9, and were asymptomatic. All had undergone the Mustard operation. The patients' data were compared to those of 61 control youngsters whose mean age was 14 years, with a range from 9 to 20 years. There was no difference between patients and control subjects for maximal systolic blood pressure response or diastolic blood pressure response. The values for maximal systolic blood pressure were, however, all in the lower range of normal.

Of the many papers on the exercise responses of patients with tetralogy of Fallot, two are of note. Hirschfeld et al. (22) reported results from 28 patients ages 7 to 30 years old who were 2 to 9 years postrepair. The maximal systolic blood pressure of the control subjects was 152 ± 2.9 (*SE*) mmHg, and of the patients, 135 ± 3.8 mmHg. This difference was significant at $p<.005$. Similarly, the peak heart rate was significantly reduced. In a study of 135 patients performing 279 exercise studies, Wessel et al. (36) reported the systemic (systolic) blood pressure in 40 selected patients postintracardiac repair. They reported a mean value for maximal systolic blood pressure of 137.5 ± 18 (*SD*) mmHg, with a range from 115 to 175. These data are not compared with control subjects from the same laboratory but appear lower than the normal values obtained in other cycle ergometer studies.

Numerous studies have included exercise data both pre- and post-Fontan operation for either tricuspid atresia or common ventricle. Alpert and Rao (7) summarized exercise blood pressure data from two institutions on 23 patients pre-Fontan. Of these, 11 showed systolic blood pressure increases that were within the normal range. Nine patients had no change in systolic blood pressure with exercise, and in 3 patients systolic blood pressure decreased to below resting values, a distinctly abnormal response. In a very high proportion of the patients from the Medical College of Georgia (9 of 13), there were signs of exercise-induced ischemia.

Driscoll and his co-workers (18) from the Mayo Clinic reported results from 81 patients pre-Fontan, 33 with tricuspid atresia, 38 with univentricular heart, and 10 with other complex congenital heart disease. They compared these results to 29 patients post-Fontan. The preoperative patients had very low working capacities (21% predicted) and exercise heart rate. The systolic blood pressure responses were also reduced ($p<.05$) compared to those of the control subjects. The systolic blood pressure values were expressed as a percentage of predicted values and, surprisingly, the pre-Fontan group achieved 90% predicted and the post-Fontan group, 85% predicted. There were similar reductions in exercise diastolic blood pressure both pre- and post-Fontan.

Annecchino et al. (10) reported exercise data from 9 of 50 consecutive Fontan patients who performed Bruce treadmill studies. The mean maximal systolic blood pressure achieved was 140 mmHg, which was normal for age and sex for their laboratory.

Data from the Mayo experience were provided by Zellers et al. in 1989 (39). They reported pre- and post-Fontan data for 20 patients. Table 4 summarizes the percent predicted systolic blood pressure and diastolic blood pressure mean values ($\pm SD$) for the patients both pre- and postoperatively. The systolic blood pressure and diastolic blood pressure were within the normal range at rest and with exercise both pre- and postoperatively. The diastolic blood pressure showed a significant increase following the Fontan operation.

Conclusion

Several studies have addressed the systolic and diastolic blood pressure levels achieved during maximal dynamic exercise. There is debate over whether a systolic pressure value can be too high and whether diastolic pressure should change. Thus, it may be necessary to develop norms for systolic blood pressure change related to variables such as cardiac output, stroke volume, work load, $\dot{V}O_2$, heart rate, and respiratory exchange ratio so that the magnitude of blood pressure response may be judged with respect to physiologic changes needed to perform work. Blood pressure is needed to perfuse exercising muscle; values too high or too low may reduce work physiology efficiency.

Table 4   Exercise Data (Mean ± SD)
Before and After Modified Fontan Operation in 20 Patients

Measurement*	Preoperative	Postoperative	P
Exercise duration (% pred)	45 ± 15	66 ± 18	0.0007
Total work (% pred)	28 ± 12	47 ± 22	0.0013
$\dot{V}O_2$max			
% pred	54 ± 15	59 ± 15	0.016
ml/kg/min	22 ± 6	27 ± 6	0.016
HR (% pred)			
Rest	98 ± 19	105 ± 18	0.21
Exercise	74 ± 14	81 ± 10	0.08
BP, systolic (% pred)			
Rest	101 ± 17	98 ± 8	0.4
Exercise	90 ± 19	87 ± 7	0.36
BP, diastolic (% pred)			
Rest	91 ± 15	101 ± 11	0.018
Exercise	86 ± 13	100 ± 17	0.012
$\dot{V}_E/\dot{V}O_2$ (%)			
Rest	58 ± 36	43 ± 16	0.136
Exercise	61 ± 19	38 ± 5	0.0001

*% pred = % of predicted value. $\dot{V}O_2$max = maximal oxygen consumption. HR = heart rate. BP = blood pressure. $\dot{V}_E/\dot{V}O_2$ = ratio of minute ventilation to oxygen consumption (ventilatory equivalent for oxygen).

Note. From "Exercise tolerance and cardiorespiratory response to exercise before and after the Fontan Operation" by T.M. Zellers, D.J. Driscoll, C.D. Mottram, F.J. Puga, H.V. Schaff, and G.K. Danielson. *Mayo Clinic Proceedings*, 64:1491, 1989. Copyright by Mayo Clinic Proceedings. Reprinted by permission.

Few studies have addressed exercise blood pressure in noncardiac diseases; more studies are needed to judge the utility of this testing. The interpretation of the existing data with respect to cardiac disease, including coarctation of the aorta, is also of debate, as demonstrated by the studies by Zellers and Driscoll (18, 38). The most important point to be stressed is the great difficulty in assessing accurately both systolic and diastolic blood pressures. Treadmill protocols lead to problems separating "hoofbeats" and heartbeats. For critical assessment of blood pressure, with the understanding that maximal exercise $\dot{V}O_2$ will be slightly lower than on a treadmill, the use of a cycle ergometer is strongly recommended. We look forward to further studies for

- greater understanding of the physiologic meaning of certain levels of exercise systolic and diastolic blood pressures;
- differences in variables at sea level versus at altitude; and

- definition of responses in ethnic minorities other than blacks, such as Hispanics and Orientals.

References

1. Alpert, B.A., E.V. Dover, D.L. Booker, A.M. Martin, and W.B. Strong. Blood pressure response to dynamic exercise in healthy children: black vs. white. *J. Pediatr.* 99:556-560, 1981.
2. Alpert, B.S., N.L. Flood, I.C. Balfour, and W.B. Strong. Automated blood pressure measurement during ergometer exercise in children. *Cathet. Cardiovasc. Diagn.* 8:525-533, 1982.
3. Alpert, B.S., N.L. Flood, W.B. Strong, E.V. Dover, R.H. DuRant, A.M. Martin, and D.L. Booker. Responses to ergometer exercise in a healthy biracial population of children. *J. Pediatr.* 101:538-545, 1982.
4. Alpert, B.S., P.A. Gilman, W.B. Strong, M.F. Ellison, M.D. Miller, J. McFarlane, and T. Hayashidera. Hemodynamic and ECG responses to exercise in children with sickle cell anemia. *Am. J. Dis. Child.* 135:362-366, 1981.
5. Alpert, B.S., W. Kartodihardjo, R. Harp, T. Izukawa, and W.B. Strong. Exercise blood pressure response: A predictor of severity of aortic stenosis in children. *J. Pediatr.* 98:763-765, 1981.
6. Alpert, B.S., D.M. Moes, R.H. DuRant, W.B. Strong, and N.L. Flood. Hemodynamic responses to ergometer exercise in children and young adults with left ventricular pressure or volume overload. *Am. J. Cardiol.* 52:563-567, 1983.
7. Alpert, B.S., and P.S. Rao. Exercise electrocardiography in tricuspid atresia. In: *Tricuspid Atresia*, P.S. Rao (Ed.). Mt. Kisco, NY: Futura, 1982, pp. 147-151.
8. Alpert, B.A., D.E. Verrill, N.L. Flood, J.P. Boineau, and W.B. Strong. Complications of ergometer exercise in children. *Pediatr. Cardiol.* 4:91-96, 1983.
9. American Heart Association Council on Cardiovascular Disease in the Young. Standards for exercise testing in the pediatric age group. *Circulation* 66:1377A-1397A, 1982.
10. Annecchino, F.P., F. Brunelli, A. Borghi, P. Albruzzesee, M. Merlo, and L. Parenzan. Fontan repair for tricuspid atresia: Experience with 50 consecutive patients. *Am. Thorac. Surg.* 45:430-436, 1988.
11. Arensman, F.W., F.A. Treiber, M.P. Gruber, and W.B. Strong. Exercise-induced differences in cardiac output, blood pressure, and systemic vascular resistance in a healthy biracial population of 10-year-old boys. *Am. J. Dis. Child.* 143:212-216, 1989.

12. Barber, G., G.K. Danielson, C.T. Heise, and D.J. Driscoll. Cardiorespiratory response to exercise in Ebstein's anomaly. *Am. J. Cardiol.* 56:509-514, 1985.

13. Barber, G., G.K. Danielson, F.J. Puga, C.T. Heise, and D.J. Driscoll. Pulmonary atresia with ventricular septal defect: Preoperative and postoperative responses to exercise. *J. Am. Coll. Cardiol.* 7:630-638, 1986.

14. Connor, T.M. Evaluation of persistent coarctation of aorta after surgery with blood pressure measurement and exercise testing. *Am. J. Cardiol.* 43:74-78, 1979.

15. Connor, T.M., and W.P. Baker. A comparison of coarctation resection and patch angioplasty using post-exercise blood pressure measurements. *Circulation* 64:567-572, 1981.

16. Cumming, G.R., and G.H. Mir. Exercise hemodynamics of coarctation of the aorta-acute effects of propranolol. *Br. Heart J.* 32:365-369, 1970.

17. Dlin, R. Blood pressure response to dynamic exercise in healthy and hypertensive youths. *Pediatrician* 13:34-43, 1986.

18. Driscoll, D.J., G.K. Danielson, F.J. Puga, H.V. Schaff, C.T. Heise, and B.A. Staats. Exercise tolerance and cardiorespiratory response to exercise after the Fontan operation for tricuspid atresia or functional single ventricle. *J. Am. Coll. Cardiol.* 7:1087-1094, 1986.

19. Earley, A., M.C. Joseph, E.A. Shinebourne, and M. DeSwiet. Blood pressure and effect of exercise in children before and after surgical correction of coarctation of aorta. *Br. Heart J.* 44:411-415, 1980.

20. Freed, M.D., A. Rocchini, A. Rosenthal, A.S. Nadas, and A.R. Castaneda. Exercise-induced hypertension after surgical repair of coarctation of the aorta. *Am. J. Cardiol.* 43:253-258, 1979.

21. Godfrey, S. *Exercise Testing in Children.* London: Saunders, 1974.

22. Hirschfeld, S., A.J. Tuboku-Metzger, G. Borkat, J. Ankeney, J. Clayman, and J. Liebman. Comparison of exercise and catheterization results following total surgical correction of tetralogy of Fallot. *J. Thorac. Cardiovasc. Surg.* 75:446-451, 1978.

23. James, F.W., and S. Kaplan. Systolic hypertension during submaximal exercise after correction of coarctation of aorta. *Circulation* 49 and 50(Suppl. II):II-27-II-33, 1974.

24. James, F.W., S. Kaplan, C.J. Glueck, J.Y. Tsay, M.J.S. Knight, and C.J. Sarwar. Responses of normal children and young adults to controlled bicycle exercise. *Circulation* 61:902-912, 1980.

25. James, F.W., D.C. Schwartz, S. Kaplan, and S.P. Spilkin. Exercise electrocardiogram, blood pressure, and working capacity in young patients with valvular or discrete subvalvular aortic stenosis. *Am. J. Cardiol.* 50:769-775, 1982.

26. Markel, H., A.P. Rocchini, R.H. Beckman, J. Martin, J. Palmisano, C. Moorehead, and A. Rosenthal. Exercise-induced hypertension after repair of coarctation of the aorta: Arm versus leg exercise. *J. Am. Coll. Cardiol.* 8:165-171, 1986.

27. Maron, B.J., J.O. Humphries, R.D. Rowe, and E.D. Mellets. Prognosis of surgically corrected coarctation of the aorta: A 20-year post-operative appraisal. *Circulation* 47:119-126, 1973.
28. Matthews, R.A., F.J. Fricker, L.B. Beerman, R.J. Stephenson, D.R. Fisher, W.H. Neches, S.C. Park, C.C. Lenox, and J.R. Zuberbuhler. Exercise studies after the Mustard operation in transposition of the great arteries. *Am. J. Cardiol.* 51:1526-1529, 1983.
29. McConnell, M.E., S.R. Daniels, J. Lobel, F.W. James, and S. Kaplan. Hemodynamic response to exercise in patients with sickle cell anemia. *Pediatr. Cardiol.* 10:141-144, 1989.
30. Riopel, D.A., A.B. Taylor, and R.A. Hohen. Blood pressure responses to treadmill exercise in children with aortic stenosis [abstract]. Paper presented at the 46th annual meeting of the American Academy of Pediatrics, New York, 1977.
31. Riopel, D.A., A.B. Taylor, and R.A. Hohen. Blood pressure, heart rate, pressure-rate product and electrocardiographic changes in healthy children during treadmill exercise. *Am. J. Cardiol.* 44:697-704, 1979.
32. Smith, R.T., Jr., R.M. Sade, D.A. Riopel, A.B. Taylor, F.A. Crawford, and R.A. Hohen. Stress testing for comparison of synthetic patch aortoplasty with resection and end-to-end anastomosis for repair of coarctation in childhood. *J. Am. Coll. Cardiol.* 4:765-770, 1984.
33. Treiber, F.A., L. Musante, W.B. Strong, and M. Levy. Racial differences in young children's blood pressure. *Am. J. Dis. Child.* 143:720-723, 1989.
34. Wanne, O.P.S., and E. Haapoja. Blood pressure during exercise in healthy children. *Eur. J. Appl. Physiol.* 58:62-67, 1988.
35. Washington, R.L., J.C. van Gundy, C. Cohen, H.M. Sondheimer, and R.R. Wolfe. Normal aerobic and anaerobic exercise data for North American school-age children. *J. Pediatr.* 112:223-233, 1988.
36. Wessel, H.Y., W.J. Cunningham, M.H. Paul, C.K. Bastanier, A.J. Muster, and F.S. Idriss. Exercise performance in tetralogy of Fallot after intra-cardiac repair. *J. Thorac. Cardiovasc. Surg.* 80:582-593, 1980.
37. Whitmer, J.T., F.W. James, S. Kaplan, D.C. Schwartz, and M.J.S. Knight. Exercise testing in children before and after surgical treatment of aortic stenosis. *Circulation* 63:254-263, 1981.
38. Zellers, T.M., and D.J. Driscoll. Utility of exercise testing to assess aortic recoarctation. *Pediatr. Exerc. Sci.* 1:163-170, 1989.
39. Zellers, T.M., D.J. Driscoll, C.D. Mottran, F.J. Puga, H.V. Schaff, and G.K. Danielson. Exercise tolerance and cardiorespiratory response to exercise before and after the Fontan operation. *Mayo Clin. Proc.* 64:1489-1497, 1989.

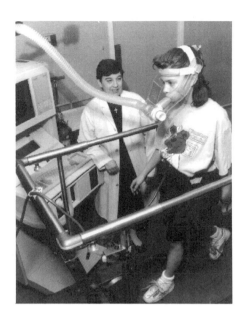

Measurement of Oxygen Consumption

Patty S. Freedson, PhD
Terri L. Goodman, MS
University of Massachusetts

In the latter part of the 18th century two French scientists, Lavoisier and Laplace, studied the nature of energy conversions in animals using a calorimeter (33). A guinea pig was placed in a cage surrounded by an ice jacket that absorbed the heat produced by the animal. This system was surrounded by another ice jacket that absorbed the heat from the outside environment. Thus, the chamber was effectively isolated, and as long as ice was present in both jackets, no heat was transferred from one to the other. The heat produced by the guinea pig melted the ice in the inner jacket at a certain rate, and the

The authors thank Sandra Carter for her assistance in preparing this manuscript.

91

scientists were able to calculate the animal's rate of heat production by measuring the amount of ice that melted over a given time. Carbon dioxide production was measured simultaneously, and Lavoisier and Laplace discovered that the energy released by the animal in the form of heat was of similar magnitude as the energy liberated in the oxidation of carbon (taken from the amount of carbon dioxide produced).

Because all aerobic energy–producing reactions in the body depend on oxygen, an indirect estimate of energy production can be obtained by measuring a person's oxygen consumption. During metabolic transformations, oxygen is consumed and heat is produced, so either of these variables can be used to estimate energy expenditure. The standard method for determining the rate of energy production during exercise is to measure oxygen consumption using open circuit indirect calorimetry.

In the early 1920s, Hill and Lupton reported that each person has a maximal level of oxygen consumption (26). In the 1950s, experimental techniques were standardized for measuring maximal oxygen consumption ($\dot{V}O_2$max). The procedure developed depends on the relationship between oxygen consumption and work rate up to a person's $\dot{V}O_2$max. Beyond this level, increases in work do not produce any further increases in $\dot{V}O_2$. At the work rate corresponding to $\dot{V}O_2$max, work time is limited, and muscle and blood lactic acid concentration accelerates, signaling a rapid increase in anaerobic metabolism.

$\dot{V}O_2$max is generally considered the best single physiologic indicator of an individual's ability to transport and utilize oxygen and is a measure of an individual's aerobic capacity. Measurement of $\dot{V}O_2$max uses a progressive incremental exercise test, usually performed on a treadmill or cycle ergometer, to the point where further increments of work are theoretically accompanied by a plateau in oxygen consumption. The test can involve either work performed continuously or rest periods interspersed between exercise bouts. A detailed analysis of $\dot{V}O_2$max test protocols that have been used in pediatric exercise testing is presented in the section on "Aerobic Exercise Testing Protocols."

This section focuses on the following topics as they pertain to measuring submaximal and maximal oxygen consumption in the pediatric population:

1. how oxygen consumption is determined,
2. measurement of $\dot{V}O_2$max,
3. measurement of submaximal $\dot{V}O_2$,
4. reliability of $\dot{V}O_2$max,
5. effect of sample selection on $\dot{V}O_2$max, and
6. norms for $\dot{V}O_2$max.

Technical Considerations: Oxygen Consumption Measurement

As mentioned earlier, open circuit indirect calorimetry may be used to assess oxygen consumption during exercise. Several procedures can be used to assess oxygen consumption with this technique. In one method, the subject breathes in ambient room air through a two-way valve, and the expired air is collected in a closed container (e.g., Douglas bag, gasometer, or meteorological balloon). The expired volume is measured with some type of volume meter, gas temperature is recorded, and oxygen and carbon dioxide concentrations are assessed with gas analyzers. The volume of expired air can also be assessed with a pneumotachometer or a turbine-based flow meter that is placed in the expired air line.

Expired air volumes must be converted to standard temperature and pressure, dry (*STPD*; 0°C, 760 mmHg, no water vapor). This conversion is necessary to standardize air volumes because the volume of a gas varies directly with temperature (Charles' law) and inversely with pressure (Boyle's law).

Expired fractions of O_2 and CO_2 are commonly measured using electronic paramagnetic O_2 and infrared CO_2 analyzers that have been calibrated using gas of known concentrations of oxygen and carbon dioxide. If the method for assessing expired volume uses the turbine or pneumotachometer, the time for sampling the composition of the expired aid must be equivalent to the time of volume assessment.

Oxygen consumption can then be calculated using the following equation:

$$\dot{V}O_2 \ (L \cdot min^{-1}) = V_E STPD \ (L \cdot min^{-1}) \cdot (F_E N_2 \cdot F_I O_2 / F_I N_2) - F_E O_2$$

where

$V_E STPD$ = expired volume STPD
$F_E N_2$ = fraction of nitrogen in the expired air $[1 - (F_E O_2 + F_E CO_2)]$
$F_I O_2$ = fraction of oxygen in the inspired air (.2093)
$F_I N_2$ = fraction of nitrogen in the inspired air (.7904)
$F_E O_2$ = fraction of oxygen in the expired air

Carbon dioxide production is calculated as follows:

$$\dot{V}CO_2 \ (L \cdot min^{-1}) = V_E STPD \cdot (F_E CO_2 - F_I CO_2)$$

where

$F_E CO_2$ = fraction of carbon dioxide in the expired air
$F_I CO_2$ = fraction of carbon dioxide in the inspired air (.0003)

The ratio of the carbon dioxide produced to oxygen consumed ($\dot{V}CO_2/\dot{V}O_2$) is called the respiratory exchange ratio (RER) and is used to calculate energy expenditure from $\dot{V}O_2$ and RER (see Table 1). Because of inherent chemical differences in the composition of carbohydrates, fats, and proteins, different amounts of oxygen are required to oxidize completely the carbon and hydrogen atoms into carbon dioxide and water. Thus, $\dot{V}CO_2/\dot{V}O_2$ varies depending on the nutrient metabolized. Table 1 presents the caloric expenditure equivalents and the corresponding proportions of carbohydrates and fats that are used. These are nonprotein equivalents and represent the portion of the total metabolic process that can be attributed to the combustion of only

Table 1   Thermal Equivalents of Oxygen
for the Nonprotein Respiratory Exchange Ratio (RER)

Nonprotein RER	Kcal per liter of O_2 consumed	% Kcal from carbohydrate	% Kcal from fat
0.707	4.686	0	100
0.71	4.690	1.10	98.9
0.72	4.702	4.76	95.2
0.73	4.714	8.40	91.6
0.74	4.727	12.0	88.0
0.75	4.739	15.6	84.4
0.76	4.751	19.2	80.8
0.77	4.764	22.8	77.2
0.78	4.776	26.3	73.7
0.79	4.788	29.9	70.1
0.80	4.801	33.4	66.6
0.81	4.813	36.9	63.1
0.82	4.825	40.3	59.7
0.83	4.838	43.8	56.2
0.84	4.850	47.2	52.8
0.85	4.862	50.7	49.3
0.86	4.875	54.1	45.9
0.87	4.887	57.5	42.5
0.88	4.899	60.8	39.2
0.89	4.911	64.2	35.8
0.90	4.924	67.5	32.5
0.91	4.936	70.8	29.2
0.92	4.948	74.1	25.9
0.93	4.961	77.4	22.6
0.94	4.973	80.7	19.3
0.95	4.985	84.0	16.0
0.96	4.998	87.2	12.8
0.97	5.010	90.4	9.58
0.98	5.022	93.6	6.37
0.99	5.035	96.8	3.18
1.00	5.047	100.0	0

carbohydrates and fats. The validity of the RER for estimating caloric expenditure is maintained at exercise intensities up to about 50% of $\dot{V}O_2$max, or below the level of exercise where there is a significant anaerobic component. At $\dot{V}O_2$max, the RER exceeds 1.0 and may be used as one of the criteria to establish a satisfactory maximal effort.

Many computer-based metabolic exercise testing systems have been developed since the late 1960s. These systems provide instantaneous assessment of whole body metabolism and generally correlate well with manual methods (29, 39, 74). However, because hardware and software differ among systems, it is necessary to test the validity of any system during both submaximal and maximal exercise conditions. These systems were developed for use with adults; depending on the system design, it may be necessary to scale down tubing diameter, mouthpiece dead space, and mixing chamber size (51). Particular attention to calibrating the ventilation measuring device at low ventilatory volumes is required because breathing frequency and tidal volume are considerably lower for children than for adults (51). These measurement issues have not been examined and should be a research focus in pediatric exercise testing.

Measurement of $\dot{V}O_2$max

The most important reason for measuring $\dot{V}O_2$ in a clinical setting is to evaluate $\dot{V}O_2$max, a measure of physiologic functional capacity. This measure can be obtained directly by exercising a child to maximal exertion or by estimation from a submaximal exercise protocol. Most university exercise physiology laboratories and some clinical laboratories have the equipment necessary to measure $\dot{V}O_2$max directly. If a highly accurate and reproducible measure is required, directly measured $\dot{V}O_2$max is necessary.

$\dot{V}O_2$max depends on the functional capacity of the pulmonary and cardiovascular systems and thus can provide the clinician or researcher with valuable information about the effects of interventions such as surgical procedures and drug therapies on maximal aerobic power. In addition, the effects of aerobic exercise training are usually quantified on the basis of changes in $\dot{V}O_2$max.

For both children and adults, $\dot{V}O_2$max is expressed either as an absolute rate ($L \cdot min^{-1}$) or relative to some measure of body size, most notably body mass ($ml \cdot kgBW^{-1} \cdot min^{-1}$) or lean body mass ($ml \cdot kgLBM^{-1} \cdot min^{-1}$). The use of relative expressions presumably normalizes $\dot{V}O_2$max for differences in body size. Selection of the best expression for $\dot{V}O_2$max in children is complicated by growth. Even though dividing $\dot{V}O_2$max by body mass or lean body mass appears to account for growth-related changes in $\dot{V}O_2$max, these body size correction factors are probably not entirely appropriate (52). For example, a basic assumption underlying the use of a $\dot{V}O_2$ ratio expression (kgBW · min^{-1}) is that the correlation between $\dot{V}O_2$max and body mass $r = 1.0$. Katch (30) has shown convincingly that the relationship between these two variables is on the order of $r = .70$. However, Bar-Or (5) argues that the use of dimensionality theory to derive more growth-appropriate expressions of $\dot{V}O_2$max, such as $\dot{V}O_2$ per height^2, does not improve the interpretation of $\dot{V}O_2$max in the growing child. Therefore, $\dot{V}O_2$max relative to body mass (ml · kgBW^{-1} · min^{-1}) remains the standard form of expression for maximal aerobic power in children.

Measurement of Submaximal $\dot{V}O_2$

Submaximal exercise oxygen consumption has also been assessed in the pediatric population. In most cases, these investigations have focused on child versus adult comparisons of metabolic efficiency or economy during walking and running. However, there is significant clinical value in assessing the submaximal energy cost of locomotion in children. For example, comparison of the energy cost of locomotion in children with gait disabilities with standard age-specific energy cost values over a wide range of walking and running speeds may be helpful to the clinician (73). This type of evaluation offers the clinician information about the effectiveness of an intervention on the child's economy of locomotion. Steady state conditions are a prerequisite for this type of application, so it is necessary to collect metabolic measurements after 3 to 5 min of locomotion at a constant speed. An analysis among the minute-by-minute values should be performed to ensure that steady state conditions have been attained.

Measurement of $\dot{V}O_2$max in Children

Many investigators have used a variety of treadmill and cycle ergometer protocols to assess $\dot{V}O_2$max in children. $\dot{V}O_2$max data for male subjects between the ages of 9 and 14 years are presented in Tables 2-12. This group was chosen because most studies focus on males in this age group, making between-study comparisons possible.

Effect of Exercise Protocol on $\dot{V}O_2$max

Many investigators have determined the maximal aerobic power of children using a cycle ergometer. The major advantage to this testing method is that the child need not learn a new skill. The greatest disadvantage is that the test may be limited by local muscle fatigue instead of cardiorespiratory capacity.

The different protocols used with the cycle ergometer include stepwise-loading, supramaximal, and discontinuous (see Tables 2-5). The range of mean $\dot{V}O_2$max values reported in the literature for a stepwise-loading protocol is 1.13 to 2.27 L · min^{-1} (35.6 to 60.6 ml · kg^{-1} · min^{-1}) in 9- to 14-year-old boys. The ranges reported for the supramaximal and discontinuous protocols are 1.46 to 2.57 L · min^{-1} (49.0 to 55.4 ml · kg^{-1} · min^{-1}) and 1.30 to

Table 2   Summary of Studies That Used a Stepwise-Loading Protocol on the Cycle Ergometer to Measure $\dot{V}O_2$max

Study	N	Age (years)	$\dot{V}O_2$max (L · min^{-1})	$\dot{V}O_2$max (ml · kg^{-1} · min^{-1})
Rodahl et al. (49)	9	10	1.13	—
	14	12	1.43	—
Nakagawa & Ishiko (45)	10	12-13	1.62 ± 0.24	40.7 ± 3.9
Ikai & Kitagawa (27)	18	10-11	1.50 ± 0.26	49.1 ± 7.9
	21	11-12	1.77 ± 0.27	51.3 ± 6.0
	14	12-13	1.90 ± 0.33	44.9 ± 4.7
Maksud et al. (35)	16	10	1.25 ± 0.26	37.5 ± 4.1
	18	11	1.43 ± 0.22	35.6 ± 5.8
Sobolova et al. (64)	11	13	1.90 ± 0.21	45
Boileau et al. (9)	21	11-14	2.27 ± 0.49	47.0 ± 6.3
Gilliam et al. (23)	28	9-10	1.52 ± 0.25	43.6 ± 6.8
	21	11-13	1.84 ± 0.33	44.7 ± 6.5
Yamaji et al. (76)	9	10-11	1.43 ± 0.22	39.9 ± 6.7
	8	13-14	2.08 ± 0.14	42.5 ± 3.6
Sundberg & Elovainio (67)	12	12	2.20 ± 0.40	59.3 ± 6.2
	19	12	2.13 ± 0.25	55.4 ± 7.7
Binkhorst et al. (6)	13	12	1.85 ± 0.32	—
Sunnegårdh & Bratteby (68)	32	12-14	2.61 ± 0.51	52.2 ± 5.3
Petzl et al. (48)	19	10	—	47.4 ± 7.0
	40	11	—	56.9 ± 7.0
	22	12	—	60.6 ± 9.0
	19	13	—	59.7 ± 11.7
	10	10	—	47.1 ± 10.2
	13	11	—	50.0 ± 13.2
	11	12	—	56.3 ± 13.5
	10	13	—	49.1 ± 9.2
Washington et al. (72)	29	9-14	2.13 ± 0.52	47 ± 10
Hansen et al. (24)	8	10-11	1.64 ± 0.20	46.2 ± 6.7
	9	10-11	1.82 ± 0.22	56.4 ± 4.6

Note. Values are means ± *SD*. All subjects were male.

Table 3   Summary of Studies That Used a Supramaximal Protocol on the Cycle Ergometer to Measure $\dot{V}O_2max$

Study	N	Age (years)	$\dot{V}O_2max$ (L · min^{-1})	$\dot{V}O_2max$ (ml · kg^{-1} · min^{-1})
Cumming & Danzinger (12)	13	10-11	1.46 ± 0.23	—
Eriksson et al. (22)	8	13-14	2.51 ± 0.11*	49
Baggley & Cumming (4)	16	9-12	2.02	50.1
Anderson et al. (1)	14	10	1.61 ± 0.19	49.3 ± 6.7
	12	12	1.89 ± 0.17	50.4 ± 7.5
Woynarowska (75)	80	11-12	2.34 ± 0.29	—
Massicotte et al. (36)	20	10	1.84 ± 0.31	55.4 ± 6.2
	21	11	1.90 ± 0.30	54.8 ± 6.4
	22	12	2.30 ± 0.20	52.7 ± 9.3
	20	13	2.57 ± 0.47	55.2 ± 7.8

Note. Values are means ± *SD* unless otherwise noted. All subjects were male.
*Mean ± SE.

Table 4   Summary of Studies That Used a Discontinuous Protocol on the Cycle Ergometer to Measure $\dot{V}O_2max$

Study	N	Age (years)	$\dot{V}O_2max$ (L · min^{-1})	$\dot{V}O_2max$ (ml · kg^{-1} · min^{-1})
Yoshizawa (77)	5	10	1.38 ± 0.20	45.1 ± 2.3
	15	10	1.30 ± 0.20	44.2 ± 3.8
	22	11	1.47 ± 0.29	41.8 ± 7.6
	21	11	1.51 ± 0.27	46.6 ± 5.8
	27	12	1.99 ± 0.48	46.3 ± 4.7
	27	12	1.76 ± 0.31	47.1 ± 6.2
	15	13	2.50 ± 0.42	49.5 ± 7.6
	15	13	2.24 ± 0.38	53.6 ± 6.3
Cunningham & Eynon (15)	10	10-12	2.17 ± 0.43	52.5 ± 4.1
	6	13	2.65 ± 0.52	52.9 ± 9.5
Cunningham et al. (18)	15	10	2.00 ± 0.30	56.6 ± 7.7

Note. Values are means ± *SD*. All subjects were male.

2.65 L · min^{-1} (41.3 to 56.6 ml · kg^{-1} · min^{-1}), respectively. The overall range of $\dot{V}O_2max$ values found with the cycle ergometer is 1.13 to 2.65 L · min^{-1} (35.6 to 60.6 ml · kg^{-1} · min^{-1}).

The major advantage of using a treadmill $\dot{V}O_2max$ test is that the cardiorespiratory system is more likely to be the limiting factor than local muscle

**Table 5   Summary of Studies That Used Other Protocols
on the Cycle Ergometer to Measure $\dot{V}O_2$max**

		Age	$\dot{V}O_2$max	
Study	N	(years)	$(L \cdot min^{-1})$	$(ml \cdot kg^{-1} \cdot min^{-1})$
Binyildiz (7)	32	11	1.16 ± 0.30	32.6 ± 7.5
	32	12	1.30 ± 0.35	33.9 ± 7.1
	32	13	1.52 ± 0.38	36.7 ± 6.4
Rutenfranz et al. (55)	31	10	2.03 ± 0.30	60.0 ± 6.5
	29	11	2.07 ± 0.30	56.9 ± 6.1
	30	12	2.31 ± 0.34	58.0 ± 8.0
	28	12	2.33 ± 0.32	57.4 ± 7.1
	29	13	2.70 ± 0.51	61.4 ± 6.7
	27	13	2.50 ± 0.46	54.1 ± 5.6

Note. Values are means $\pm$ *SD*. All subjects were male.

fatigue. The major disadvantage is that most children have not previously run on a treadmill and may find it intimidating.

Treadmill testing has been conducted with various stepwise-loading protocols and also with walking, discontinuous, and supramaximal protocols (see Tables 6-11). The ranges of mean values for these protocols are as follows:

- Stepwise-loading, increase grade—1.75 to 3.03 L $\cdot$ min^{-1} (47.7 to 61.0 ml $\cdot$ kg^{-1} $\cdot$ min^{-1})
- Stepwise-loading, increase speed—1.77 to 2.79 L $\cdot$ min^{-1} (45.7 to 58.2 ml $\cdot$ kg^{-1} $\cdot$ min^{-1})
- Stepwise-loading, increase grade and speed—1.76 to 2.49 L $\cdot$ min^{-1} (45.9 to 61.3 ml $\cdot$ kg^{-1} $\cdot$ min^{-1})
- Walking—1.61 to 2.45 L $\cdot$ min^{-1} (43.1 to 55.5 ml $\cdot$ kg^{-1} $\cdot$ min^{-1})
- Discontinuous—1.83 to 2.55 L $\cdot$ min^{-1} (47.4 to 59.4 ml $\cdot$ kg^{-1} $\cdot$ min^{-1})
- Supramaximal—1.79 to 2.72 L $\cdot$ min^{-1} (47.8 to 60.6 ml $\cdot$ kg^{-1} $\cdot$ min^{-1})

Table 12 presents $\dot{V}O_2$max values obtained with various protocols in 10- to 13-year-old boys. Although the ranges are similar, it cannot be determined if different protocols would elicit similar values in the same subjects. In studies that specifically examined this issue, higher values were obtained with the treadmill compared to the cycle ergometer in the same group of subjects, and higher values were found with a running than with a walking protocol.

For example, Boileau et al. (9) reported mean $\dot{V}O_2$max ($\pm$ *SD*) values of 2.45 (± 0.58) L $\cdot$ min^{-1} and 2.27 ± 0.49 L $\cdot$ min^{-1} for treadmill and cycle ergometer tests, respectively, in a group of 11- to 14-year-old boys. Values relative to body mass ($\pm$ *SD*) were 50.5 ± 5.9 ml $\cdot$ kg^{-1} $\cdot$ min^{-1} for the treadmill test and 47.0 ± 6.3 ml $\cdot$ kg^{-1} $\cdot$ min^{-1} for the cycle ergometer test. The coefficients

Table 6   Summary of Studies That Used an Increasing-Grade, Stepwise-Loading Protocol on the Treadmill to Measure $\dot{V}O_2$max

		Age	$\dot{V}O_2$max	
Study	N	(years)	(L · min⁻¹)	(ml · kg⁻¹ · min⁻¹)
Blimkie et al. (8)	20	10-11	2.32 ± 0.04*	61.0 ± 1.6*
	19	10-11	1.75 ± 0.06*	56.1 ± 1.1*
	20	12-13	2.88 ± 0.07*	59.4 ± 1.2*
	19	12-13	2.21 ± 0.06*	57.6 ± 1.5*
Cunningham et al. (17)	28	12-13	2.47 ± 0.36	57.2 ± 7.0
Cunningham & Paterson (16)	62	10	1.96 ± 0.28	—
	62	11	2.28 ± 0.58	—
	62	12	2.62 ± 0.45	—
	62	13	3.03 ± 0.52	—
van Mechelen et al. (71)	41	12-14	—	53.2 ± 5.4
Sheehan et al. (57)	16	10-12	1.80 ± 0.26	47.7 ± 4.2

Note. Values are means ± *SD* unless otherwise noted. All subjects were male.

*Mean ± *SE*.

Table 7   Summary of Studies That Used an Increasing-Speed, Stepwise-Loading Protocol on the Treadmill to Measure $\dot{V}O_2$max

		Age	$\dot{V}O_2$max	
Study	N	(years)	(L · min⁻¹)	(ml · kg⁻¹ · min⁻¹)
Sprynarova (65)	114	10	1.77 ± 0.15	48.0 ± 5.2
	114	11	2.06 ± 0.33	50.7 ± 5.9
	114	12	2.25 ± 0.33	50.4 ± 4.9
Matsui et al. (37)	18	12	1.93 ± 0.20	46.4 ± 5.2
	54	13	2.04 ± 0.33	45.7 ± 6.3
	8	12-14	2.79 ± 0.36	47.5 ± 5.4
Miyamura et al. (43)	69	13-14	2.75 ± 0.06*	58.2 ± 0.7*

Note. Values are means ± *SD* unless otherwise noted. All subjects were male.

*Mean ± *SE*.

of variation for the two tests were 4.4% (treadmill) and 5.3% (cycle ergometer). Sixteen of the 21 subjects (76%) met an oxygen consumption leveling-off criterion (<150 ml · min⁻¹ with increasing work) with the treadmill protocol, whereas 8 subjects (38%) met this criterion with the cycle ergometer protocol. Correlation coefficients of r = .95 (L · min⁻¹) and r = .84 (ml · kg⁻¹ · min⁻¹)

Table 8   Summary of Studies That Used an Increasing-Grade and Increasing-Speed, Stepwise-Loading Protocol on the Treadmill to Measure $\dot{V}O_2$max

Study	N	Age (years)	$\dot{V}O_2$max (L · min⁻¹)	$\dot{V}O_2$max (ml · kg⁻¹ · min⁻¹)
Vodak & Wilmore (71)	69	9-12	1.90 ± 0.40	53.6 ± 5.6
Mayers & Gutin (38)	7	9-11	—	56.6 ± 2.0
	8	9-11	—	45.9 ± 2.7
Jetté et al. (28)	20	11-14	2.49 ± 0.49	56.9 ± 5.8
Saris et al. (56)	8	10	1.76 ± 0.23	52.7 ± 5.5
	6	12	1.88 ± 0.33	53.0 ± 4.7
Binkhorst et al. (6)	24	10	—	52.2 ± 5.1
	18	12	—	50.4 ± 6.2
Rowland et al. (53)	28	9-14	—	61.3 ± 8.3

Note. Values are means ± *SD*. All subjects were male.

Table 9   Summary of Studies That Used a Walking Protocol on the Treadmill to Measure $\dot{V}O_2$max

Study	N	Age (years)	$\dot{V}O_2$max (L · min⁻¹)	$\dot{V}O_2$max (ml · kg⁻¹ · min⁻¹)
Boileau et al. (9)	21	11-14	2.45 ± 0.58	50.5 ± 5.9
Paterson et al. (47)	8	10-12	2.04 ± 0.27	55.5 ± 5.9
Spurr et al. (67)	24	10-11	1.79 ± 0.26	53.5 ± 7.3
	45	10-11	1.74 ± 0.21	52.5 ± 5.4
	15	10-11	1.65 ± 0.29	51.4 ± 5.2
	24	12-13	2.26 ± 0.23	51.7 ± 4.2
	31	12-13	2.07 ± 0.24	52.0 ± 5.7
	10	12-13	2.26 ± 0.33	51.4 ± 7.2
Sheehan et al. (57)	16	10-12	1.61 ± 0.23	43.1 ± 6.3

Note. Values are means ± *SD*. All subjects were male.

were reported between $\dot{V}O_2$max values from cycle ergometer and treadmill tests.

Cumming and Langford (14) examined five cycle ergometer protocols and three treadmill protocols in 9- to 13-year-old children. Twenty-three subjects completed all eight tests (random order) within a 4-week period. Mean $\dot{V}O_2$max values (± *SD*) for the five cycle ergometer protocols (Godfrey, James, rapid loading, upright, supine) were 47.9 ± 8.3, 48.5 ± 7.2, 48.2 ± 8.3, 47.4 ± 7.0, and 40.4 ± 7.4 ml · kg⁻¹ · min⁻¹). For the treadmill protocols, the

Table 10   Summary of Studies That Used a Discontinuous Protocol on the Treadmill to Measure $\dot{V}O_2$max

Study	N	Age (years)	$\dot{V}O_2$max (L · min^{-1})	$\dot{V}O_2$max (ml · kg^{-1} · min^{-1})
Maksud & Coutts (34)	17	11-14	2.21 ± 0.41	47.4 ± 4.0
Metz & Alexander (41)	30	12-13	2.55 ± 0.56	50.9
Thiart & Wessels (69)	36	10-11	2.01 ± 0.26	56.1 ± 4.7
	38	12-13	2.35 ± 0.26	59.4 ± 4.7
Krahenbuhl & Pangrazi (31)	10	9-10	—	55.1 ± 3.6
	11	9-10	—	48.6 ± 4.5
Sheehan et al. (57)	16	10-12	1.83 ± 0.24	48.7 ± 5.0

Note. Values are means ± *SD*. All subjects were male.

highest mean values were found with the Bruce protocol (52.9 ± 7.7 ml · kg^{-1} · min^{-1}) and the Carolina Balke walking protocol (48.2 ± 6.6 ml · kg^{-1} · min^{-1}). The Carolina Balke protocol produced values equivalent to those obtained with any of the cycle ergometer protocols, whereas the Bruce protocol produced higher values than any obtained with the cycle ergometer protocols. Mean maximal heart rate (± *SD*) for the eight protocols, respectively, were 195 ± 5, 197 ± 7, 192 ± 6, 198 ± 5, 182 ± 11, 204 ± 5, 201 ± 6, and 198 ± 5 beats per minute (bpm). As with mean $\dot{V}O_2$max values, mean maximal heart rate values were highest with the two Bruce treadmill protocols. Cumming and Langford (14) recommend treadmill protocols over cycle ergometer protocols and running over walking protocols for children.

Armstrong et al. (2) also found higher $\dot{V}O_2$max values with a treadmill protocol versus a cycle ergometer protocol in 11- to 16-year-old boys who were in two comparable groups of 7th- to 10th-grade students. The mean $\dot{V}O_2$max (± *SD*) from the group that used the treadmill protocol to determine aerobic capacity ($N = 28$) was 2.35 ± 0.58 L · min^{-1} or 48.0 ± 6.0 ml · kg^{-1} · min^{-1}, whereas the mean $\dot{V}O_2$max (± *SD*) from the cycle ergometer group ($N = 57$) was 1.98 ± 0.44 L · min^{-1} or 42.0 ± 5.0 ml · kg^{-1} · min^{-1}. Both the treadmill and cycle ergometer protocols were discontinuous with 1-min rest periods between work loads. Peak heart rates (± *SD*) were 202 ± 10 bpm (treadmill) and 196 ± 9 bpm (cycle ergometer). No criteria to assess the attainment of $\dot{V}O_2$max were reported.

A few investigators have looked at walking versus running treadmill protocols. In a study by Paterson et al. (47), three different treadmill speeds were used to determine $\dot{V}O_2$max in the same group of 10- to 12-year-old boys ($N = 8$). A walking speed of 5.5 kilometers per hour (kph) produced a mean $\dot{V}O_2$max (± *SD*) of 2.04 ± 0.27 L · min^{-1} or 55.5 ± 5.9 ml · kg^{-1} · min^{-1}, a jogging speed (6.75 kph) produced a mean $\dot{V}O_2$max (± *SD*) of 2.14 ± 0.39 L

Table 11   Summary of Studies That Used a Supramaximal Protocol on the Treadmill to Measure $\dot{V}O_2$max

Study	N	Age (years)	$\dot{V}O_2$max (L · min^{-1})	$\dot{V}O_2$max (ml · kg^{-1} · min^{-1})
Morse et al. (44)	22	10-12	—	47.8 ± 5.0
Shephard et al. (60, 61)	10	10-12	1.79 ± 0.32	47.9 ± 6.3
	6	10-12	1.91 ± 0.29	48.1 ± 5.3
	7	10-12	1.80 ± 0.46	47.9 ± 5.9
Daniels & Oldridge (20)	6	12.1	2.33 ± 0.55	59.5 ± 4.8
	6	12.4	2.38 ± 0.59	59.7 ± 5.1
	6	13.1	2.56 ± 0.74	59.6 ± 6.8
	6	13.5	2.72 ± 0.76	59.3 ± 6.3
	14	13.5	2.74 ± 0.74	60.6 ± 5.6
Hermansen & Oseid (25)	20	10	1.96	54.3
	20	11	2.17	54.7
	20	12	2.52	58.1

Note. Values are means ± *SD*. All subjects were male.

Table 12 $\dot{V}O_2$max Ranges Obtained With Different Testing Protocols in 10- to 13-Year-Old Boys

Protocol	$\dot{V}O_2$max (ml · kg^{-1} · min^{-1})
Cycle ergometer	
Stepwise-loading	35.6-59.3
Supramaximal	49.0-55.4
Discontinuous	41.8-56.6
Other	32.6-61.4
Treadmill	
Stepwise-loading, increase grade	47.7-61.0
Stepwise-loading, increase speed	45.7-58.2
Stepwise-loading, increase grade & speed	45.9-61.3
Walking	43.1-55.5
Discontinuous	47.4-59.4
Supramaximal	47.8-59.4

· min^{-1} or 57.9 ± 4.4 ml · kg^{-1} · min^{-1}, and a running speed (7.9 kph) produced a mean $\dot{V}O_2$max (± *SD*) of 2.18 ± 0.29 L · min^{-1} or 59.5 ± 5.4 ml · kg^{-1} · min^{-1}. Mean maximal heart rates (± *SD*) for these three speeds were 191 ± 7, 195 ± 7, and 197 ± 7 bpm, respectively.

Zauner and Benson (78) used the Balke walking protocol and an intermittent running protocol to determine $\dot{V}O_2$max in 8- to 16-year-old competitive swimmers ($N = 21$). Mean $\dot{V}O_2$max values ($\pm$ SD) were again higher using the running protocol (52.0 ± 14.1 versus 49.3 ± 14.6 ml $\cdot$ kg^{-1} $\cdot$ min^{-1}, [$p<.05$]). Mean maximal heart rate was also higher with the running protocol (202 bpm) compared to the walking protocol (183 bpm). Nineteen of the 21 subjects (90%) met an oxygen consumption leveling-off criterion (no increase in oxygen consumption with an increase in work load) with the running test, whereas just 7 (33%) satisfied this criterion with the walking protocol. Also, all but one subject terminated the running test at a heart rate of 200 bpm, whereas no subjects reached a heart rate of 200 bpm with the walking test.

When comparing continuous walking and continuous running protocols to determine $\dot{V}O_2$max in 10- to 12-year-old boys, Sheehan et al. (57) found a significant difference between the mean values ($\pm$ SD) of 1.61 ± 0.23 L $\cdot$ min^{-1} or 43.1 ± 6.3 ml $\cdot$ kg^{-1} $\cdot$ min^{-1} obtained with the walking test and 1.80 ± 0.26 L $\cdot$ min^{-1} or 47.7 ± 4.2 ml $\cdot$ kg^{-1} $\cdot$ min^{-1} obtained with the running test in the same subjects ($n = 16$). The difference in mean maximal heart rate ($\pm$ SD) was also significant (194 ± 12 versus 202 ± 7 bpm for the walking and running protocols, respectively). More subjects met the criterion of a $\dot{V}O_2$ plateau, a heart rate greater than 198 bpm, and a respiratory exchange ratio greater than 1.0 with the running test than with the walking test.

Sheehan et al. also looked at the difference between a continuous and an intermittent treadmill running protocol. Although not statistically significant, slightly higher values were obtained using the intermittent protocol (1.83 ± 0.24 L $\cdot$ min^{-1} or 48.7 ± 5.0 ml $\cdot$ kg^{-1} $\cdot$ min^{-1} for the intermittent protocol versus 1.80 ± 0.26 L $\cdot$ min^{-1} or 47.7 ± 4.2 ml $\cdot$ kg^{-1} $\cdot$ min^{-1} for the continuous protocol). Also, 12% more subjects met both the oxygen plateau criterion and the RER criterion of greater than 1.15 with the intermittent protocol than with the continuous protocol. The intermittent protocol took twice as long to complete as the continuous protocol. Similar results were found by Skinner et al. (63) with continuous and discontinuous walking protocols. Mean $\dot{V}O_2$max values ($\pm$ SD) of 53.0 ± 4.3 ml $\cdot$ kg^{-1} $\cdot$ min^{-1} and 51.6 ± 7.0 ml $\cdot$ kg^{-1} $\cdot$ min^{-1} were obtained using intermittent and continuous tests, respectively, in two comparable groups of 6- to 15-year-old boys. These values were not significantly different, but the intermittent test took more than three times as long to complete as the continuous test.

Reliability of $\dot{V}O_2$max

Reliability of $\dot{V}O_2$max in children has been investigated using several approaches. Baggley and Cumming (4) reported a reliability coefficient of $r = .92$ in 14- to 17-year-olds when $\dot{V}O_2$max was measured four times over an 8-month period using a cycle ergometer. This is similar to the reliability coefficient of $r = .95$ reported by Boileau et al. (9). A lower reliability coefficient ($r = .81$) was reported by Cunningham et al. (19) for 10-year-old boys using a cycle ergometer test with the two tests conducted 24 to 48 hr apart.

Reliability coefficients using treadmill $\dot{V}O_2max$ protocols range from $r = .53$ to $r = .99$. Metz and Alexander (42) reported a reliability coefficient for maximal oxygen consumption values of $r = .99$; however, no details were given on how this value was obtained. Miyamura et al. (43) repeated a treadmill $\dot{V}O_2max$ test one week after a first test ($n = 38$) and found a correlation of $r = .90$ between the two tests in 13- to 14-year-old boys. Boileau et al. (9) also found a high correlation ($r = .97$) between two treadmill $\dot{V}O_2max$ tests in 11- to 14-year-old boys. The second test was completed 3 weeks after the first. Bonen et al. (10) found high correlations between two $\dot{V}O_2max$ tests in 7- to 15-year-old boys ($r = .97$ for $L \cdot min^{-1}$; $r = .87$ for $ml \cdot kg^{-1} \cdot min^{-1}$, $n = 21$).

Paterson et al. (47) examined the reliability of walking, jogging, and running protocols by repeating each test three times in 8 boys ages 10 to 12. All tests were completed within a 4-week period. Reliability coefficients were $r = .56$ ($L \cdot min^{-1}$) and $r = .47$ ($ml \cdot kg^{-1} \cdot min^{-1}$) for the walking protocol, $r = .91$ ($L \cdot min^{-1}$) and $r = .87$ ($ml \cdot kg^{-1} \cdot min^{-1}$) for the jogging protocol, and $r = .90$ ($L \cdot min^{-1}$) and $r = .95$ ($ml \cdot kg^{-1} \cdot min^{-1}$) for the running protocol. The running protocol produced the least variable results (3% to 6%) followed by the jogging protocol (5% to 8%); the most variability was found with the walking protocol (10% to 14%).

Cunningham et al. (19) reported a higher correlation between two treadmill $\dot{V}O_2max$ tests of 10-year-old boys conducted 4 to 5 months apart when a plateau was reached in both tests. When all subjects were examined, the test-retest correlation was $r = .53$. For the 18% of the subjects who showed an oxygen plateau in both tests, the reliability coefficient was $r = .74$. In those subjects who had an oxygen plateau in one of the tests (38%), the correlation between the two tests was $r = .60$; when no oxygen plateau was seen (38%), the correlation between the two tests was $r = .27$.

Adequate test-retest reliability for $\dot{V}O_2max$ has been reported for jogging, running, and cycling $\dot{V}O_2max$ among 10- to 14-year-old boys. Although it has been suggested that better $\dot{V}O_2max$ reliability is achieved when a $\dot{V}O_2$ plateau criterion is used, further research is needed to adequately address this issue.

Subject Selection

When comparing values from different studies, one should consider how the sample was selected (i.e., volunteers, random selection, or athletes). There appears to be bias toward physically fit subjects because people who are active and fit are more likely to volunteer for and cooperate in a study than are unfit individuals (56). Studies using volunteers have reported a greater percentage of values in the higher ranges (55 to 65 ml · kg^{-1} · min^{-1}) than have studies using randomly selected subjects. Studies using volunteers reported 15% from 45 to 50 ml · kg^{-1} · min^{-1}, 37% from 50 to 55 ml · kg^{-1} · min^{-1}, 37% from 55 to 60 ml · kg^{-1} · min^{-1}, and 11% from 60 to 65 ml · kg^{-1} · min^{-1}. Studies using random selection reported 11% from 45 to 50 ml · kg^{-1} · min^{-1}, 69% from 50 to 55 ml · kg^{-1} · min^{-1}, 21% from 55 to 60 ml · kg^{-1} · min^{-1}, and 0% from 60 to 65 ml · kg^{-1} · min^{-1}).

Endurance-trained children tend to have higher $\dot{V}O_2$max values than do those without strenuous endurance training. The majority of $\dot{V}O_2$max values reported for trained children were in the 55 to 60 ml · kg^{-1} · min^{-1} range (7% from 50 to 55 ml · kg^{-1} · min^{-1}, 64% from 55 to 60 ml · kg^{-1} · min^{-1}, and 29% from 60 to 65 ml · kg^{-1} · min^{-1}). For untrained children, 25% were from 45 to 50 ml · kg^{-1} · min^{-1}, 47% from 50 to 55 ml · kg^{-1} · min^{-1}, and 28% from 55 to 60 ml · kg^{-1} · min^{-1}. These untrained groups may have included some trained children, but subjects were randomly selected and did not contain exclusively one athletic group.

Criteria for $\dot{V}O_2$max

The use of criteria to establish if a true maximal oxygen consumption is obtained during a test is important. Cunningham et al. (19) found that $\dot{V}O_2$max was more reliable over two trials if a plateau was seen. Also, slightly higher lactate and respiratory exchange ratios were seen in subjects who showed a plateau. Because not all children show a plateau (62), more than one criterion is needed. In fact, Rowland and Cunningham suggested that a plateau in $\dot{V}O_2$ should not be used as a criterion measure in children because few children demonstrate a plateau during maximal testing (54). Perhaps a combination of criteria should be established as guidelines. A maximal heart rate above 190 bpm and a heart rate plateau appear to be good criteria; this allows for the population variation in maximal heart rate and assures that the cardiorespiratory system is stressed maximally. This may or may not pertain to trained child athletes; high $\dot{V}O_2$max values have been obtained in this group with maximal heart rates lower than expected (67). Also, when both a heart plateau and an oxygen consumption plateau were achieved during the same maximal test of a child, the heart rate plateau occurred first and was 100 to 300 kg · m below the oxygen consumption plateau (67).

Norms for $\dot{V}O_2$max in Children

Figures 1 and 2 illustrate the relationship between $\dot{V}O_2$max and age among boys and girls from 6 to 18 years of age. This represents a cross-sectional

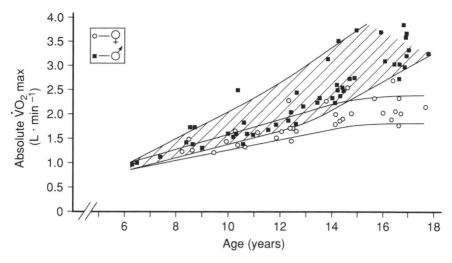

Figure 1: Absolute V̇O₂max (L · min⁻¹) versus chronological age.

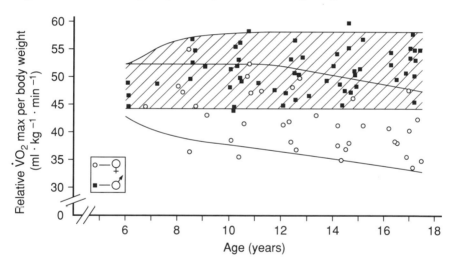

Figure 2: Relative V̇O₂max (ml · kg⁻¹ · min⁻¹) versus chronological age. *Note.* Figures 1 and 2 are from *Pediatric Sports Medicine for the Practitioner* (pp. 4, 5) by O. Bar-Or, 1983, New York: Springer-Verlag. Copyright 1983 by Springer-Verlag. Reprinted by permission.

analysis from several different studies that has been compiled by Bar-Or (5). When V̇O₂max is expressed as an absolute score (L · min⁻¹ in Figure 1), the rate of increase is similar between boys and girls up to age 12. Gender differences are present even before puberty, but the magnitude of this difference nearly doubles after puberty. These gender differences are related to a number of factors, including muscle mass, hemoglobin concentration, and physical activity (32).

Relative $\dot{V}O_2$max (ml · kg^{-1} · min^{-1}) versus age is presented in Figure 2. Relative $\dot{V}O_2$max remains relatively stable over the age span for boys and decreases for girls. This decrease is most likely explained by an increase in body fat among girls (5).

Although the database used to develop these norms is large, caution must be exercised in their interpretation. Growth and maturation influence $\dot{V}O_2$max in children and at any given chronological age, the maturity level may be very different between children. Therefore, these data must be considered as general trends in $\dot{V}O_2$max; large variations may exist between individuals. Growth and maturation greatly influence $\dot{V}O_2$max in children (but not in adults). One must consider this factor when interpreting normative $\dot{V}O_2$max responses in children.

Conclusion

Measurement of oxygen uptake ($\dot{V}O_2$) during exercise testing can provide useful information beyond that obtained by electrocardiographic monitoring and observation for symptoms. Because oxygen uptake is the product of cardiac output and peripheral oxygen uptake, determination of $\dot{V}O_2$max provides an indirect estimation of maximal cardiac output and functional reserve. In this manner, $\dot{V}O_2$max gives a numerical assessment of cardiovascular fitness and can be used to serially assess changes in training athletes, responses to rehabilitation programs, and clinical course of young patients with cardiac and pulmonary disease. Because the maximal oxygen uptake measured during a progressive exercise test is dependent on patient effort, it is important to verify that criteria for a true maximal test have been attained. $\dot{V}O_2$max values are also affected by mode of exercise and type of protocol, with treadmill running producing the highest levels. There are no accepted norms for $\dot{V}O_2$max in children; a wide range of values have been reported from various laboratories. Values for $\dot{V}O_2$max remain essentially stable relative to body weight during the prepubertal years.

References

1. Anderson, K.L. , V. Seliger, J. Rutenfranz, and R. Mocellin. Physical performance capacity of children in Norway: I. Population parameters in a rural inland community with regard to maximal aerobic power. *Eur. J. Appl. Physiol.* 33:177-195, 1974.
2. Armstrong, N., J. Balding, P. Gentle, J. Williams, and B. Kirby. Peak oxygen uptake and physical activity in 11- to 16-year-olds. *Pediatr. Exerc. Sci.* 2:349-358, 1990.

3. Astrand, P.O. Definitions, testing procedures, accuracy, and reproducibility. *Acta Paediatr. Scand.* 217(Suppl.):9-12, 1971.

4. Baggley, G., and G.R. Cumming. Serial measurement of working and aerobic capacity of Winnipeg school children during a school year. In: *Environmental Effects of Work Performance,* G.R. Cumming, A.W. Taylor, and D. Snidal (Eds.). AB: Canadian Association of Sport Sciences, 1972, pp. 173-186.

5. Bar-Or, O. *Pediatric Sports Medicine for the Practitioner.* New York: Springer-Verlag, 1983.

6. Binkhorst, R.A., W.H.M. Saris, A.M. Noordeloos, M.A. Van't Hof, and A.F.J. De Haan. Maximal oxygen consumption of children (6 to 18 years) predicted from maximal and submaximal values in treadmill and bicycle tests. In: *Children and Exercise XII,* J. Rutenfranz, R. Mocellin, and F. Klimt (Eds.). Champaign, IL: Human Kinetics, 1986, pp. 227-232.

7. Binyildiz, P.O. Prediction of maximal oxygen uptake in boys 11-13 years of age. *Eur. J. Appl. Physiol.* 43:213-219, 1980.

8. Blimkie, C.J.R., D.A. Cunningham, and P.M. Nichol. Gas transport capacity and echocardiographically determined cardiac size in children. *J. Appl. Physiol.* 49:994-999, 1980.

9. Boileau, R.A., A. Bonen, V.H. Heyward, and B.H. Massey. Maximal aerobic capacity on the treadmill and bicycle ergometer of boys 11-14 years of age. *J. Sports Med.* 17:153-162, 1977.

10. Bonen, A., V.H., Heyward, K.J. Cureton, R.A. Boileau, and B.H. Massey. Prediction of maximal oxygen uptake in boys, ages 7-15 years. *Med. Sci. Sports* 11:24-29, 1979.

11. Cumming, G.R. Maximal treadmill endurance times of children with heart defects. In: *Children and Exercise IX,* K. Berg and B.O. Eriksson (Eds.). Baltimore: University Park Press, 1980, pp. 354-368.

12. Cumming, G.R., and R. Danzinger. Bicycle ergometer studies in children. *Pediatrics* 32:202-208, 1963.

13. Cumming, G.R., and W. Friesen. Bicycle ergometer measurement of maximal oxygen uptake in children. *Can. J. Physiol. Pharmacol.* 45:937-946, 1967.

14. Cumming, G.R., and S. Langford. Comparison of nine exercise tests used in pediatric cardiology. In: *Children and Exercise XI,* R.A. Binkhorst, H.C.G. Kemper, and W.H.M. Saris (Eds.). Champaign, IL: Human Kinetics, 1985, pp. 58-68.

15. Cunningham, D.A., and R.B. Eynon. The working capacity of young competitive swimmers, 10-16 years of age. *Med. Sci. Sports* 5:227-231, 1973.

16. Cunningham, D.A., and D.H. Paterson. Age specific prediction of maximal oxygen uptake in boys. *Can. J. Appl. Sport Sci.* 10:75-80, 1985.

17. Cunningham, D.A., J.J. Stapleton, I.C. MacDonald, and D.H. Paterson. Daily energy expenditure of young boys as related to maximal aerobic power. *Can. J. Appl. Sport Sci.* 6:207-211, 1981.

18. Cunningham, D.A., P. Telford, and G.T. Swart. The cardiopulmonary capacities of young hockey players: Age 10. *Med. Sci. Sports* 8:23-25, 1976.
19. Cunningham, D.A., B.M.V. Waterschoot, D.H. Paterson, M. Lefcoe, and S.P. Sangal. Reliability and reproducibility of maximal oxygen uptake measurement in children. *Med. Sci. Sports* 9:104-108, 1977.
20. Daniels, J., and N. Oldridge. Changes in oxygen consumption of young boys during growth and running training. *Med. Sci. Sports* 3:161-165, 1971.
21. Devries, H.A., and C.E. Klafs. Prediction of maximal oxygen intake from submaximal tests. *J. Sports Med.* 16:207-214, 1976.
22. Eriksson, B.O., G. Grimby, and B. Saltin. Cardiac output and arterial blood gases during exercise in pubertal boys. *J. Appl. Physiol.* 31:348-352, 1971.
23. Gilliam, T.B., S. Sady, W.G. Thorland, and A.L. Weltman. Comparison of peak performance measures in children ages 6 to 8, 9 to 10, and 11 to 13 years. *Res. Q.* 48:695-702, 1977.
24. Hansen, H.S., K. Froberg, J.R. Nielsen, and N. Hyldebrandt. A new approach to assessing maximal aerobic power in children: The Odense School Child Study. *Eur. J. Appl. Physiol.* 58:618-624, 1989.
25. Hermansen, L., and S. Oseid. Direct and indirect estimation of maximal oxygen uptake in pre-pubertal boys. *Acta Paediatr. Scand.* 217(Suppl.): 18-23, 1971.
26. Hill, A.V., and H. Lupton. Muscular exercise, lactic acid and the supply and utilization of oxygen. *Q. J. Med.* 16:135-139, 1923.
27. Ikai, M., and K. Kitagawa. Maximum oxygen uptake of Japanese related to sex and age. *Med. Sci. Sports* 4:127-131, 1972.
28. Jetté, M., J. Campbell, J. Mongeon, and R. Routhier. The Canadian Home Fitness Test as a predictor of aerobic capacity. *Can. Med. Assoc. J.* 114:680-682, 1976.
29. Kannagi, T., R.A. Bruce, K.F. Hossack, K. Chang, F. Kusumi, and S. Trimble. An evaluation of the Beckman metabolic cart for measuring ventilation and aerobic requirements during exercise. *J. Cardiac Rehabil.* 3:38-53, 1983.
30. Katch, V.L. Use of the oxygen/body weight ratio in correlation analyses: Spurious correlations and statistical considerations. *Med. Sci. Sports* 5:253-257, 1973.
31. Krahenbuhl, G.S., and R.P. Pangrazi. Characteristics associated with running performance in young boys. *Med. Sci. Sports Exerc.* 15:486-490, 1983.
32. Krahenbuhl, G.S., J.S. Skinner, and W.M. Kohrt. Developmental aspects of maximal aerobic power in children. In: *Exercise Sport Science Reviews*, R.L. Terjung (Ed.). New York: Macmillan, 1985, pp. 503-538.
33. Lavoisier, A.L., and P.S. Laplace. Memoire sur la chaleur. *Memoires, de l'Academic Royale.* p. 355, 1780.

34. Maksud, M.G.,and K.D. Coutts. Application of the Cooper twelve-minute run-walk test to young males. *Res. Q.* 42:54-59, 1971.
35. Maksud, M.G., K.D. Coutts, and L.H. Hamilton. Oxygen uptake, ventilation, and heart rate: Study in negro children during strenuous exercise. *Arch. Environ. Health* 23:23-28, 1971.
36. Massicotte, D.R., R. Gauthier, and P. Markon. Prediction of VO₂max from the running performance in children aged 10-17 years. *J. Sports Med.* 25:10-17, 1985.
37. Matsui, H., M. Miyashita, M. Miura, K. Kobayashi, T. Hoshikawa, and S. Kamei. Maximum oxygen intake and its relationship to body weight of Japanese adolescents. *Med. Sci. Sports* 4:29-32, 1972.
38. Mayers, N., and B. Gutin. Physiological characteristics of elite prepubertal cross-country runners. *Med. Sci. Sports* 11:172-176, 1979.
39. McArdle, W.D., F.I. Katch, and V.L. Katch. *Exercise Physiology: Energy Nutrition and Human Performance.* Philadelphia: Lea & Febiger, 1986.
40. McKay, G.A., and E.W. Banister. A comparison of maximum oxygen uptake determination by bicycle ergometry at various pedaling frequencies and by treadmill running at various speeds. *Eur. J. Appl. Physiol.* 35:191-200, 1976.
41. Metz, K.F., and J.F. Alexander. An investigation of the relationship between maximum aerobic work capacity and physical fitness in twelve- to fifteen-year-old boys. *Res. Q.* 41:75-81, 1970.
42. Metz, K.F., and J.F. Alexander. Estimation of maximal oxygen intake from submaximal work parameters. *Res. Q.* 42:187-193, 1971.
43. Miyamura, M., H. Kuroda, K. Hirata, and Y. Honda. Evaluations of the step test scores based on the measurements of maximal aerobic powers. *J. Sports Med.* 15:316-322, 1975.
44. Morse, M., F.W. Schultz, and D.E. Cassels. Relation of age to physiological response of the older boy (10-17 years) to exercise. *J. Appl. Physiol.* 1:683-709, 1949.
45. Nakagawa, A., and T. Ishiko. Assessment of aerobic capacity with special reference to sex and age of junior and senior high school students in Japan. *Jpn. J. Physiol.* 20:118-129, 1970.
46. Nixon, P.A., and D.M. Orenstein. Exercise testing in children. *Pediatr. Pulmonol.* 5:107-122, 1988.
47. Paterson, D.H., D.A. Cunningham, and A. Donner. The effect of different treadmill speeds on the variability of VO₂ max in children. *Eur. J. Appl. Physiol.* 47:113-122, 1981.
48. Petzl, D.H., P. Haver, E. Schuster, C. Popow, and F. Haschke. Reliability of estimation of maximum performance capacity on the basis of submaximum ergometric stress tests in children 10-14 years old. *Eur. J. Pediatr.* 147:174-178, 1988.
49. Rodahl, K., P.O. Astrand, N.C., Birkhead, T., Hettinger, B. Issekutz, D.M. Jones, and R. Weaver. Physical working capacity: A study of some

children and young adults in the United States. *Arch. Environ. Health* 2:499-510, 1961.
50. Rowland, T.W. Oxygen uptake and endurance fitness in children: A developmental perspective. *Pediatr. Exerc. Sci.* 1:313-328, 1989.
51. Rowland, T.W. *Exercise and Children's Health.* Champaign, IL: Human Kinetics, 1990.
52. Rowland, T. "Normalizing" maximal oxygen uptake or the search for the holy grail (per kg). *Pediatr. Exerc. Sci.* 3:95-102, 1991.
53. Rowland, T.W., J.A. Auchinachie, T.J. Keenan, and G.M. Green. Submaximal aerobic running economy and treadmill performance in prepubertal boys. *Int. J. Sports Med.* 9:201-204, 1988.
54. Rowland, T.W., and L.N. Cunningham. Oxygen uptake plateau during maximal treadmill exercise in children. *Chest* (in press).
55. Rutenfranz, J., K.L. Andersen, V. Seliger, F. Klimmer, I. Berndt, and M. Ruppel. Maximum aerobic power and body composition during the puberty growth period: Similarities and differences between children of two European countries. *Eur. J. Pediatr.* 136:123-133, 1981.
56. Saris, W.H.M., A.M. Noordeloos, B.E.M. Ringhalda, M.A. Van't Hof, and R.A. Binkhorst. Reference values for aerobic power of healthy 4- to 18-year-old Dutch children: Preliminary results. In: *Children and Exercise XI.*, R.A. Binkhorst, H.C.G. Kemper, and W.H.M. Saris (Eds.). Champaign, IL: Human Kinetics, 1985, pp. 151-160.
57. Sheehan, J.M., T.W. Rowland, and E.J. Burke. A comparison of four treadmill protocols for determination of maximum oxygen uptake in 10- to 12-year-old boys. *Int. J. Sports Med.* 8:31-34, 1987.
58. Shephard, R.J. The working capacity of schoolchildren. In: *Frontiers of Fitness*, R.J. Shephard (Ed.). Springfield, IL: Charles C. Thomas, 1971, pp. 319-344.
59. Shephard, R.J. Tests of maximum oxygen intake: A critical review. *Sports Med.* 1:99-124, 1984.
60. Shephard, R.J., C. Allen, O. Bar-Or, C.T.M. Davies, S. Degre, R. Hedman, K. Ishii, M. Kaneko, J.R. La Cour, P.E. Di Prampero, and V. Seliger. The working capacity of Toronto schoolchildren: I. *Can. Med. Assoc. J.* 100:560-566, 1969.
61. Shephard, R.J., C. Allen, O. Bar-Or, C.T.M. Davies, S. Degre, R. Hedman, K. Ishii, M. Kaneko, J.R. La Cour, P.E. Di Prampero, and V. Seliger. The working capacity of Toronto schoolchildren. II. *Can. Med. Assoc. J.* 100:705-714, 1969.
62. Shephard, R.J., C.H. Weese, and J.E. Merriman. Prediction of maximal oxygen intake from anthropometric data: Some observations on preadolescent schoolchildren. *Int. Z. Angew. Physiol.* 29:119-130, 1971.
63. Skinner, J.S., O. Bar-Or, V. Bergsteinova, C.W. Bell, D. Royer, and E.R. Buskirk. Comparison of continuous and intermittent tests for determining maximal oxygen intake in children. *Acta Paediatr. Scand.* 217(Suppl.): 24-28, 1971.

64. Sobolova, V., V. Seliger, D. Grussova, J. Machovcova, and V. Zelenka. The influence of age and sports training in swimming on physical fitness. *Acta Paediatr. Scand.* 217(Suppl.):63-67, 1971.

65. Sprynarova, S. Development of the relationship between aerobic capacity and the circulatory and respiratory reaction to moderate activity in boys 11-13 years old. *Physiol. Bohemoslov.* 15:253-264, 1966.

66. Spurr, G.B., J.C. Reina, M. Barac-Nieto, and M.G. Maksud. Maximum oxygen consumption of nutritionally normal white, mestizo, and black Columbian boys 6-16 years of age. *Hum. Biol.* 54:553-574, 1982.

67. Sundberg, S., and R. Elovainio. Cardiorespiratory function in competitive endurance runners aged 12-16 years compared with ordinary boys. *Acta Paediatr. Scand.* 71:987-992.

68. Sunnegårdh, J., and L.E. Bratteby. Maximal oxygen uptake, anthropometry and physical activity in a randomly selected sample of 8 and 13 year old children in Sweden. *Eur. J. Appl. Physiol.* 56:266-272, 1987.

69. Thiart, B.F., and C.T. Wessels. The maximal oxygen intake of physically active boys, 8-13 years of age. *Acta Paediatr. Belg.* 28(Suppl.):48-53, 1974.

70. van Mechelen, W., H. Hlobil, and H.C.G. Kemper. Validation of two running tests as estimates of maximal aerobic power in children. *Eur. J. Appl. Physiol.* 55:503-506, 1986.

71. Vodak, P.A., and J.H. Wilmore. Validity of the 6-minute jog-walk and the 600-yard run-walk in estimating endurance capacity in boys, 9-12 years of age. *Res. Q.* 46:230-234, 1975.

72. Washington, R.L., J.C. Van Gundy, C. Cohen, H.M. Sondheimer, and R.R. Wolfe. Normal aerobic and anaerobic exercise data for North American school-age children. *J. Pediatr.* 122:223-233, 1988.

73. Waters, R.L., B.R. Lunsford, J. Perry, and R. Byrd. Energy-speed relationship of walking: Standard tables. *Orthop. Res.* 6:215-222, 1988.

74. Wilmore, J.H., J.A. Davis, and A.C. Norton. An automated system for assessing metabolic and respiratory function during exercise. *J. Appl. Physiol.* 40:619-624, 1976.

75. Woynarowska, B. The validity of indirect estimations of maximal oxygen uptake in children 11-12 years of age. *Eur. J. Appl. Physiol.* 43:19-23, 1980.

76. Yamaji, K., M. Miyashita, and R.J. Shephard. Relationship between heart rate and relative oxygen intake in male subjects aged 10 to 27 years. *J. Hum. Ergol.* 7:29-39, 1978.

77. Yoshizawa, S. A comparative study of aerobic work capacity of urban and rural adolescents. *J. Hum. Ergol.* 1:45-65, 1972.

78. Zauner, C.W., and N.Y. Benson. Continuous treadmill walking versus intermittent treadmill running as maximal exercise tests for young competitive swimmers. *J. Sports Med.* 21:173-178, 1981.

Anaerobic Threshold

Reginald L. Washington, MD
Rocky Mountain Pediatric Cardiology

The term *anaerobic threshold* (AT) historically has been used to describe the point at which oxygen supply is thought to no longer meet the oxygen demands of exercising muscle. This concept has been extensively debated in the literature, and the highlights of this debate are presented in this section. Relatively little research has been completed evaluating the use of anaerobic threshold in children. This review discusses the concept of the ventilatory anaerobic threshold (VAT) and its applications to pediatric exercise.

Anaerobiosis, Lactate, and Gas Exchange During Exercise

At very low exercise intensities, the concentration of blood lactate is nearly identical to levels recorded at rest. At some particular level of exercise

Note. Portions of this chapter are from ''Anaerobic Threshold in Children'' by R.L. Washington, 1989, *Pediatric Exercise Science, 1*(3), pp. 244-256. Copyright 1989 by Human Kinetics Publishers, Inc. Reprinted by permission.

intensity, which varies among subjects, blood lactate concentration begins to increase. As the oxygen demand of exercising muscle exceeds the oxygen supply, anaerobic metabolism is used to supply the energy required to continue work. Lactic acid is a by-product of this anaerobic metabolism. Once formed, lactic acid will be almost completely disassociated in the serum, and it is buffered predominantly by the bicarbonate system.

$$Na^+HCO_3^- + H^+LA^- \rightarrow Na^+LA^- + H_2CO_3 \rightarrow (-H_2O + CO_2)$$

Consequent to the buffering of lactic acid, the partial pressure of CO_2 in the venous capillary blood increases. The ventilatory control mechanisms try to maintain homeostasis of PCO_2, resulting in an increase in ventilation. Thus, as lactic acid increases during exercise, ventilation responds to two different CO_2 sources: (a) the metabolic CO_2 generated from aerobic metabolism and (b) the excess CO_2 resulting from buffered lactic acid (6).

Recently investigators have challenged the idea that muscle hypoxia during exercise is the cause of the increase in blood lactate at a particular work rate (13, 19). These investigators emphasize that blood lactate concentration is the net result of lactate production countered by lactate clearance. The rise in lactate concentration may not necessarily indicate the onset of increased production per se. An increase in lactate production could have occurred much earlier but may not have caused an immediate increase in the blood lactate concentration, because lactate clearance also increased.

In resting individuals, lactic acid is formed in several tissues: intestines, skeletal muscle, red blood cells, and even some regions of the liver. Glucose breakdown appears to be a major source of lactic acid formation at rest. Much of the lactic acid that is formed by conversion of dietary glucose is converted to liver glycogen or is oxidized directly as an energy source. The significant role of lactic acid as an oxidizable fuel in both resting and exercising subjects was not recognized until isotope tracers were used to study lactic acid metabolism (29).

Until recently, the study of lactate metabolism in humans during exercise has been limited to measurements of lactate concentration in the blood and the muscle and to the arteriovenous lactate differences across specific tissue beds. These measurements yield valuable but incomplete information regarding the rates and pathways of lactate turnover during oxidation. Mazzeo et al. (24) used the stable, nonradioactive tracer[1-^{13}C] lactate to evaluate the magnitude and extent of blood lactate disposal and oxidation in humans at rest and during two different exercise intensities. They found that blood lactate disposal rates were significantly correlated to oxygen consumption (VO_2) and that the lactate oxidation rate was similarly related to VO_2. Mazzeo et al. concluded that blood lactate concentration is not an accurate indicator of lactate disposal or oxidation during exercise.

It appears that the increase in lactate above baseline depends on the balance between the rate of production and the rate of catabolism. The blood lactate concentration during exercise is dependent upon increased lactate production, which is countered by increased lactate clearance (by the liver and other lactate-consuming tissues). Factors controlling the balance of the formation, uptake, and release of lactate are complex. These factors include beta-adrenergic stimulation, prior endurance training, glucose uptake and utilization, and the role of decreased oxygen tension (hypoxia). The regulation of this production versus clearance deserves further research.

The original concept of a sharp increase in serum concentration of lactate corresponding to the point at which exercising muscle cells become anaerobic is not valid. Lactate is more than a dead-end metabolite that accumulates during exercise. The lactate level in serum is the result of a complex interaction between production and clearance, which is, as of yet, poorly understood and deserves further investigation.

Onset of Blood Lactate Accumulation

Blood lactate concentrations can be measured during exercise. There is a point at which the blood lactate concentration sharply rises, and this point has been termed the onset of blood lactate accumulation (OBLA). Green et al. (19) investigated the interrelationship between the acute increase in ventilation during exercise and the OBLA. They found that the oxygen consumption at the point of increased ventilation expressed in terms of power output occurred at a higher value than the OBLA, also expressed in terms of power output. Green et al. concluded that the hyperventilation that occurs during exercise, and the AT as determined by blood lactate accumulation, do not represent identical biochemical events. This observation suggests, then, that an increase in anaerobic metabolism by exercising muscle precedes both the onset of hyperventilation during exercise and the OBLA. Similar observations have been reported by others (3, 24).

Some investigators use an absolute blood lactate level of 2 mmol $\cdot$ L^{-1} or 4 mmol $\cdot$ L^{-1} as a definition of AT. This concept was evaluated by Davis et al. (9), who found that the VAT did not correspond with the fixed absolute lactate concentration of 2 mmol $\cdot$ L^{-1} or 4 mmol $\cdot$ L^{-1}. Other studies (11) have shown that the AT occurs at the same oxygen uptake whether measured by gas exchange or absolute blood lactate concentration. This finding was thought to eliminate the need for blood sampling (and subsequent lactate analysis) and thus allowed noninvasive determination of AT during standard incremental exercise testing.

Brooks (3), in an extensive review of the concept of AT, remarked that lactate production occurs in contracting muscle for reasons other than oxygen limitation on mitochondrial adenosine triphosphate (ATP) production. He concluded by remarking that several groups of investigators have produced results indicating that parameters associated with changes in pulmonary minute ventilation do not always track changes in blood lactate concentration.

To confuse the picture, recent data (11) suggest that the increase of serum lactate level begins immediately after the onset of graded exercise and continues throughout a graded exercise study. This observation suggests that the acute increase in blood lactate levels actually represents a point at which clearance of lactate from the body is exceeded by production of lactate at the muscular level, and it implies that hypoxia and anaerobic metabolism begin at the cellular level long before the accumulation of the lactic acid in the serum. For this reason, the threshold of Wasserman and McIlroy (43) discussed in the next paragraph may represent the point at which the clearance of lactate from the serum is too slow to keep pace with production. The lactate that accumulates then is buffered by HCO_3 and results in hyperventilation—the VAT.

Ventilatory Anaerobic Threshold

If respiratory chemoreceptors are intact, the increased CO_2 production associated with an increase in the blood level of lactate and a reciprocal decrease in bicarbonate results in an increase in ventilatory drive. The point at which ventilation increases was termed the *anaerobic threshold* by Wasserman and McIlroy (43) in 1964. They observed that ventilation (V_E) increases out of proportion to VO_2 at work rates above the AT. The increase in V_E reflects an increase in respiratory frequency without an increase in tidal volume. The AT described by Wasserman and McIlroy is now referred to as the VAT.

Work performed at levels above VAT is associated with an increased oxygen debt (47). The VAT also demarks the work rate above which VO_2 kinetics are slowed, resulting in a delay of steady state after changes in work rate during an incremental test.

Methods

Several methods have been proposed for determining AT. As discussed above, the definition of AT is not at all clear and, therefore, comparison of various methodologies becomes cumbersome. To some, the AT marks the point at which the exercising muscle begins to use predominantly anaerobic metabolism for its energy supply (8). Others define the AT as that point at which the concentration of lactate in the serum abruptly increases (the OBLA). Still others define AT as that point at which the production of lactate exceeds the lactate clearance from the serum. Methods have been described that determine the AT using any of the definitions above. Caution must be used when comparing one method with another.

The VAT probably occurs at a time slightly later than the abrupt increase of lactic acid in the serum during exercise. It is not accurate to compare a technique that attempts to determine the VAT to one that measures lactate levels. Several studies that have reviewed the methods for determining AT and VAT are reviewed here.

The classic concept of lactate threshold has been used by exercise physiologists for years. It has been demonstrated that this threshold can be repeatedly obtained in individuals (11), can be used in training (10), and can predict athletic performance (38). Traditionally, this threshold is said to occur at 4 mmol $\cdot$ L^{-1} in adults (1). Annola and Rusko (1) found poor reproducibility of blood lactate concentration at the AT if this threshold is fixed at 2 or 4 mmol $\cdot$ L^{-1}. Mazzeo et al. (24), using tracer techniques, suggested that blood lactate concentration is not an accurate indicator of lactate disposal and oxidation. This could explain why it may not be helpful to use a set concentration of lactate to define the AT.

The normal range for the VO_2 at which plasma lactate abruptly increases is not easy to determine. The results are extremely variable. Davis et al. found the range to be from 39.6 to 62.1 ml $\cdot$ kg^{-1} $\cdot$ min^{-1} in 39 adult males (11). In untrained healthy children, Washington et al. found the range to be equally varied (16 to 55 ml $\cdot$ kg^{-1} $\cdot$ min^{-1}) or 75% $\pm$ 13% of $\dot{V}O_2$max (41).

Plasma lactate concentrations at a given level of exercise are variable and are sensitive to various clinical conditions including anemia (20), pedal speed (20), and hypoxia. They are even influenced by the composition of the preexercise meal (46). Wasserman (42) has suggested the use of a ramp test with rapid power increases to determine the lactate threshold. Such a test allows little time for plasma concentration to be altered by lactate diffusion into nonexercising muscle. However, ramp tests are not useful if other parameters are to be measured and evaluated (dysrhythmias, peak blood pressure, peak oxygen consumption, etc.).

During progressive exercise, V_E increases linearly with VO_2. The ventilatory equivalent for oxygen (V_E/VO_2) and the ventilatory equivalent for CO_2 (V_E/VCO_2) may be plotted against time. There occurs a point at which the V_E/VO_2 increases without a change in the V_E/VCO_2, and this is VAT as described by Wasserman and McIlroy (43) (see Figure 1). Numerous investigators have since refined the techniques used to noninvasively determine the VAT. The VAT has been identified by nonlinear increases in minute ventilation (11), nonlinear increases in CO_2 production (42), and abrupt systematic increases in the respiratory exchange ratio (36). Ciozzo et al. (4) compared several of these gas exchange indexes and favored the V_E/VO_2 for the noninvasive determination of VAT. Washington et al. (41) found that if the respiratory exchange ratio (VCO_2/VO_2) is plotted against time, frequently the slope changes abruptly at the VAT as determined by plotting the V_E/VO_2 and VE/VCO$_2$ versus time (see Figure 1). If both parameters are used, the reproducibility of this technique is improved.

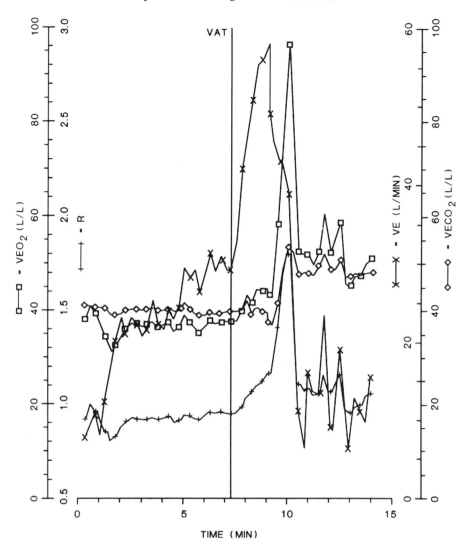

Figure 1: Determination of ventilatory anaerobic threshold (VAT), which occurs when the slope of ventilatory equivalent for oxygen (V_E/VO_2) increases without a simultaneous change in the slope for ventilatory equivalent for carbon dioxide (V_E/VCO_2). (R denotes respiratory exchange ratio.) *Note.* From "Anaerobic Threshold in Children" by R.L. Washington. *Pediatr. Exerc. Sci.* 1:249, 1989. Copyright 1989 by Human Kinetics Publishers, Inc. Reprinted by permission.

Several investigators have studied the range of reviewer variability obtained with these ventilation techniques to determine the VAT. Yeh et al. (48) concluded that the noninvasive gas response determinations had such a wide range of variability (average range 16%) that these techniques should be abandoned. Gladden (18) agreed with this concern and offered the suggestion that breath-by-breath technology would be useful in eliminating this variability. Washington (unpublished data) evaluated the use of breath-by-breath analyzers in determining the VAT and found that if all data are used, there are too many points, which makes an exact determination nearly impossible. If the data are averaged in 10- to 15-s intervals, a clear deflection point is usually discernible. The VAT cannot be determined in certain subjects (approximately 20%) during exercise because of an erratic breathing pattern (11, 41).

Conconi et al. (5) proposed a noninvasive method for evaluating the AT. The heart rate during exercise is plotted against time. At a certain point during exercise, the slope of the heart rate decreases rather acutely; this point of tapering has been termed the heart rate deflection point. This deflection point is thought by some to coincide with the OBLA. Gaisl and Wiesspeiner (17) evaluated this noninvasive technique in children 11 years of age. According to their data, the heart rate determined using ventilatory techniques and the heart rate determined by using the OBLA were similar, which suggested the use of the heart rate deflection point in children. Further studies using this technique will be required before firm conclusions can be drawn and before this technique can be recommended for children.

The use of ventilatory techniques to determine the VAT is in part dependence on the type of exercise being performed. Davis et al. (11) have shown that the VAT varies when the same subjects are tested with different exercise protocols. The best method for expressing the phenomenon of VAT is not clear. Several investigators (4, 41) suggest that VAT is most useful when expressed as a percent of maximum VO_2 at VAT.

Normal Values

There are few published studies establishing normal values for VAT in children. Data presented in Table 1 have been extrapolated from several articles and reflect the wide variability of normal values reported. Two larger studies reported normal values for treadmill and bicycle ergometers. Reybrouck et al. reported normal values for children 5.7 to 18.5 years old using the treadmill (33). Washington et al. published normal values for children from 6 to 13 years of age using the bicycle ergometer (41).

The VAT is observed at a significantly lower $\dot{V}O_2$ in girls compared to boys of the same age; this suggests that anaerobiosis begins at a lower exercise intensity in girls.

When these data are compared to normal standards for adults, it appears that the VAT (expressed in $ml \cdot kg^{-1} \cdot min^{-1}$ or percent $\dot{V}O_2max$) decreases with age. This finding suggests that an increase in the ability to exercise anaerobically occurs during growth. The AT of children and adolescents, when expressed as a percent of $\dot{V}O_2max$, is higher than that found in adults. This would imply that the VAT occurs later in time during exercise and, once

Table 1   Normal Values for VAT in Children

Study	VAT % $\dot{V}O_2$max		HR at VAT		R at VAT cc/min/kg		VO_2 at VAT		Comments
	M	F	M	F	M	F	M	F	
Washington (41)	75	71	169	167	0.98	0.99	34	30	151 children; 7.5-12.5 years old
	±13	±9	±15	±16	±0.04	±0.04	±7	±5	
Cooper (6)	60 ± 9						M	F	109 children; 6-17 years old
							27	19	
							±6	±6	
Reybrouck (32)	M 58-74	F 61-70					M 29-35	F 24-29	95 children; 5-14 years old

Note. HR = heart rate. R = respiratory exchange ratio. M = male. F = female. From "Anaerobic Threshold in Children" by R.L. Washington. *Pediatr. Exerc. Sci.* 1:251, 1989. Copyright by Human Kinetics Publishers, Inc. Adapted by permission.

it occurs, is not well tolerated by young children. Maximal lactate levels are lower in children than in adults during exercise (26). Eriksson et al. (16) have suggested that the ability to produce lactate during maximal exercise depends on sexual maturity. This may be because children have a lower concentration of the glycolytic enzyme phosphofructokinase than is found in adults (15). Therefore, the fixed blood lactate level used to indicate the anaerobic threshold may be close to the maximal blood lactate value that can be reached in young children and therefore should not be used.

Studies comparing VAT for arm exercise versus VAT for leg exercise have not been carried out in children. Data established in adults (11) show that VAT for arm exercise occurs earlier. Davis et al. (11) suggest that this difference is related to differences in recruitment patterns of motor units during arm crank tests versus leg tests. At some point during exercise, arm muscles are taxed beyond their capability to supply energy entirely aerobically, and thus lactate is produced. Jones and Ehrsam (21) believe that the exercising muscle mass does not influence ventilatory threshold when expressed relative to the $\dot{V}O_2$max. It is possible, therefore, that discrepancies between studies are caused by the criteria used to define the ventilatory threshold and the $\dot{V}O_2$max.

VAT, Training, and Endurance Performance

VAT has been used to predict marathon time performance in adults (38). AT was found to be more closely associated with marathon running performance than was $\dot{V}O_2max$. Tanaka et al. (38) also found that the changes in distance running performance were more directly accounted for by changes in $\dot{V}O_2$ at AT than were any other parameters studied. Becker and Vaccaro found that, during an 8-week training period, children demonstrated an increase in $\dot{V}O_2$ at AT from 25.9 to 33.2 ml $\cdot$ kg^{-1} $\cdot$ min^{-1} (2).

Tanaka et al. (38) found that in adults the VAT is a more accurate predictor of endurance performance than is the OBLA (at 4 mmol $\cdot$ L^{-1}). Vago et al. (40) established that the VAT actually reflects endurance capacity and that VAT should be determined systematically in addition to $\dot{V}O_2max$ during maximal exercise tests to better evaluate physical fitness. Wolfe et al. (46) predicted athletic performance in trained and untrained adolescents using $\dot{V}O_2$ at AT or heart rate at VAT.

Reybrouck (32) found that maximal endurance performance was best predicted by the ventilatory threshold for long-term exercise. Combining variables could not improve the prediction.

In adults, the VAT is sensitive to endurance training. Denis et al. (12) and Smith and O'Donnell (36) found that if the VAT was expressed as a percent of $\dot{V}O_2max$, it was more sensitive to training than $\dot{V}O_2max$. Ready and Quinney (31) found that during de-training in adults the VAT changes more rapidly than $\dot{V}O_2max$. The effects of training on VAT in children are not known.

Kindermann et al. (22) evaluated the lactate level obtained in adults during exercise performed with constant running speeds and demonstrated that the work load selected by the runners resulted in a serum lactate concentration of approximately 4 mmol $\cdot$ L^{-1}. They observed that exercise could be performed at this level for 45 to 60 min with a stable heart rate. Kindermann et al. concluded that during training the exercising heart rate should be approximately at the AT.

Weltman and Katch (44) studied the relationship in adults between maximum heart rate obtained during exercise and the heart rate at AT and concluded that the two heart rates are not related in the same subject, which suggests that an extrapolation cannot be made between maximum heart rate and heart rate at AT. Several investigators (14, 25) have suggested that the heart rate at VAT be used for training or rehabilitation in adults. Dwyer and Bibee (14) suggested that more uniform activity prescriptions could be obtained if the work performed was equated to the VAT and that this heart rate must be determined for each individual. Wolfe et al. (46) and Washington et al. (41) have demonstrated that, in children, the heart rate at VAT is variable in subjects of similar physical fitness, suggesting that the heart rate at VAT cannot be predicted and must be individually measured. Rowland and Green (35) found that in healthy children the heart rate at VAT often exceeded that predicted by standard formulas for calculating target heart rates in adults by over 10 bpm in a majority of girls studied. This study would indicate that target heart rate guidelines designed for training older individuals may not adequately stress oxygen delivery systems in prepubertal subjects.

In the past, exercise prescriptions have been based on specific percentages of either $\dot{V}O_2$max or maximum heart rate. These exercise prescriptions, however, cannot distinguish between exercise levels above or below the AT. Therefore, assigning an exercise prescription based solely on these parameters will produce a variety of metabolic responses.

Yoshida (49) observed that the absolute concentration of blood lactate during graded exercise is somewhat dependent on substrate availability (diet) in adults. Yoshida found that if one uses the blood lactate concentration for evaluating endurance, the OBLA would be altered. On the other hand, the lactate inflection point (and thus the VAT) is not influenced by diet in spite of altered blood lactate levels during graded exercise. This situation needs further investigation and has not been evaluated in children.

The VAT does not appear to be affected by exercise at altitude (45) or during other conditions that produce relative hypoxia (18). Stephenson et al. (37) evaluated the AT during phases of the menstrual cycle in women and reported that this cycle had no effect on the AT or $\dot{V}O_2$max.

Effects of Cardiac Malformations on the Anaerobic Threshold

Several studies have assessed the use of the AT in evaluating adults with heart disease. Matsumura et al. (23) demonstrated that the determination of AT by respiratory measurements is a safe, accurate, and objective method for measuring aerobic capacity in patients with coronary artery disease. Coyle et al. (7) evaluated the blood lactate threshold in well-trained patients with ischemic heart disease. These subjects demonstrated, after training, a relatively high VAT relative to $\dot{V}O_2$max. This suggests that some individuals with a $\dot{V}O_2$max that is limited by impaired cardiac function can undergo adaptations with training that enable them to maintain close to a steady metabolic state during exercise.

Opasich et al. (30) studied the relationship between VAT and hemodynamic patterns during a maximal symptom-limited stress test in adults. This study concluded that patients with a normal exercise wedge pressure showed a higher VAT than patients with abnormal exercise wedge pressures. If patients had their exercise tests evaluated using the concept of VAT and their VAT was normal, their exercise wedge pressures were also normal. Finally, patients with abnormal exercise hemodynamic patterns, classified according to VAT, showed different hemodynamics and different responses in ventricular function. In these patients, the level of AT seems to be related to cardiac impairment. Tanaka and Yoshimura (39) showed that in untrained individuals the stroke volume during exercise was relatively diminished above the work rate corresponding to the AT. This difference in stroke volume may be attributed to inadequate filling or diastolic dysfunction with impaired cardiac function secondary to disease states. Niemela et al. (28) was able to predict the effects of aortic valve replacement on exercise capacity. The patients likely to improve with valve replacement had a lower VAT preoperatively. Niemela et al. suggested that repeat determinations of VAT give additional data regarding functional status after surgery. Sequential exercise testing, in their opinion, did not require the patient to be exercised past the VAT.

Very little work has been done evaluating the usefulness of VAT in children who have congenital heart disease. Reybrouck et al. (34) evaluated 50 children with congenital heart disease and showed that VAT can easily be determined in most children over the age of 5 years. They reported that children with ventricular or atrial septal defects had no correlation between VAT and the size of the left-to-right shunt. The VAT, however, correlated significantly with morphologic variables and the habitual level of physical activity. This study also suggested that VAT is a more sensitive indicator of physical performance than $\dot{V}O_2$max in this population of patients.

A more sensitive indicator of physical performance is required in children who have undergone cardiac surgery because it appears that heart rate in this population is not an accurate predictor of physical performance or even of effort. Very often the chronotropic mechanism is altered either by the disease or the surgical treatment used to treat the disease. The use of the VAT measurement in this population is more sensitive in discriminating subnormal exercise capacity than normal standards. This is because its measurement is independent of maximal heart rate response if the VAT is expressed as a percentage of peak heart rate during the exercise study.

The heart rate at VAT can be determined using a submaximal test as long as the break point is identified; thus, the VAT is useful in studying children in whom it is not desirable to perform repeated maximal tests.

VAT and Exercise Intolerance

Wasserman (42) reviewed the applications of VAT in assessing patients with the subjective complaint of exercise intolerance. He suggests that in testing patients who complain of exercise intolerance, the VAT should be used to complement $\dot{V}O_2$max. If the $\dot{V}O_2$max and VAT are normal, Wasserman concludes that the patient is normal, is limited by obesity, or perhaps has mild lung disease. If the $\dot{V}O_2$max is low and the VAT is low, conditions that limit cardiac output during exercise should be considered (primary heart disease, pulmonary vascular disease, peripheral vascular disease, or anemia). If the $\dot{V}O_2$max is low and the VAT is normal, then the cardiovascular system is not the limiting factor. Instead, this patient is possibly limited by lung disease or is not willing to put forth the effort needed to generate a normal $\dot{V}O_2$max.

Conclusion

Whereas the biochemical interpretation of the AT is uncertain, a growing body of experimental data indicates the utility of measuring AT, usually indirectly as the VAT, during exercise testing. Because it typically correlates well with $\dot{V}O_2max$, AT may serve as an effective submaximal marker of aerobic fitness. The use of AT as an aerobic training threshold for improving cardiovascular fitness is conceptually attractive and would appear to be more appropriate than the traditionally used target heart rate. Further research is needed before the full clinical application of estimating AT during exercise testing in children can be identified.

References

1. Annola, S., and H. Rusko. Reproducibility of the aerobic and anaerobic threshold in 20-50 year old. *Eur. J. Appl. Physiol.* 53:260-266, 1984.
2. Becker, D.M., and P. Vaccaro. Anaerobic threshold alterations caused by endurance training in young children. *J. Sports Med.* 23:445-449, 1983.
3. Brooks, G.A. Anaerobic threshold: Review of the concept and directions for future research. *Med. Sci. Sports Exerc.* 17:22-31, 1985.
4. Ciozzo, V.J., J. David, J.F. Ellis, J.L. Azus, R. Vandagriff, C.A. Prietto, and W.C. McMaster. A comparison of gas exchange indices used to detect the anaerobic threshold. *J. Appl. Physiol.* 53:1184-1189, 1982.
5. Conconi, F., M. Ferrari, P.G. Ziglio, P. Droghetti, and L. Codeca. Determination of the anaerobic threshold by a noninvasive field test in runners. *J. Appl. Physiol.* 52:869-873, 1982.
6. Cooper, D.M., D. Weiler-Ravell, B.J. Whipp, and K. Wasserman. Aerobic parameters of exercise as a function of body size during growth in children. *J. Appl. Physiol.* 56(3):628-634, 1984.
7. Coyle, E., W. Martin, A. Ehsani, J. Hagberg, S. Bloomberg, D. Sinacore, and J. Holloszy. Blood lactate threshold in some well-trained ischemic heart disease patients. *J. Appl. Physiol.* 54:18-23, 1983.
8. Davis, J.A. Anaerobic threshold: Review of the concept and directions for further research. *Med. Sci. Sports Exerc.* 17:6-18, 1985.
9. Davis, J.A., V.J. Ciozzo, N. Lamara, J. Ellis, R. Vandagriff, C. Prietto, and W. McMaster. Does the gas exchange anaerobic threshold occur at a fixed blood lactate concentration of 2 or 4mM? *Int. J. Sports Med.* 4:89-98, 1983.
10. Davis, J.A., M.H. Frank, B.J. Whipp, and K. Wasserman. Anaerobic threshold alterations caused by endurance training in middle-aged men. *J. Appl. Physiol.* 46:1039-1046, 1979.

11. Davis, J.A., P. Vodak, J. Wilmore, J. Vodak, and P. Kurtz. Anaerobic threshold and maximal aerobic power for three modes of exercise. *J. Appl. Physiol.* 41:544-550, 1976.

12. Denis, C., R. Fourquet, P. Poty, A. Geyssant, and J.R. Lacour. Effect of 40 weeks of endurance training on the anaerobic threshold. *Int. J. Sports Med.* 3:208-214, 1982.

13. Donavan, C.M., and G.A. Brooks. Endurance training affects lactate clearance, not lactate production. *Am. J. Physiol.* 244:E83-E92, 1983.

14. Dwyer, J., and R. Bibee. Heart rate indices of the anaerobic threshold. *Med. Sci. Sports Exerc.* 15:72-76, 1983.

15. Eriksson, B.O., P.D. Gollnick, and B. Saltin. Muscle metabolism and enzyme activities after training in boys 11-13 y.o. *Acta Paediatr. Scand.* 87:485-487, 1973.

16. Eriksson, B.O., J. Karlsson, and B. Saltin. Muscle metabolites during exercise in pubertal boys. *Acta Paediatr. Scand.* 217:154-157, 1971.

17. Gaisl, G., and G. Wiesspeiner. A noninvasive method of determining the anaerobic threshold in children. *Pediatr. Exerc. Sci.* 2:29-36, 1990.

18. Gladden, L.B. Current anaerobic threshold controversies. *Physiologist* 27:312-318, 1984.

19. Green, J.J., R.L. Hughson, G.W. Orr, and D.A. Rainey. Anaerobic threshold, blood lactate and muscle metabolites in progressive exercise. *J. Appl. Physiol.* 54:1032-1038, 1983.

20. Hughes, R.L., M. Clode, R. Edwards, T.J. Goodwin, and N. Jones. Effect of inspired oxygen on cardiopulmonary and metabolic responses to exercise in man. *J. Appl. Physiol.* 42:25-34, 1979.

21. Jones, N., and R. Ehrsam. The anaerobic threshold. *Exerc. Sport Sci. Rev.* 10:49-83, 1982.

22. Kindermann, W., G. Simon, and J. Keul. The significance of the aerobic-anaerobic transition for the determination of workload intensities during endurance training. *Eur. J. Appl. Physiol.* 42:25-34, 1979.

23. Matsumura, N., H. Nishijima, S. Kojima, F. Hashimoto, M. Minami, and H. Yasuda. Determination of anaerobic threshold for assessment of functional state in patients with chronic heart failure. *Circulation* 68:360-367, 1983.

24. Mazzeo, R.S., G.A. Brooks, D.A. Schoeller, and T.F. Budinger. Disposal of blood lactate in humans during rest and exercise. *J. Appl. Physiol.* 60:232-241, 1986.

25. Michelson, T., and F. Hagerman. Anaerobic threshold measurements of elite oarsmen. *Med. Sci. Sports Exerc.* 14:440-444, 1982.

26. Morse, M., F.W. Schulz, and D.E. Cassels. Relation of age to physiologic responses of the older boy (10-17 years) to exercise. *J. Appl. Physiol.* 1:683-709, 1949.

27. Naimark, A., K. Wasserman, and M.B. McIlroy. Continuous measurement of ventilatory exchange ratio during exercise. *J. Appl. Physiol.* 19:644-652, 1964.

28. Neimela, K., M. Ikaheimo, and J. Takkunen. Determination of the anaerobic threshold in the evaluation of functional studies before and following valve replacement for aortic regurgitation. *Cardiology* 72:165-173, 1985.

29. Newgard, C.B., L.J. Hirsch, D.W. Foster, and J.D. McGarry. Studies on the mechanisms by which exogenous glucose is converted into liver glycogen in the rat: A director of indirect pathway. *J. Biol. Chem.* 258: 8046-8052, 1983.

30. Opasich, C., F. Cobelli, G. Riccardi, R. Aquilani, and G. Specchia. Relationships between anaerobic threshold and exercise hemodynamic pattern in patients with previous myocardial infarction. *Cardiology* 75:32-44, 1988.

31. Ready, A.E., and H. Quinney. Alterations in anaerobic threshold as the result of endurance training and detraining. *Med. Sci. Sports Exerc.* 14: 292-296, 1982.

32. Reybrouck, T., J. Ghesquiere, M. Weymans, and A. Amery. Ventilatory threshold measurement to evaluate maximal endurance performance. *Int. J. Sports Med.* 7:26-29, 1986.

33. Reybrouck, T., M. Weymans, J. Ghesquiere, D. van Gerven, and H. Stijns. Ventilatory anaerobic threshold during treadmill exercise in kindergarten children. *Eur. J. Appl. Physiol.* 50:79-86, 1982.

34. Reybrouck, T., M. Weymans, H. Stijns, and L. vanderHauwaert. Ventilatory anaerobic threshold for evaluating exercise performance in children with congenital left to right intracardiac shunt. *Pediatr. Cardiol.* 7:19-24, 1986.

35. Rowland, T., and G. Green. Anaerobic threshold and the determination of training target heart rates in premenstrual girls. *Pediatr. Cardiol.* 10: 75-79, 1989.

36. Smith, D.A., and T.V. O'Donnell. The time course during 36 weeks endurance training of changes in $\dot{V}O_2$max and anaerobic threshold as determined with a new computerized method. *Clin. Sci.* 67:229-236, 1984.

37. Stephenson, L.A., M.A. Kolka, and J. Wilkerson. Anaerobic threshold, work capacity, and perceived exertion during the menstrual cycle. *Med. Sci. Sports Exerc.* 12:87, 1980.

38. Tanaka, K., Y. Matsumura, A. Matsuzaka, K. Hirakoba, S. Kumagai, S.O. Sun, and K. Asano. A longitudinal assessment of anaerobic threshold and distance running performance. *Med. Sci. Sports Exerc.* 16:278-282, 1984.

39. Tanaka, K., and T. Yoshimura. Transient response in cardiac function below, at and above anaerobic threshold. *Eur. J. Appl. Physiol.* 54:356-361, 1986.

40. Vago, P., J. Mercier, M. Ramonatxo, and C. Prefaut. Is ventilatory anaerobic threshold a good index of endurance capacity? *Int. J. Sports Med.* 8:190-195, 1987.

41. Washington, R.L., J.C. VanGundy, C. Cohen, H. Sondheimer, and R. Wolfe. Normal aerobic and anaerobic exercise data for North American school-age children. *J. Pediatr.* 112:223-233, 1988.
42. Wasserman, K. The anaerobic threshold measurement to evaluate exercise performance. *Am. Rev. Respir. Dis.* 129:S35-S40, 1984.
43. Wasserman, K., and M.B. McIlroy. Detecting the threshold of anaerobic threshold in cardiac patients during exercise. *Am. J. Cardiol.* 14:844-852, 1964.
44. Weltman, A., and V. Katch. Relationship between the onset of metabolic acidosis and maximal oxidation uptake. *J. Sports Med.* 19:135-142, 1979.
45. West, J.B. Lactate during exercise at extreme altitude. *Fed. Proc.* 45: 2953-2957, 1986.
46. Wolfe, R.R., R.L. Washington, E.D. Daberkow, J.R. Murphy, and H.L. Brammel. Anaerobic threshold as a predictor of athletic performance in young female runners. *Am. J. Dis. Child.* 140:922-925, 1986.
47. Yano, T., and K. Asano. Oxygen deficit and anaerobic threshold in the incremental exercise in normoxia and hypoxia. *Jpn. J. Physiol.* 34:1129-1133, 1984.
48. Yeh, M.P., R.M. Gardner, T.D. Adams, F.G. Yanowitz, and C. Ro. Anaerobic threshold: Problems of determination and validation. *J. Appl. Physiol.* 55:1178-1186, 1983.
49. Yoshida, T. Effect of dietary modification on anaerobic threshold. *Sports Med.* 3:4-9, 1986.

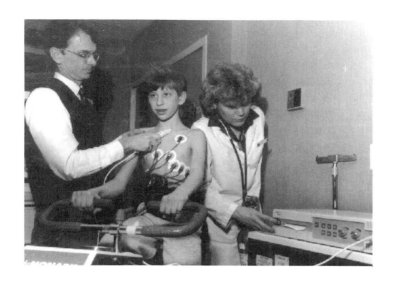

Measurement
of Cardiac Output

Reginald L. Washington, MD
Rocky Mountain Pediatric Cardiology

The cardiovascular system links the lungs (where gas exchange occurs with the atmosphere) and various organs (where oxygen is utilized and carbon dioxide is produced). In healthy individuals a maximum exercise effort is reached when the cardiovascular system has attained its maximum capacity to move blood to the exercising muscles. Knowledge of cardiac output changes during exercise is helpful for understanding exercise physiology and the effect of disease on exercise performance (5). This section reviews several noninvasive techniques used to measure cardiac output; each technique requires substantial operator experience to attain reliable and reproducible results.

Basic Physiology

Cardiac output is determined by the equation $CO = SV \times HR$: Cardiac output (CO), the amount of blood pumped out of the heart per minute, is determined by multiplying stroke volume (SV) by the heart rate (HR). The stroke volume is the amount of blood pumped out of the heart with each beat and is determined by the preload (the amount of blood in the heart at the beginning of a heartbeat), afterload (the resistance to blood flow during contraction), and contractility (the force of the contracting heart muscle during the heartbeat).

Cardiac output increases in an almost linear manner during exercise concomitant with increasing oxygen consumption. There is a three- to fivefold increase in cardiac output from rest to maximum exercise. Table 1 lists the values for cardiac index derived from two studies in healthy children performed in either the supine or sitting position using a cycle ergometer.

Increase in cardiac output occurs at the beginning of exercise and in transition to higher exercise levels during a graded exercise test. A steady state cardiac output is usually achieved within 2 min of each work load. Cardiac output increases by approximately 20 cc per minute for every centimeter of increase in height for children working at the same $\dot{V}O_2$ (10).

Cardiac output is dependent on the type of exercise being performed. Upright exercise yields higher values from maximum cardiac output than does supine exercise, and treadmill ergometry causes higher maximum cardiac output than does cycle ergometry (3).

Children typically have a markedly lower stroke volume relative to body size than do adults at all levels of exercise. This lower stroke volume, however, is compensated for by the higher heart rate at a given exercise level. But this compensation is not complete, so children typically have a lower cardiac output than do adults at any given metabolic level ($\dot{V}O_2$) (2, 7). It is not clear if this somewhat lower cardiac output in children has any biological significance (1). It is possible that the concomitant higher arterial-mixed venous O_2 difference is sufficient to compensate the oxygen transport system

Table 1   Cardiac Response

| Author/year | Age (years) | Value ($L \cdot min^{-1} \cdot min^{-2}$) | | Instrument | Protocol |
		Rest	Max		
Eriksson et al., 1973 (7)	11-13	3.9	12.5	Seated cycle in cath lab	Continuous
Eriksson et al., 1971 (8)	13-14	5.25 ± 0.50	17.41 ± 0.88	Cycle	Continuous

during submaximal exercise. However, low cardiac output may cause a handicap during maximal exercise when peripheral oxygen extraction can no longer rise (8) or when the child is exposed to combined stresses of exercise, heat, altitude, or relative hypoxia (as in congenital heart disease or pulmonary disease).

The amount of decrease in cardiac output depends on the age or the developmental stage of the child. The lower stroke volume of young children is compensated for by a higher heart rate such that the cardiac output of a young child is only slightly lower than that of adolescents (1). Wirth et al. (27) evaluated the relationship between heart volume, maximal aerobic power, and developmental status. They found that at equal levels of maximal oxygen uptake (liters per minute) the heart volume in the prepubertal child is the smallest of any age group. This fact may help explain the finding that prepubescents have lower cardiac output at any given work rate and at peak exercise.

Measuring Cardiac Output

Several techniques have been described for measuring cardiac output in children noninvasively during exercise. These techniques were recently reviewed by Driscoll et al. (5); only the highlights of each test are presented here. Caution should be used when one compares cardiac outputs measured by different techniques and in different laboratories. The measurements are sensitive to small changes in methodology and protocol. No single test is highly accurate (i.e., there is *no* "gold standard").

Carbon Dioxide Rebreathing

Cardiac output can be determined easily if oxygen uptake and carbon dioxide production are measured at the mouth and arterial-mixed venous oxygen content differences of oxygen and carbon dioxide are measured in the blood. This is known as the Fick method (9). If carbon dioxide output, mixed venous carbon dioxide content, and arterial carbon dioxide content are known, the Fick equation also will calculate cardiac output.

When all measurements are obtained in the gas phase, the Fick technique is called indirect.

$$CO = \frac{\dot{V}_{CO_2}}{C_{vCO_2} - C_{aCO_2}}$$

($\dot{V}_{CO_2}$ is carbon dioxide output, C_{vCO_2} is mixed venous carbon dioxide content, and C_{aCO_2} is arterial carbon dioxide content). This carbon dioxide technique is often used to measure cardiac output during exercise testing.

Carbon dioxide output is usually measured in a steady state by analysis of a timed collection of expired gases, taken immediately preceding the determination of the cardiac output. The arterial PCO_2 also can be estimated by using the end-tidal PCO_2. Equations are available to relate the arterial PCO_2 to the end-tidal PCO_2 (13, 14). Or the arterial PCO_2 can be estimated using the Bohr equation and tidal volume, mixed expired PCO_2, volume of respiratory equipment dead space, and an assumed value of the subject's physiologic dead space (13). A mixed venous carbon dioxide content can be obtained if the alveolar PCO_2 is used as an estimate for the mixed venous PCO_2 under conditions that allow an equilibrium of the two gas phases. The most common method for achieving this equilibrium is CO_2 rebreathing (13). During the rebreathing phase, the PCO_2 is continually monitored at the mouth until a plateau or equilibrium value is obtained. When using this technique, the subject rebreathes a gas mixture that includes 8% to 15% carbon dioxide and the balance in oxygen.

The technique of indirect carbon dioxide measurement of cardiac output with rebreathing has been incorporated in several commercially available metabolic carts. The values obtained from cardiac output compare favorably with both dye dilution and indirect Fick measurements (19, 22, 24, 28). Disadvantages of the indirect Fick method include the time required to carefully select the rebreathing bag volume and gas concentrations necessary to produce a plateau value for PCO_2. If the bag volume is too large, a plateau is never obtained. Considerable experience is required to select the proper bag volume and carbon dioxide concentrations. Some children find the rebreathing of carbon dioxide to be particularly disagreeable at higher work levels. Finally, this technique is useful only in exercise studies that result in a brief steady state.

Hargreaves and Jennings (11) compared the CO_2 rebreathing and thermodilution techniques for determining cardiac output. They found that the end-tidal PCO_2 accurately predicted arterial PCO_2 in all patients except those with liver disease, in whom a direct arterial measurement is recommended. They concluded that the indirect Fick technique is valid in adult subjects with cardiovascular disease.

Marks et al. (16) suggested that this technique should not be used in patients with mitral insufficiency or chronic pulmonary disease because of the potential for large errors. A large study of children to validate this technique has not been done.

Acetylene Rebreathing

Oxygen and carbon dioxide may be used to indirectly measure cardiac output, as discussed previously. Other gases, however, may enter or leave the bloodstream via the lungs. If these gases do not interact with the blood constituents and are transported in purely physical solution, they are termed inert gases. If the diffusion of such a gas is very rapid compared with the transportation by the flow of blood, the uptake of that gas is said to be "blood flow limited" (5). When the transportation of a particular gas is flow limited, the gas can be used to estimate cardiac output. The most common gases used this way are acetylene and nitrous oxide, although dimethyl ether and freon also have been used.

Several reviews have described techniques using acetylene rebreathing to determine cardiac output (26). Most methods use a mass spectrometer for measuring gas concentrations. Helium serves as an indicator of mixing and system volume. The disappearance rate of acetylene is proportional to pulmonary capillary blood flow, which is taken as an index of cardiac output.

The breathing cycle used in this technique is only an approximation of the continuous and complete mixing of gas within the lungs. To ensure adequate mixing, the rebreathing bag must be nearly emptied with each breath (23). Rapid breathing rates facilitate this mixing process but may also alter cardiac output.

The volume of gas in a rebreathing bag can affect the measurement of cardiac output. If the volume is too small, adequate equilibration cannot occur and cardiac output is underestimated (23). Patients with lung disease may have difficulty obtaining adequate mixing with normal bag volumes, in which case smaller volumes must be used.

Cardiac output measurements obtained using acetylene rebreathing compare well with the measurements obtained using either direct Fick (4) or dye dilution (26) in healthy subjects. Acetylene rebreathing, however, measures only effective pulmonary blood flow; these measurements differ from true cardiac output if intracardiac or intrapulmonary shunting is present, so this technique should be used with caution in those patients. The variation observed may increase in patients with cardiovascular disease or intracardiac or intrapulmonary shunting.

Electrical Bioimpedance

Impedance cardiography is a noninvasive technique that has numerous potential clinical applications (6, 12). Cardiac output is measured by detecting changes in transthoracic electrical impedance associated with the cardiac cycle. The method relies on the oversimplified assumption that the thorax is a homogeneous column of blood, the volume of which increases by the left ventricular stroke volume during each systole.

The validity of this technique in adults has been well studied. Edmunds et al. (6) found that transthoracic impedance cardiography is a rapid, feasible, noninvasive technique for measuring cardiac output. It requires little active cooperation from the subject and gives reliable results in patients with respiratory illnesses such as asthma or bronchiolitis. Edmunds et al. found that changes in lung volume due to breath holding did not affect cardiac output measurement. Their results, however, were consistently higher than the indirect Fick measurements of cardiac output, making a correction factor necessary (6).

Smith et al. (25) found a poor correlation between the impedance technique and the CO_2 rebreathing technique and discussed extensively the pitfalls of the impedance method. A thorough, extensive study evaluating comparisons between electrical bioimpedance and a criterion standard in children are necessary before the bioimpedance technique can be recommended.

Doppler Method

The Doppler frequency shift created by the moving cellular components of blood is proportional to blood flow velocity. This frequency shift is measured by ultrasound (commercially manufactured units are available). The flow is derived from the product of the mean velocity of blood flow and the cross-sectional area of the vessel where the flow velocity is measured.

Several investigators have demonstrated the feasibility of this method and have compared the results of cardiac output measurements by Doppler frequency shift with other methods. High correlations have been described ($r = .94$) (18, 21) in adults as well as in children.

Measurements of cardiac output during exercise are possible but are more difficult to obtain and less reliable than measurements made at rest. During exercise it is more difficult to ensure consistency of the angle between the ultrasound beam and the direction of blood flow. Also increased movements of heart and lung during exercise make it difficult to record reliable and reproducible Doppler signals (15).

Limited studies have been done in children during exercise. Marx et al. (17) found a correlation of .86 when comparing the Doppler method to rebreathing techniques, but in 15% of their subjects, adequate Doppler signal could not be obtained. Nicolosi et al. (20) warned that the intrinsic variability of each single measurement of cardiac output using the Doppler technique was 25% and cautioned that a single value of cardiac output in an individual subject should be interpreted with extreme caution.

Further substantiation of the reliability of this technique is needed before it can be recommended for widespread use.

Clinical Value of Cardiac Output Determination

Several techniques can be used to measure cardiac output during exercise. All the techniques reviewed here have advantages and disadvantages. It is difficult to determine which technique is most accurate because there is no pure criterion standard that is noninvasive. All of the techniques described have at least a 10% variation from test to test. This variation may be due in part to a natural variation in cardiac output during exercise.

The technique selected is perhaps not critical, if the same technique is used on the same individual for serial testing (to evaluate the effects of a rehabilitation program, for example). Comparisons of cardiac output that use different techniques in the same individual should be avoided. Techniques that measure pulmonary blood flow may not be accurate in individuals with left-to-right or right-to-left shunting in the heart or lung. In addition, the effect of previous thoracotomies and alterations in lung function on cardiac output are not well described in children.

A single measurement of cardiac output without simultaneous measurement of activity is not interpretable. The best measure of activity is oxygen uptake. Whenever possible, oxygen uptake should be recorded along with cardiac output; only when these two values are recorded simultaneously can individuals be compared to one another or to a control population. Cardiac outputs of individuals or control populations that were obtained using different noninvasive techniques should not be compared. Each technique measures indirectly an estimation of cardiac output, and each is subject to a variable degree of error. In fact, the techniques measure different parameters. It is unlikely that these parameters are comparable in their estimation of cardiac output.

Driscoll et al. reported several clinical uses for the noninvasive determination of cardiac output (5). Patients who had undergone a Fontan operation demonstrated decreased stroke volume and decreased heart rate. Similarly, patients with transposition of the great vessels who had undergone a Mustard or Senning procedure demonstrated decreased stroke volume and decreased heart rate. Patients with tetralogy of Fallot demonstrated a decreased heart rate for a given amount of work, implying a decrease in cardiac output. The indirect measurement of cardiac output is useful in patients who are undergoing rehabilitation to improve cardiac output and exercise performance. In this setting, the patients are compared to themselves during the rehabilitative process, and any error in measurement is likely to be reproduced each time the test is performed (minimizing the importance of the error). On the other hand, these techniques should not be used in population studies comparing healthy persons with individuals with various cardiovascular or pulmonary disorders.

Conclusion

Direct measurement of cardiac output during exercise testing can provide important information about cardiac reserve in many clinical settings. Routine assessment of cardiac output in the testing laboratory is, however, hindered by the lack of a safe, accurate method for its measurement during exercise. The most commonly used techniques, carbon dioxide rebreathing (indirect Fick) and thermodilution, require either intravascular catheters or exercise steady state, whereas the validity of other methods, such as thoracic bio-impedance, has not been fully established. The development of methods for measuring cardiac output during exercise is further impeded by the lack of a standard against which new techniques can be validated. Further study is needed on the means by which information obtained during exercise testing about cardiac output and stroke volume can be applied to clinical decision making.

References

1. Bar-Or, O. *Pediatric Sports Medicine for the Practitioner*. New York: Springer-Verlag, 1983.
2. Bar-Or, O., R.J. Shephard, and C.L. Allen. Cardiac output of 10-13 year old boys and girls during submaximal exercise. *J. Appl. Physiol.* 30:219-223, 1971.
3. Braden, D.S., and W.B. Strong. Cardiovascular responses and adaptations to exercise in childhood. In: C.V. Gisolfi and D.R. Lamb (Eds.). *Prospectives in Exercise Science and Sports Medicine: Vol. 2 Youth Exercise and Sport*, Indianapolis: Benchmark Press, 1989, pp. 293-333.
4. Chapman, C.B., H.L. Taylor, C. Borden, R.V. Ebert, and A. Keys. Simultaneous determinations for the resting arterio-venous oxygen difference by the acetylene and direct Fick methods. *J. Clin. Invest.* 29:651-659, 1950.
5. Driscoll, D.J., B.A. Staats, and K.C. Beck. Measurement of cardiac output during exercise: A review. *Pediatr. Exerc. Sci.* 1:102-115, 1989.
6. Edmunds, A.T., S. Godfrey, and M. Tooley. Cardiac output measured by trends thoracic impedance cardiography at rest, during exercise and at various lung volumes. *Clin. Sci.* 63:107-113, 1982.
7. Eriksson, B.O. Cardiac output during exercise in prepubertal boys. *Acta Paediatr. Scand.* 217(Suppl.):53-55, 1971.
8. Eriksson, B.O., and G. Koch. Cardiac output and inter-arterial blood pressure at rest and during sub-maximal and maximal exercise in 11-13 year old boys before and after physical training. In: *Pediatric Work Physiology*, O. Bar-Or (Ed.). Natanya, Israel: Wingate Institute, 1973, pp. 139-150.
9. Fick, A. Measuring the quantity of blood in the heart ventricles. In: *Congenital Heart Disease*, W. Pashkind (Ed. and Trans.). Strudsburg, PA: Hutchinson Ross, 1982.

10. Godfrey, S. The growth and development of cardiopulmonary responses in exercise. In: *Scientific Foundations of Pediatrics*, J.A. David and J. Dobbing (Eds.). Philadelphia: Saunders, 1974, pp. 271-280.

11. Hargreaves, M., and G. Jennings. The evaluation of CO_2 rebreathing method for the noninvasive measurement of resting cardiac output in man. *Clin. Exp. Pharmacol. Physiol.* 10:609-614, 1983.

12. Heatherington, M., K.K. Teo, R. Haennel, P. Greenwood, R.E. Rossall, and T. Kappagoda. Use of impedance cardiography in evaluating the exercise response of patients with left ventricular dysfunction. *Eur. Heart J.* 6:1016-1024, 1985.

13. Jones, N.L., and A.S. Rebuck. Rebreathing equilibration of CO_2 during exercise. *J. Appl. Physiol.* 35:538-541, 1973.

14. Jones, N.L., D.G. Robertson, and J.W. Kane. Differences between end-tidal and arterial PCO_2 in exercise. *J. Appl. Physiol.* 47:954-960, 1979.

15. Lamb, T.W., N.R. Anthonisen, and S.M. Tenney. Control frequency of breathing during muscular exercise. *J. Appl. Physiol.* 20:244-248, 1965.

16. Marks, C., V. Ketch, A. Rocchini, R. Beekman, and A. Rosenthal. Validity and reliability of cardiac ouput by CO_2 rebreathing. *Sports Med.* 2:432-446, 1985.

17. Marx, G.R., R.W. Hicks, H.D. Allen, and S.M. Kinzer. Measurement of cardiac output and exercise factor by pulsed Doppler echocardiography during supine bicycle ergometry in normal, young adolescent males. *J. Am. Coll. Cardiol.* 10:430-434, 1987.

18. Morrow, W.R., D.J. Murphy, Jr., D.J. Fisher, J.C. Huta, L.S. Jefferson, and E. O'Briansmith. Continuous wave Doppler cardiac output and use in pediatric patients receiving inotropic support. *Pediatr. Cardiol.* 9:131-136, 1988.

19. Muiesan, G., C.A. Sorbini, E. Solines, V. Garssi, G. Casucci, and E. Petz. Comparison of CO_2 rebreathing and direct Fick methods for determining cardiac output. *J. Appl. Physiol.* 24:424-429, 1968.

20. Nicolosi, G.L., E.G. Pungercic, E. Cervesato, D. Pavan, L. Modena, E. Mofo, V. Dallaglio, and D. Zanattini. Feasibility and variability of six methods for the echocardiographic Doppler determination of cardiac outputs. *Brit. Heart J.* 59:299-303, 1988.

21. Nishimura, R.A., M.J. Callahan, H.V. Schaff, D.M. Illstrup, F.A. Miller, and A.J. Tajik. Noninvasive measurement of cardiac output by continuous wave Doppler echocardiography: Initial experience and review of literature. *Mayo Clin. Proc.* 59:484-489, 1984.

22. Paterson, D.H., and D.A. Cunningham. Comparison of methods to calculate cardiac output using the CO_2 rebreathing method. *Eur. J. Appl. Physiol.* 35:223-230, 1976.

23. Petroni, M.F., B.T. Peterson, and R.W. Hyde. Lung tissue volume and blood flow by rebreathing: Theory. *J. Appl. Physiol.* 44:795-802, 1978.

24. Reybrouck, T., A. Amery, L. Billiet, R. Fagard, and H. Stijns. Comparison of cardiac output determined by carbon dioxide-rebreathing and direct

Fick method at rest and during exercise. *Clin. Sci. Mol. Med.* 55:445-452, 1978.

25. Smith, S.A., A.E. Russell, M.J. West, and J. Chalmers. Automated non-invasive measurement of cardiac output: Comparison of electrical bio-impedance and carbon dioxide rebreathing techniques. *Brit. Heart J.* 59: 292-298, 1988.

26. Treiebwasser, J.H., R.L. Johnson, R.P. Burpo, J.C. Campbell, W.C. Reardon, and C.G. Blomqvist. Noninvasive determination of cardiac output via a modified acetylene rebreathing procedure utilizing mass spectrometer measurements. *Aviat. Space Environ. Med.* 48:203-209, 1977.

27. Wirth, A., E. Trager, K. Scheele, D. Mayer, K. Diehm, K. Reischle, and H. Weiker. Cardiopulmonary adjustment and metabolic response to maximal and submaximal physical exercise in boys and girls at different stages of maturity. *Eur. J. Appl. Physiol.* 29:229-240, 1978.

28. Ziedifard, E., M. Silverman, and S. Godfrey. Reproducibility of indirect Fick method for calculation of cardiac output. *J. Appl. Physiol.* 33:141-143, 1972.

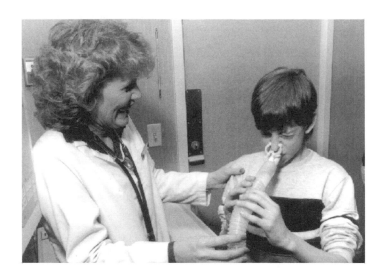

Assessment of Exercise Pulmonary Function

David M. Orenstein, MD
Children's Hospital of Pittsburgh
University of Pittsburgh

The metabolic demands of maximal exercise are substantial, with cardiac output increasing some 5-fold over resting values, and minute ventilation increasing as much as 12-fold (21). Despite these tremendous changes, homeostasis is maintained with, for example, little change in arterial oxygen tension (21).

Even with the huge demands on the respiratory system, it seldom limits exercise tolerance in children or adults. Perhaps because of this, many traditional exercise laboratories have chosen not to make even the most rudimentary respiratory measurements.

Portions of this chapter are adapted from Nixon, P.A., Orenstein, D.M. Exercise Testing in Children. *Pediatr. Pulmonol.*, 5:107-122, 1988. Copyright © 1988 by John Wiley and Sons. Reprinted by permission of Wiley-Liss, a division of John Wiley and Sons, Inc.

Nonetheless, children with respiratory ailments may well be limited by pulmonary factors, and the exercise test offers an excellent setting for discovering these limiting factors. In fact, the exercise test may even enable the clinician to diagnose a pulmonary problem that standard resting pulmonary function tests and roentgenograms do not reveal. This can be accomplished with equipment that is now available commercially and is within the financial means of most clinical facilities.

This chapter discusses the contributions of the respiratory system to exercise tolerance, which parts of these contributions may serve as the weak links in the exercise tolerance chain in children with respiratory disorders, and how these links can be identified.

Normal Responses to Exercise

Before addressing the responses to exercise in children with respiratory disorders, I will cover some of the normal physiological responses to exercise.

Exercise Tolerance

Exercise tolerance depends largely on respiration, both whole-body and cellular: Efficient muscle contraction requires oxygen delivery to the muscle, oxygen uptake by the muscle, and the removal of metabolically produced carbon dioxide. If any of these processes fails, local and even systemic acidosis will ensue, and exercise will cease. Nonpulmonary problems can interfere with these processes: After the lungs have provided oxygen to the bloodstream, a compromised cardiovascular system may be unable to deliver the oxygenated blood to the exercising muscles; anemia may limit the oxygen-carrying capacity of the circulating blood; and abnormal muscle may be unable to process the delivered oxygen for muscle contraction. These nonpulmonary problems are discussed in other sections.

Exercise Ventilation

As one begins to exercise, oxygen must be supplied to the newly exercising muscle, and—soon—carbon dioxide must be removed. These processes require an increase in minute ventilation ($\dot{V}_E$) almost immediately on beginning exercise. Early in progressive exercise, $\dot{V}_E$, the oxygen consumed ($\dot{V}O_2$), and the carbon dioxide produced ($\dot{V}CO_2$), all increase in parallel (49). The ratio of $\dot{V}CO_2/\dot{V}O_2$, or the respiratory exchange ratio (variously abbreviated R or

RER), is in the range of 0.85 to 0.95 during rest or light exercise. However, after about 60% of maximum $\dot{V}O_2$, as muscle energy demand outstrips oxygen supply and increasing amounts of energy are produced anaerobically, the $\dot{V}CO_2$ increases out of proportion to the $\dot{V}O_2$ (see the section "Anaerobic Threshold") and R values rise to 1.05 or 1.10 or even greater. Because $\dot{V}_E$ is tied much more closely to $\dot{V}CO_2$ than to $\dot{V}O_2$ (48), $\dot{V}_E$, too, increases above the anaerobic threshold. The relationship of the amount of air breathed to the amount of oxygen consumed, or to the amount of carbon dioxide produced, is an interesting one, and its measurement can give useful information. These relationships are expressed as the ratios of minute ventilation to oxygen consumption ($\dot{V}_E/\dot{V}O_2$) and to carbon dioxide production ($V_E/\dot{V}CO_2$); they are referred to as the ventilatory equivalents for oxygen and carbon dioxide, respectively. It can be seen from the preceding discussion that $\dot{V}_E/\dot{V}O_2$ increases at the anaerobic threshold, whereas $\dot{V}_E/\dot{V}CO_2$ does not.

Increases in minute ventilation are made up by increases in both tidal volume (V_T) and breathing frequency (f_b) (Figure 1). Tidal volume increases until it reaches 50% to 60% of the resting vital capacity, after which further increases in ventilation are accounted for by greater f_b. The actual breathing frequency achieved and the absolute exercise tidal volume depend on age, with greater tidal volume and lower respiratory rates in older children

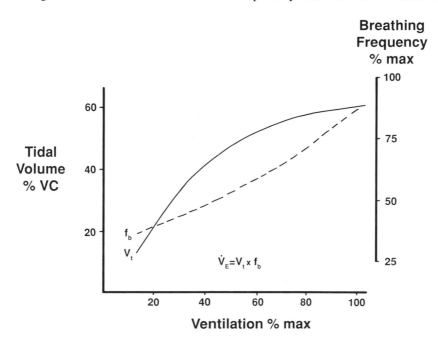

Figure 1:   Increases in minute ventilation are made up by increases in both tidal volume (V_T) (until tidal volume reaches approximately 50% of vital capacity) and breathing frequency (f_b). *Note*. From Nixon and Orenstein (34). Copyright © 1988 by John Wiley and Sons. Adapted by permission of Wiley-Liss, a division of John Wiley and Sons, Inc.

(Figure 2). During an individual breath, the time for inspiration (T_i) is about 40% of the total time for a breath. The ratio of inspiratory time to total time for a breath, T_i/T_{tot}, is useful in assessing the response to exercise in some children with respiratory disorders, such as when expiratory obstruction (and therefore prolonged expiratory time) forces a shortened T_i and therefore a greater T_i/T_{tot}.

During steady state exercise below the anaerobic threshold (about 50% to 70% of each person's maximum), minute ventilation remains stable after the first few minutes. During progressively increasing exercise, or during constant work loads above the anaerobic threshold, ventilation steadily increases. However, even at exhaustion, there is probably considerable ventilatory reserve in normal subjects. Breathing reserve has been estimated in a number of different ways (Table 1).

Maximal Voluntary Ventilation

In healthy subjects, minute ventilation seldom exceeds 60% to 70% of maximal voluntary ventilation (MVV), even as a subject nears exhaustion during progressive exercise (20, 27, 47).

Gas Exchange

Along with increased alveolar ventilation, exercise elicits an increase in cardiac output and increased pulmonary blood flow. The matching of ventilation and perfusion is one of the most impressive aspects of adaptation to

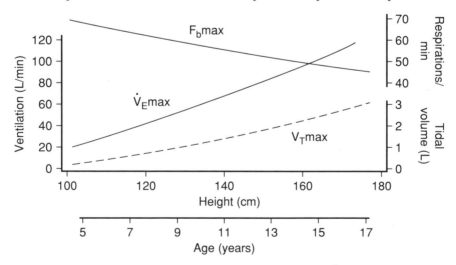

Figure 2: Maximal tidal volume (V_T) and minute ventilation ($\dot{V}_E$) increase with age, whereas maximal breathing frequency (f_b) decreases with age. *Note.* From *Exercise testing in children* (p. 80) by S. Godfrey, 1974, London: W.B. Saunders. Copyright 1974 by W.B. Saunders. Reprinted by permission.

Table 1   Breathing Reserve Terms

Term employed	Definition	Reference
Pulmonary reserve	$\dot{V}_E max - \dot{V}_E rest$	Sturgis (46)
		Peabody (39)
Breathing reserve	$MVV - \dot{V}_E$	Wasserman (47)
—	$MVV/(MVV - \dot{V}_E)$	Wasserman (47)
—	$\dot{V}_E/MVV$	Jones (27)
—	$\dot{V}_E/(FEV_1 \times 35)$	Godfrey (19)
Dyspnea index	$\dot{V}_E/MVV$	

Note. MVV = maximum voluntary ventilation. $\dot{V}_E$ = minute ventilation during highest work rate. FEV_1 = forced expired volume in 1 s.

exercise, because systemic arterial oxygen tensions remain unchanged during exercise in healthy children (18) and may even improve in some children with lung disorders (22). Similarly, carbon dioxide levels seldom increase during exercise and actually fall slightly at the end of vigorous exercise in healthy children (18).

Breathing Sensation

Subjective sensations are important in determining how much exercise can be performed. Almost always, even vigorous exercise in very sick patients ends because the exercising subject decides it should end, and not because of a catastrophic event. Extreme muscle fatigue often contributes to the inability to continue exercise during a progressively increasing test, and sensation of this fatigue is an important factor. The ventilatory muscles are among the important muscles determining exercise tolerance, especially in children with a respiratory disorder. Breathing sensation depends on several factors, including respiratory muscle power and impedance to breathing (28). Several tools are available to determine ratings of perceived exertion (RPE), or symptom intensity. The most common of these tools is the Borg scale (7). Using the Borg scale (Figure 3, a and b) the subject rates his or her perception of exertion at various work rates. This scale can be used to estimate the intensity of leg work, chest pain, or breathing effort. Although this tool has been used mainly with adults, it has been used with success in some pediatric laboratories (2).

Abnormal Responses to Exercise

Respiratory disorders can influence the response to exercise in several ways. This discussion provides a framework for understanding these altered responses in the most important pediatric obstructive (asthma and cystic fibrosis) and restrictive (scoliosis, pectus excavatum, and neuromuscular disease) pulmonary disorders.

6	
7	Very, very light
8	
9	Very light
10	
11	Fairly light
12	
13	Somewhat hard
14	
15	Hard
16	
17	Very hard
18	
19	Very, very hard
20	

0	Nothing at all
0.5	Very, very weak (just noticeable)
1	Very weak
2	Weak (light)
3	Moderate
4	Somewhat strong
5	Strong (heavy)
6	
7	Very strong
8	
9	
10	Very, very strong (almost maximal)
●	Maximal

Figure 3: Two versions of the Borg scale, with which the subject rates his or her perception of exertion at various work rates. *Note.* From ''Perceived Exertion: A Note on History and Methods'' by G.V. Borg. *Med. Sci. Sports* 5(2):90-93, 1973. Copyright © 1973 by the American College of Sports Medicine. Reprinted by permission.

Asthma

It has been known for centuries that strenuous exercise can elicit respiratory difficulty in children with asthma. Recent studies have begun to clarify the pathophysiology of this troublesome and common situation (for a summary of the field, see Lemanske and Henke [31]).

Exercise-induced asthma (EIA) appears to be more easily provoked under certain environmental conditions and with particular forms of exercise. Airway cooling seems to play an important role in the genesis of EIA (45); high minute ventilation is more likely to provoke an attack in cold, dry air than in warm, humid air. In fact, the EIA response is largely abolished if the inspired air is warmed and humidified (16). Running or cycling is more likely to elicit an attack than swimming (23). Exercise of moderate to high intensity and relatively short duration (6 to 8 min) is more provocative than high- or low-intensity exercise of shorter or longer duration (13). Typically, the symptoms appear shortly after, and not during, exercise (1). During the first 1 to 2 hr after exercise (the refractory period) a repeated bout of exercise will cause much less EIA than the first bout (17). In most children and adolescents with asthma, EIA can be prevented with the inhalation of cromolyn sodium or beta agonist bronchodilators (e.g., albuterol), or both, just prior to exercise (31). In some patients, a further decline in pulmonary function is noted 4 to 6 hr after exercise, the so-called late asthmatic response (4).

Cystic Fibrosis

Cystic fibrosis (CF) is characterized by the production of abnormally thick mucus, bronchiolar obstruction and infection, and progressive loss of pulmonary function (6). Many patients with mild lung dysfunction have normal exercise tolerance, but as the disease progresses and pulmonary function deteriorates, with ever-increasing obstruction to expiratory airflow, exercise tolerance diminishes (14). Although decreasing exercise tolerance is directly related to decreasing pulmonary function, it is not possible to predict exercise tolerance from the results of standard pulmonary function tests (26).

The patient with CF meets the increasing metabolic demands of exercise by employing larger-than-normal minute ventilation, in part to compensate for larger-than-normal dead space (10, 22). The minute ventilation in patients with CF increases through increases in both tidal volume, up to about 50% to 60% of vital capacity (38), and respiratory rate. Unpublished studies from our laboratory have shown that the maximal respiratory rate correlates significantly (and inversely) with the patient's age, more than with disease severity. Increasing the respiratory rate when there is substantial expiratory airflow obstruction requires adjustments in the timing of each breath. Some evidence suggests that CF patients with severe obstruction shorten their inspiratory time, giving more time for expiration; this adjustment is measured as a lower T_i/T_{tot} (9). The minute ventilation required by the large dead space means greater-than-normal ventilation for any given amount of oxygen consumed or carbon dioxide produced, which is measurable as large $\dot{V}_E/\dot{V}O_2$ and $\dot{V}_E/\dot{V}CO_2$ (10). It is not uncommon for the peak minute ventilation of such a patient to approach or even exceed MVV, whereas in the healthy individual, peak minute ventilation seldom exceeds 60% to 70% of MVV (22). The oxygen cost of breathing associated with excessive minute ventilation may further reduce exercise capacity by using oxygen that could otherwise go to exercising leg muscles to provide for the needs of the ventilatory muscles.

Cardiovascular responses (e.g., heart rate) may not reach predicted maximal values because the ventilatory limitation may cause the patient to stop exercising before the cardiovascular system reaches its maximal capacity (10). Although peak heart rate may be below age-predicted maximal levels, heart rate at submaximal work levels may be higher because of hypoxemia, decreased fitness, the increased work of breathing, or any combination of the three (10). Sensations of dyspnea may likewise cause a patient to terminate exercise before the heart rate or any other physiologic marker (e.g., respiratory exchange ratio) reaches maximal levels (34).

Most patients with CF are able to maintain adequate blood oxygen and carbon dioxide levels (26). In some patients, oxygenation may even improve with exercise because of improved ventilation-to-perfusion ($\dot{V}_A/\dot{Q}$) matching (22). However, in some patients with severe disease (forced expiratory volume in 1 s [FEV_1] < 50% of forced vital capacity), $\dot{V}_A/\dot{Q}$ mismatching will result in oxyhemoglobin desaturation with or without carbon dioxide retention (14, 26, 29). Oxygen supplementation improves oxyhemoglobin saturation and decreases heart rate and minute ventilation during submaximal work while not increasing peak-exercise capacity (12, 35).

Restrictive Chest Wall Disorders

Scoliosis.   Scoliosis can deform the thoracic cage, causing a restrictive pulmonary defect with decreased vital capacity and total lung capacity (3). With severe curves (Cobb angle greater than 100° to 120°), exertional dyspnea and diminished exercise tolerance are common. Some regions of the lung may be underventilated, resulting in poor $\dot{V}_A/\dot{Q}$ matching. At submaximal levels of work, minute ventilation may be higher than normal, and the arterial-venous O_2 difference may be greater to compensate for the $\dot{V}_A/\dot{Q}$ imbalance (33). Oxygen uptake at submaximal levels may also be higher because of the increased oxygen requirements of the respiratory muscles, which are forced to work at a mechanical disadvantage because of the misshapen thorax. At higher work loads, patients with severe restriction may be limited by the mechanics of the ventilatory pump. Because they have limited vital capacity, their ability to increase tidal volume during exercise is limited and tidal volume often approaches vital capacity, instead of leveling off at 50% of vital capacity as would be normal (47). Because tidal volume is limited, increases in minute ventilation demand higher-than-normal respiratory rates (47). Oxygen uptake and minute ventilation at maximal levels of work are lower than normal, because the work loads achieved are low (42). Although the deformity may limit maximal work capacity, much of the diminished work capacity and lower fitness may be attributed to decreased habitual physical activity and can be improved with exercise conditioning (5). Furthermore, surgical correction may decrease the minute ventilation and oxygen uptake required for submaximal levels of work (33, 42). With mild degrees of scoliosis (Cobb angle 3° to 46°), no physiologic abnormality is detectable either with resting pulmonary function tests or exercise tests (30).

Pectus Excavatum.   In children and adolescents with pectus excavatum, the chest wall defect—even when severe from the cosmetic point of view— seldom has physiologic impact (25). In the rare cases in which it does, there may be slightly diminished cardiac stroke volume and therefore a lower-than-normal cardiac output (40). The psychologic effect of a severe pectus deformity may be crippling. Decreased exercise tolerance is not uncommon (8, 40) and may be associated with decreased habitual activity.

Neuromuscular Disease.   These disorders (e.g., Duchenne muscular dystrophy) can cause restrictive pulmonary defects. They are discussed more fully in the next section, "Noncardiopulmonary Pediatric Exercise Tests."

Performing the Exercise Test

The choice of exercise test protocol depends on the condition to be investigated. The choices include maximal and submaximal exercise tests as well as tests for special circumstances.

Maximal Exercise Tests

For assessing functional exercise capacity and aerobic fitness, progressive maximal test protocols are appropriate. In each of these protocols, exercise intensity is increased at even intervals, and the test ends when the subject is unable or unwilling to continue or (rarely) when the physician or technician feels that it would be unsafe to continue (34). See the section "Aerobic Exercise Testing Protocols" for details about various maximal test protocols on the cycle ergometer and treadmill.

Submaximal Exercise Tests

Daily life, even for competitive athletes, seldom approaches maximal levels. Therefore, submaximal tests often provide valuable information about a patient's exercise tolerance and adaptive responses to exercise levels that are achieved in real-life situations. Such submaximal tests are much less taxing than maximal tests, especially for the sick child, and are ideally suited for evaluating responses to exercise repeatedly over a course of treatment (surgical, pharmacologic, exercise conditioning, etc.). The submaximal test can also be used as part of a short-term evaluation of an intervention (oxygen supplementation for cystic fibrosis, chest bracing for scoliosis, etc.) in which two tests can be performed, one with and one without the intervention, within an hour or so of each other.

With the typical submaximal protocol, the work rate increases gradually until a level is reached that elicits a heart rate that is about 75% of peak (or age-predicted peak); that level is maintained for 5 to 8 min (34). Caution must be exercised in designing such a test for the child or adolescent with proven or suspected respiratory impairment, because these children's target heart rates cannot be based on predictions from healthy populations (see the earlier discussion on cystic fibrosis); a heart rate of 75% of age-predicted maximum may actually be greater than an individual patient's own maximal exercise heart rate.

Tests for Special Circumstances

Exercise-Induced Asthma.   If the exercise test is used to diagnose EIA, standard protocols should be followed (13). The test should be performed on the treadmill or cycle ergometer with the patient exercising for 6 to 8 min. Exercise of longer duration will not induce greater bronchoconstriction and may even lessen it—the run-through phenomenon (43). The intensity of exercise should be great enough to elicit heart rates of around 170 beats per minute (bpm) in children and 150 bpm in adults (13). Measurement of expiratory flow rates with standard spirometry, ideally with flow-volume loops (Figure 4), should be performed immediately before and every 3 min after the exercise challenge for at least 15 min. The test results are considered positive if peak expiratory flow (PEF) or FEV_1 decreases by 10% to 15% from preexercise measurements (13). False-negative tests are not uncommon, and retesting should be performed within a week. The sensitivity of the test can be increased if the inspired air is cold (< 2 °C) and dry. In fact, some laboratories substitute a resting cold air inhalation challenge for the standard exercise test to diagnose EIA (50). Results from our laboratory have not borne out the published success rates of 80% or more in detecting EIA with either the exercise tests or the cold air challenge tests.

In general, laboratory tests for diagnosing EIA are not necessary in a child with known asthma who develops exercise-related symptoms of cough, chest tightness, or dyspnea (see Table 2). One can assume that the symptoms are caused by EIA, and the child can be treated accordingly. Even in a youngster not previously recognized as having asthma, symptoms suggestive of EIA may appropriately prompt a therapeutic trial of preexercise albuterol, for example, without the more taxing (emotionally, financially, and energetically) formal EIA test in the exercise laboratory. If the child does not respond to EIA treatment, a test can be done to confirm the diagnosis. If other information is desired, such as the effectiveness of a particular preexercise medication or the degree of oxygen desaturation that accompanies an EIA attack, then

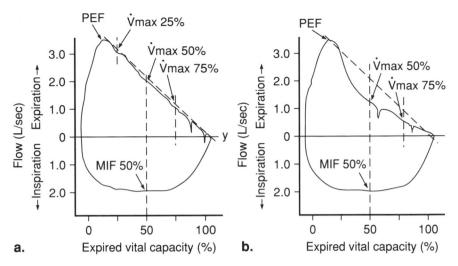

Figure 4: Measurement of expiratory flow rates with spirometry, including flow-volume loops. The left extreme represents full inspiration, when the lung volume is at total lung capacity. The right extreme of the curve represents full expiration; the lung volume at this point is residual volume. The expiratory portion of the flow-volume curve is above the abscissa. The first 50% of the expiratory curve (up to $\dot{V}$max 50% or the flow at 50% of vital capacity), including PEF (peak expiratory flow), is believed to depend on effort and to reflect large airway function. The remainder of the expiratory curve is relatively independent of effort and reflects small airway patency. The inspiratory portion of the curve lies below the abscissa. MIF 50% is maximal flow at 50% of vital capacity. Panel a is from a normal child. Panel b is from a child with expiratory obstruction. *Note.* From "Pulmonary function testing in the office, clinic, and home" by R. Lemen. In: *Kendig's disorders of the respiratory tract in children* (5th ed.) (p. 151), 1990, Philadelphia: W.B. Saunders. Copyright 1990 by W.B. Saunders. Reprinted by permission.

testing is appropriate. Finally, there may be reasons other than diagnosing EIA for performing an exercise test in children or adolescents with asthma, such as determining aerobic fitness. In these cases, a standard progressive maximal test should be performed, just as in the child without asthma.

Documenting Unusual Complaints.   Occasionally a child has an unusual respiratory complaint associated with exercise. To diagnose the cause, special tests may have to be designed to mimic the real-life situation in which the problems reportedly occur. For example, our laboratory tested a college basketball player who developed disabling dyspnea with inspiratory stridor during games and practices. Because inspiratory stridor suggests extrathoracic obstruction, we tested her with high-intensity exercise preceded and followed by pulmonary function testing with flow-volume loops concentrating on the inspiratory limb. On another occasion, the exercise challenge was followed immediately with special fluoroscopic examination of her upper airway, demonstrating inspiratory collapse of the proximal trachea.

Table 2   Situations in Which to Consider Exercise-Induced Asthma

History of asthma
Symptoms with exercise
  Cough
  Shortness of breath
  Chest tightness
Symptoms worse immediately after exercise
Symptoms worse with cold air
History of allergies
History of newborn respiratory disease requiring mechanical ventilation
Cystic fibrosis

Some children without cardiac disease complain of chest pain associated with exercise. These children can be tested in the exercise laboratory to see if their symptoms can be duplicated. A normal ECG and normal pulmonary responses to exercise can reassure the physician, parents, and child that no dangerous pathology is present. In testing these children, it is especially important to include measurements of expiratory flow rates before, during, and after exercise, because many of them suffer from undetected and unsuspected EIA (36) (see Table 3).

Table 3   Respiratory Measurements Before, During, and After Exercise

Before	During	After
Spirometry	Heart rate	Heart rate
Oxyhemoglobin saturation	Minute ventilation	Spirometry
	Ratings of perceived effort (RPE)	Oxyhemoglobin saturation
	Oxyhemoglobin saturation	

Respiratory Measurements
Before, During, and After Exercise

Before.   Although the intimidating setting of exercise laboratories (with daunting machines, strangers, etc.) precludes truly resting measurements, it is nonetheless useful to note several physiologic parameters before the test begins.

In exercise tests of most patients with known or suspected respiratory compromise, baseline pulmonary function measurements are useful. These should include vital capacity, FEV_1, and MVV. This last measurement, MVV, is usually determined during a "sprint" maneuver, in which the child is coached to "blow, blow, blow" as hard and fast as possible for 12 or 15 s; values are extrapolated to liters per minute. If the laboratory is not equipped to measure MVV, or if the patient is too sick for this somewhat tiring maneuver, an acceptable estimate can be made (11):

$$MVV = FEV_1 \times 35$$

In situations in which EIA should be considered (see Table 2), expiratory airflow must be measured prior to exercise. Ideally this is done with full spirometry, including flow-volume loops, which allows quantification of large airway and small airway flow rates (Figure 4). However, substitutes are possible, ranging from simple auscultation to document wheezing or prolonged expiration (least sensitive) to peak expiratory flow with an inexpensive peak flow meter (more sensitive), to water-seal spirometers (most sensitive). Water-seal spirometers allow quantification of vital capacity, FEV_1, peak expiratory flow rate (PEFR), maximal midexpiratory flow rate, maximal expiratory flow at 50% of vital capacity, and maximal expiratory flow at 25% of vital capacity. The last three measurements are thought to reflect patency of the smallest airways (32) and are relatively independent of small differences in effort, whereas the preceding values reflect larger airway flows and are highly effort-dependent (32).

In most cases of respiratory disease, the level of oxygenation of arterial blood is of interest. Ear and finger pulse oximeters offer continuous and noninvasive measurement of arterial oxyhemoglobin saturation (S_aO_2). These instruments are immeasurably more humane than the trauma of direct arterial puncture for measurement of arterial blood gases, and they are very accurate in children at rest. Several studies have demonstrated their usefulness in exercising adults (41, 44). Arterial oxygenation can also be estimated with fair accuracy from "arterialized" blood taken from a warmed earlobe (19, 24), a procedure that is much less painful than arterial puncture.

During.   Once again, which measurements are helpful will depend on the clinical setting. In some patients, it may be helpful simply to document a normal maximal work rate. However, especially when exercise tolerance is below normal, other measurements are useful. These include indexes of ventilation, oxygen consumption and carbon dioxide production, gas exchange, and perceived effort. It is important to be able to tell whether the effort on a progressive "maximal" was truly maximal. Several ventilatory measurements help make this judgment (Table 4). Heart rate is also helpful, both to document degree of effort and to judge the adequacy of the cardiovascular response.

Table 4   Indications That a Test Was Maximal

Heart rate reached maximal values (either age-predicted maximum or previously measured individual patient maximum)

Respiratory exchange ratio ($\dot{V}CO_2/\dot{V}O_2$) > 1.10 at highest work rate* (indicates anaerobic threshold has been passed)

$\dot{V}_E$/MVV > 75%

V_T/VC > 70%

f_b > age-predicted maximum

Apparent severe dyspnea in the absence of objective criteria (uncommon)

Fall in S_aO_2 greater than 15%, despite absence of other objective criteria (rare)

Note. $\dot{V}CO_2$ = carbon dioxide production. $\dot{V}O_2$ = oxygen consumption. $\dot{V}_E$ = minute ventilation. V_T = tidal volume. f_b = breathing frequency. S_aO_2 = oxyhemoglobin saturation.

*A value of RER greater than 1.10 indicates maximal effort only *during* exercise, not in the recovery period. High RER values are common in recovery, because the denominator of the fraction ($\dot{V}O_2$) falls very quickly when exercise stops; the numerator ($\dot{V}CO_2$) continues at high levels for a few minutes while carbon dioxide produced during exercise is being eliminated.

Ventilation.   The most basic index of exercise ventilation is the amount of air breathed in one min, V_E. As I discussed earlier, the resting MVV can be compared with the maximal value of V_E to give an indication of breathing reserve. Many patients with pulmonary or chest wall disorders use much more of their reserve than healthy subjects. Clearly a $\dot{V}_E$max/MVV greater than 80% suggests that there is little or no ventilatory reserve. The components of minute ventilation, V_T and f_b, can also be instructive. V_T can be compared with resting vital capacity (VC) to give another indication of how much the patient pushes each breath toward the absolute limit presumably defined by the VC. V_T/VC values above 60% are abnormal. Similarly, for a given $\dot{V}_E$ required for exercise, limitations in V_T must be compensated for by increases in f_b. Patients with limited V_T must increase f_b to above normal levels to achieve a given V_E. Therefore, f_b above that expected for a given age also suggests a ventilatory limit to exercise (Figure 2). The tidal breath itself can be examined further: The time spent in inspiration (T_i) will of necessity be shortened if there is expiratory obstruction prolonging T_E, and the ratio of inspiratory to total time for an individual breath (T_i/T_{tot}) will shorten.

Oxygen Consumption and Carbon Dioxide Production.   These reflections of metabolic activity are often helpful in judging aerobic fitness and ventilatory status. As I discussed earlier, $\dot{V}O_2$ and $\dot{V}CO_2$ generally increase in parallel during progressive exercise up to the anaerobic threshold, at which point $\dot{V}CO_2$ begins to increase at a faster rate than $\dot{V}O_2$. Since $\dot{V}_E$ is tied closely to $\dot{V}CO_2$, it too shows an inflection point at the anaerobic threshold. In fact, some laboratories choose to measure only $\dot{V}_E$, and not $\dot{V}O_2$ or $\dot{V}CO_2$, reasoning that the anaerobic threshold is as easily identified with the shape of the $\dot{V}_E$ curve as with $\dot{V}O_2$ or $\dot{V}CO_2$. Laboratories can also examine $\dot{V}_E$ in relation to $\dot{V}O_2$ or $\dot{V}CO_2$ to find the ventilatory equivalent for oxygen ($\dot{V}_E/\dot{V}O_2$) or carbon dioxide ($\dot{V}_E/\dot{V}CO_2$), which increases during exercise in patients who have large dead space ventilation (that is, they have to move more air than normal in and out for the same amount of oxygen that is extracted and used). The inflection point may be difficult to identify with any precision, especially if the proper techniques are not employed (see the section "Anaerobic Threshold" for details).

Gas Exchange.   Gas exchange should be measured during exercise in patients with abnormal blood gases at rest and in those at risk of altered gas exchange during exercise. The latter category includes those with severe pulmonary dysfunction of any etiology. Data are particularly compelling in CF; patients with CF whose resting FEV_1 is less than 50% of vital capacity are at risk of desaturation during exercise, whereas those with better resting pulmonary function are not at risk. Gas exchange is measured most accurately by sampling arterial blood, either with individual arterial punctures or by withdrawing blood from an indwelling plastic catheter inserted prior to exercise, usually in a radial artery. Either of these methods is painful, even with local anesthetic, and the results are not available until after the test is completed. Sampling arterialized earlobe blood is considerably less painful and frightening but similarly does not yield results in less than several minutes at best.

Ear oximeters and pulse oximeters, which have come into use within the past decade, work well for measuring S_aO_2 at rest. They may be acceptable for estimating S_aO_2 during exercise in adults, but their accuracy during exercise in children has yet to be demonstrated. Some preliminary studies have suggested that these instruments may give misleading values during exercise in children (15). Nonetheless, these instruments are used widely. In our experience, the pulse reading provides at least a rough guide as to when the saturation is reliably reflected by the oximeter: In most cases where the S_aO_2 reading has been inaccurate, the pulse oximeter's heart rate readout has not corresponded to that measured with the ECG. Arterial carbon dioxide tension can be approximated by measuring the tension of carbon dioxide in expired air at the end of a breath (ET_{CO2}).

Perception of Effort.   RPE can be determined during progressive exercise using the modified Borg scale (7) (Figure 3). The child can be asked to rate the leg effort, overall effort, or—most relevant to those with respiratory compromise—breathlessness. Children younger than 9 years old are unlikely to be able to give useful ratings (2); in fact, many older subjects also have trouble understanding the concept of perceived exertion, but some children and adolescents can give useful information with these tools. One practical (and crude) way to decide which subjects' RPE reports are worth keeping is to see if RPE increases with increasing work rate or longer time at a particular work rate. If not, the RPE reports are unlikely to be of value.

After.   At the end of an exercise test, and during the first several minutes of recovery, continued monitoring of several parameters may be of interest. Because the nadir in expiratory flow rates in EIA occurs some 10 to 20 min after exercise, pulmonary function tests must be repeated every 3 min or so after a test for EIA (13). As with the preexercise tests, these measurements may range from the very crude auscultation to the sophisticated and sensitive spirometry with flow-volume loops.

In a patient whose oxygenation falls during exercise, it is essential to track S_aO_2 or arterial oxygen tensions in recovery, to see how long it takes the patient to recover his or her baseline oxygenation. Most patients recover quickly or even overshoot to higher-than-baseline S_aO_2. However, if someone does not recover quickly, it is important to know this so that supplemental oxygen or modified exercise programs can be prescribed.

Different report forms are available for organizing and recording the child's responses, including pulmonary responses, to exercise tests. Figure 5 illustrates a sample form.

Equipment

A dizzying array of equipment is available for furnishing the pediatric exercise laboratory (see "Conducting the Pediatric Exercise Test" for a discussion of laboratory equipment in general). Next I will review equipment needed specifically for respiratory tests.

Pulmonary Function Equipment

At a minimum, the full exercise laboratory should have access to equipment for performing basic spirometry to measure forced vital capacity, FEV_1, and PEFR. A number of commercially available systems, ranging from the time-honored water-seal spirometer to the computerized systems based on pneumotachographic measurement of airflow, are available at prices most laboratories can afford.

Exercise Equipment

Both the cycle ergometer and treadmill have advantages for testing children. Collection of expired gases is considerably easier with the ergometer because

Graded Exercise Test Report

| Patient name |
| Acc. no. |
| Unit no. |

Test date:	In☐ Out☐ Patient
Dx:	Birth date
Test Reason:	MD

| Medications: |

| Sex: M☐ F☐ | Age (yrs.): | Ht (cm): | Wt (kg): | Protocol: |

Variable	Rest	1	2	3	4	5	Minute 6	7	8	9	10	11	12	13	Peak
Work rate (W)															
$\dot{V}O_2$ (ml·kg^{-1}·min^{-1})															
$\dot{V}O_2$ (ml/min)															
$\dot{V}CO_2$ (ml/min)															
$\dot{V}_E$ (L/min)															
$\dot{V}_T$ (ml)															
RR (br/min)															
Ins time (sec)															
Exp time (sec)															
PETO$_2$ (mmHg)															
PETCO$_2$ (mmHg)															
$\dot{V}_E/\dot{V}O_2$ (%)															
RER															
$\dot{V}_E$/MVV (%)															
HR (b/min)															
SaO$_2$ (%)															
BP (mmHg)															

| Length of exercise test: (min:sec): | Reason for termination: |

PWC =	W	Pred. PWC (Godfrey) =	W	% Pred. =
Peak $\dot{V}O_2$ (ml/min) =	ml/min	Pred.Peak $\dot{V}O_2$ (DMO)=	ml/min	% Pred. =
Peak HR (b/min) =	b/min	Age Pred. Peak HR =	b/min	% Pred. =

Comments:

Technician _____   Physician signature _____

Figure 5:   An example of an exercise test report form, including explanations for terms. The explanations are printed on the back of each form. This report form was developed in and is currently used in the exercise laboratory of Children's Hospital of Pittsburgh.

(Cont.)

Glossary of Abbreviations

PWC (W)	Peak work capacity	The highest work rate sustained for 1 min (expressed in Watts)
$\dot{V}O_2$ (ml/min)	Oxygen consumption	The volume of oxygen consumed per minute: VO_2 = cardiac output × arterial-mixed venous oxygen difference
$\dot{V}O_2$ (ml · kg^{-1} · mm^{-1})	Oxygen consumption	VO_2 expressed per kilogram of body weight
$\dot{V}CO_2$ (ml/min)	Carbon dioxide production	The volume of carbon dioxide produced per minute
$\dot{V}_E$ (L/min)	Minute ventilation	The volume of air expired per minute
$\dot{V}_T$ (ml)	Tidal volume	The volume of air inspired or expired per breath
RR (br/min)	Respiration rate	The number of breaths per minute
Ins time (sec)	Inspiratory time	The time taken to inspire a breath
Exp time (sec)	Expiratory time	The time taken to expire a breath
PETO$_2$ (mmHg)	End tidal O_2 tension	Tension of oxygen at the end of a tidal breath
PETCO$_2$ (mmHg)	End tidal CO_2 tension	Tension of carbon dioxide at the end of a tidal breath
$\dot{V}_E/\dot{V}O_2$ (%)	Ventilatory equivalent for O_2	The minute ventilation required for a given oxygen consumption
RER	Respiratory exchange ratio	The ratio of the amount of carbon dioxide produced to the amount of oxygen consumed ($\dot{V}CO_2/\dot{V}O_2$)
$\dot{V}_E/MVV$ (%)	Minute ventilation/ maximal voluntary ventilation	The percentage of the maximal voluntary ventilation (obtained at rest) used for ventilation during exercise
S_aO_2 (%)	Oxyhemoglobin saturation	The percentage of hemoglobin saturated with oxygen
HR (b/min)	Heart rate	
BP (mmHg)	Blood pressure	

Figure 5:   (Continued)

Prediction Equations

1. PWC (Godfrey) → $\begin{cases} \text{(male) Watts} = 2.87 \text{ (height in cm)} - 291 \\ \text{(female) Watts} = 2.38 \text{ (height in cm)} - 238 \end{cases}$

2. Peak $\dot{V}O_2$ (DMO) → $\begin{cases} \text{(male) } VO_2 \text{ (L/min)} = 0.044955 \text{ (height in cm)} - 4.64 \\ \text{(female) } VO_2 \text{ (L/min)} = 0.0308806 \text{ (height in cm)} - 2.877 \end{cases}$

3. Age-predicted peak heart rate: HR (b/min) = 220 − age (years)

Exercise Protocols

1. Godfrey (<125 cm)   A cycle ergometer test that starts at zero resistance and increases by 10 W each minute; used for subjects who are shorter than 125 cm or have an $FEV_1\%$ predicted of 30 or less

2. Godfrey (125-150 cm)   A cycle ergometer test that starts at zero resistance and increases by 15 W each minute; used for subjects whose height is between 125 and 150 cm

3. Godfrey (>150 cm)   A cycle ergometer test that starts at zero resistance and increases by 20 W each minute; used for subjects who are taller than 150 cm

Figure 5:   (Continued)

the child's head moves much less than on the treadmill. In our laboratory, we prefer the ergometer also because of the easier estimation of work rate and the independence of work rate from body weight. Finally, we believe that a child feels quite awkward the first few times on a treadmill, so the ergometer entails a smaller learning effect and less danger of falling. However, for very small children, the treadmill may be better (37).

Gas Analysis Equipment

Many commercially available computerized systems are in use, with varying degrees of reliability. Also, many laboratories have put together their own systems. In most systems, determination of oxygen uptake requires the measurement of ventilation and the analysis of oxygen and carbon dioxide tensions. Several devices can assess ventilation or airflow. Dry gas meters, spirometers, and turbine transducers measure volume, whereas pneumotachographs measure airflow. Each has advantages and disadvantages to consider when one is choosing the appropriate system for measuring parameters of interest (e.g., minute ventilation vs. inspiratory time for individual breaths).

Several carbon dioxide and oxygen analyzers are also available. Most CO_2 analyzers use infrared light, whereas oxygen analyzers are generally either the paramagnetic or fuel cell type. Oxygen and carbon dioxide concentrations can also be measured by mass spectrometry. It is important to check the analyzers for linearity and to account for the presence of water vapor. It is also important to consider how much airflow is required in their use, especially if small children are to be tested. If a system draws 200 ml/min for gas analysis, it is probably not as appropriate for pediatric testing as one that requires flows of less than 50 ml/min. Similarly, for testing children, masks or mouthpieces and valving systems must have minimal dead space, so that gas analysis will reflect the dead space of the child and not that of the machine.

References

1. Anderson, S., J. McEvoy, and S. Biance. Changes in lung volumes and airway resistance after exercise in asthmatic subjects. *Am. Rev. Respir. Dis.* 106:30-37, 1972.
2. Bar-Or, O., and D. Ward. Rating of perceived exertion in children. In: *Advances in Pediatric Sport Sciences: Biologic Issues*, O. Bar-Or (Ed.). Champaign, IL: Human Kinetics, 1989, pp. 151-168.
3. Bergofsky, E., G. Turino, and A. Fishman. Cardiorespiratory failure in kyphoscoliosis. *Medicine* 38:263-317, 1959.
4. Bierman, C., S. Spiro, and I. Petheram. Characteristics of the late response in exercise-induced asthma. *J. Allergy Clin. Immunol.* 74:701-706, 1984.
5. Bjure, J., G. Grimby, and A. Nachemson. The effect of physical training in girls with idiopathic scoliosis. *Acta Orthop. Scand.* 40:325-333, 1969.
6. Boat, T., M. Welsh, and A. Beaudet. Cystic fibrosis. In: *The Metabolic Basis of Inherited Disease*, C.R. Scriver, A.L. Beaudet, W.S. Sly, & D. Valle (Eds.) (6th ed.). New York: McGraw-Hill, 1989, pp. 2649-2680.
7. Borg, G. Psychophysical bases of perceived exertion. *Med. Sci. Sports Exerc.* 14:377-381, 1982.
8. Castile, R., B. Staats, and P. Westbrook. Symptomatic pectus deformities of the chest. *Am. Rev. Respir. Dis.* 126:564-568, 1982.
9. Cerny, F. Ventilatory control during exercise in children with cystic fibrosis [Abstract]. *Am. Rev. Respir. Dis.* 123(4, p.2):195, 1981.
10. Cerny, F.J., T.P. Pullano, and G.C. Cropp. Cardiorespiratory adaptations to exercise in cystic fibrosis. *Am. Rev. Respir. Dis.* 126(2):217-220, 1982.
11. Clark, T., S. Freedman, E. Campbell, and R. Winn. The ventilatory capacity of patients with chronic airways obstruction. *Clin. Sci.* 36:307-316, 1969.
12. Coates, A., P. Boyce, D. Muller, M. Mearns, and S. Godfrey. The role of nutritional status, airway obstruction, hypoxia, and abnormalities in

serum lipid composition in limiting exercise tolerance in children with cystic fibrosis. *Acta Paediatr. Scand.* 69:353-358, 1980.

13. Cropp, G. The exercise bronchoprovocation test: Standardization of procedures and evaluation of response. *J. Allergy Clin. Immunol.* 64(6, p.2):627-633, 1979.

14. Cropp, G.J., T.P. Pullano, F.J. Cerny, and I.T. Nathanson. Exercise tolerance and cardiorespiratory adjustments at peak work capacity in cystic fibrosis. *Am. Rev. Respir. Dis.* 126(2):211-216, 1982.

15. Curtis, S., D. Orenstein, P. Nixon, and E. Ross. Accuracy of SaO$_2$ monitors during exercise testing in pediatrics patients with cystic fibrosis [Abstract]. *Am. Rev. Respir. Dis.* 137:305, 1988.

16. Deal, E., E. McFadden, R. Ingram, Jr., R. Strauss, and J. Jaeger. Role of respiratory heat exchange in production of exercise-induced asthma. *J. Appl. Physiol.* 46:467-475, 1979.

17. Edmunds, A., M. Tooley, and S. Godfrey. The refractory period after exercise-induced asthma: Its duration and relation to the severity of exercise. *Am. Rev. Respir. Dis.* 117:247-254, 1978.

18. Eriksson, B., G. Grimby, and B. Saltin. Cardiac output and arterial blood gases during exercise in pubertal boys. *J. Appl. Physiol.* 31:348-352, 1971.

19. Godfrey, S. *Exercise Testing in Children.* London: Saunders, 1974.

20. Godfrey, S. Growth and development of cardio-pulmonary responses to exercise. In: *Scientific Foundations of Paediatrics*, J. Davies and J. Dobbing (Eds.). London: Heinemenn, 1974, pp. 271-280.

21. Godfrey, S., C. Davies, E. Wozniak, and C. Barnes. Cardiorespiratory response to exercise in normal children. *Clin. Sci.* 40:419-431, 1971.

22. Godfrey, S., and M. Mearns. Pulmonary function and response to exercise in cystic fibrosis. *Arch. Dis. Child.* 46:144-151, 1971.

23. Godfrey, S., M. Silverman, and S. Anderson. Problems of interpreting exercise induced asthma. *J. Allergy Clin. Immunol.* 52:199-209, 1973.

24. Godfrey, S., E. Wozniak, R. Courtnay Evans, and C. Samuels. Ear lobe blood samples for blood gas analysis at rest and during exercise. *B. J. Dis. Chest* 65:58-64, 1971.

25. Gyllensward, A., L. Irnell, M. Michaelsson, O. Qvist, and B. Sahlstedt. Pectus excavatum: A clinical study with long term postoperative follow-up. *Acta Paediatr. Scand.* 255(Suppl.):1-14, 1975.

26. Henke, K.G., and D.M. Orenstein. Oxygen saturation during exercise in cystic fibrosis. *Am. Rev. Respir. Dis.* 129:708-711, 1984.

27. Jones, J. *Clinical Exercise Testing* (3rd Ed.). Philadelphia: Saunders, 1988.

28. Killian, K., and N. Jones. The use of exercise testing and other methods in the investigation of dyspnea. *Clin. Chest Med.* 5:99-108, 1984.

29. Lebecque, P., J.G. Lapierre, A. Lamarre, and A. Coates. Diffusion capacity and oxygen desaturation effects on exercise in patients with cystic fibrosis. *Chest* 91:693-697, 1987.

30. Leech, J., P. Ernst, E.J. Rogala, J. Gurr, I. Gordon, and M.R. Becklake. Cardiorespiratory status in relation to mild deformity in adolescent idiopathic scoliosis. *Pediatrics* 106:143-149, 1985.

31. Lemanske, R., Jr., and K. Henke. Exercise-induced asthma. In: *Youth, Exercise, and Sport*, C. Gisolfi and D. Lamb (Eds.). Indianapolis: Benchmark Press, 1989, pp. 465-511.

32. Lemen, R. Pulmonary function testing in the office, clinic, and home. *Kendig's Disorders of the Respiratory Tract in Children* (5th ed.). Philadelphia: Saunders, 1990, pp. 147-154.

33. Lindh, M. Energy expenditure during walking in patients with scoliosis. *Spine* 3(2):122-134, 1978.

34. Nixon, P.A. and D.M. Orenstein. Exercise testing in children. *Pediatr. Pulmonol.* 5:107-122, 1988.

35. Nixon, P.A., D.M. Orenstein, S.E. Curtis, and E.A. Ross. Oxygen supplementation during exercise in cystic fibrosis. *Am. Rev. Respir. Dis.* 142(4): 807-811, 1990.

36. Nudel, D.B., S. Diamants, T. Brady, M. Jarenwattananon, B.J. Buckley, N. Gootman. Chest pain, dyspnea on exertion and exercise induced asthma in children and adolescents. *Clin. Pediatrics* 26:388-392, 1987.

37. Orenstein, D., and F. Cerny. *Exercise Testing*. Bethesda, MD: Cystic Fibrosis Foundation, 1984.

38. Orenstein, D.M., and P.A. Nixon. Exercise performance and breathing patterns in cystic fibrosis: Male-female differences and influence of resting pulmonary function. *Pediatr. Pulmonol.* 10:101-105, 1991.

39. Peabody, F. Cardiac dyspnea. *Harvey Lect.* 12:248-271, 1916-17.

40. Peterson, R., W. Young, Jr., J. Godwin, D. Sabiston, Jr., and R. Jones. Noninvasive assessment of exercise cardiac function before and after pectus excavatum repair. *J. Thorac. Cardiovasc. Surg.* 90:251-260, 1985.

41. Ries, A., J. Farrow, and J. Clausen. Accuracy of two ear oximeters at rest and during exercise in pulmonary patients. *Am. Rev. Respir. Dis.* 132:685-689, 1985.

42. Shneerson, J. Cardiac and respiratory responses to exercise in adolescent idiopathic scoliosis. *Thorax* 35:347-350, 1980.

43. Silverman, M., and S. Anderson. Standardization of exercise tests in asthmatic children. *Arch. Dis. Child.* 47:882-889, 1972.

44. Smyth, R., A. C'Urzo, A. Slutsky, B. Galko, and A. Rebuck. Ear oximetry during combined hypoxia and exercise. *J. Appl. Physiol.* 60:716-719, 1986.

45. Strauss, R., E. McFadden, R. Ingram, Jr., and J. Jaeger. Enhancement of exercise-induced asthma by cold air. *N. Engl. J. Med.* 297:743-747, 1977.

46. Sturgis, C., F. Peabody, F. Hall, and F. Fremont-Smith, Jr. Clinical studies on the respiration: VIII. The relation of dyspnea to the maximum minute volume of pulmonary ventilation. *Arch. Intern. Med.* 29:236-244, 1922.

47. Wasserman, K., J. Hansen, D. Sue, and B. Whipp. *Principles of Exercise Testing and Interpretation*. Philadelphia: Lea & Febiger, 1987.

48. Wasserman, K., A. VanEssel, and G. Burton. Interaction of physiological mechanisms during exercise. *J. Appl. Physiol.* 22:71-85, 1967.
49. Wasserman, K., and B. Whipp. Exercise physiology in health and disease. *Am. Rev. Respir. Dis.* 112:219-249, 1975.
50. Zach, M., G. Polgar, H. Kump, and P. Kroisel. Cold air challenge of airway hyper-reactivity in children: Practical application and theoretical aspects. *Pediatr. Res.* 18:469-478, 1984.

Noncardiopulmonary Pediatric Exercise Tests

Oded Bar-Or, MD
McMaster University

Traditionally, clinical exercise testing of adults (38) and children (24) has focused on the cardiovascular and respiratory systems. Likewise, measurement of fitness in the laboratory has almost exclusively focused on the O_2 transport system. In fact, fitness testing has become synonymous with testing of aerobic fitness. This section discusses laboratory-based exercise tests in pediatrics that are not centered around the O_2 transport system. Some are used to aid in a pediatric diagnostic procedure; others assess the child's physical fitness. Emphasis is placed on the rationale for each test, the pediatric diseases to which it is relevant, a description of the procedure, and discussion of its characteristics.

Muscle Endurance and Peak Power

In various pediatric disorders, peak muscle power and local muscle endurance are deficient (3, 46, 53). In disorders such as muscular dystrophies and atrophies, cerebral palsy, spina bifida, and McArdle's syndrome, it is probably not the maximal aerobic power that limits the child's ability to exercise, but rather the local muscle endurance and peak mechanical power (collectively called *anaerobic characteristics*) (5). In other conditions (e.g., cystic fibrosis with advanced muscle wasting, anorexia nervosa), a decrease in local muscle performance may accompany a reduction in maximal aerobic power. Knowledge of changes with time in peak muscle power and muscle endurance can help in evaluating the progression of a disease (Duchenne muscle dystrophy) or the effects of a rehabilitation program.

Peak muscle power and muscle endurance have been ignored in most exercise laboratories, mostly because of the absence of a standardized, valid, and reliable test to assess these functions. Until the early 1980s, the only clinically oriented test of muscle endurance for pediatric patients was the maximal time that a supine child could hold her or his neck, or a straight leg, at 45° from the ground (20, 29). This test lacked standardization and had a low reliability (29). The 30-s all-out Wingate Anaerobic Test (WAnT) was developed in the mid-1970s at the Wingate Institute in Israel. It has been used extensively with able-bodied children and adults (6) to assess performance of their lower (cycling) or upper (arm-cranking) limbs. As recently documented (53), the WAnT is also feasible for use with children and adolescents with neuromuscular disabilities such as cerebral palsy, muscular dystrophy, muscular atrophy, and spina bifida.

The Test

Equipment.   The WAnT requires a cycle ergometer in which the braking force can be kept constant, a timing device (e.g., a stopwatch), and a means of counting pedal revolutions (a mechanical or photoelectric counter). An increasing number of laboratories are using an on-line automated data collection system to retrieve the number of revolutions and calculate the performance indexes (see Figure 1). However, these indexes can also be calculated manually and off-line. Because the braking force must remain constant throughout the test, mechanically braked bikes are preferred. The commonly available Monark ergometer has often been used. Its drawback, however, is that it takes several seconds to adjust the braking force of the pendulum to the required level and then the pendulum may not be stable during the test. An alternative (which is provided by the manufacturer but can also be modified locally) is for weights, rather than a pendulum, to provide resistance.

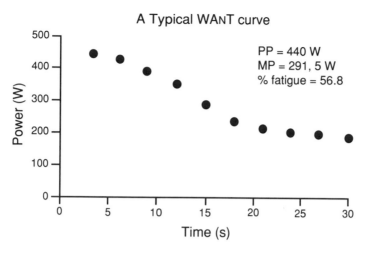

Figure 1:   A typical curve of mechanical power over time during the Wingate Anaerobic Test (PP = peak power; MP = mean power).

Several laboratories, including ours, have been using the Fleisch-Metabo ergometer (Lausanne, Switzerland). It uses weights to induce the braking force and allows smaller increments of force than the Monark ergometer. This is particularly important for children with motor disabilities, or with weak muscles, whose muscle power is low. An electronically braked bike, in which the force changes as a function of pedaling speed, is not suitable. There are, however, electronic ergometers with a constant force mode, which are suitable for the WAnT.

The Protocol.   This is a 30-s all-out cycling, or arm cranking, test. Because of the constant braking force, mechanical power can be calculated by counting the pedal revolutions. In the original version of the WAnT, power was calculated for each 5-s interval. With the greater sophistication of counting devices, counting intervals have been reduced. Our routine is to calculate power every 3 s. The protocol of the WAnT is identical for able-bodied and physically challenged individuals. The only difference is in the braking force against which the subject or patient has to cycle or arm crank. Power is calculated the same way as in aerobic testing, by multiplying the friction force at the flywheel by the velocity at which the perimeter of the flywheel is turning.

The test is preceded by a warm-up period on the bike for 3 to 4 min and then a 3-min rest. The intensity of the warm-up should be such that heart rate reaches 145 to 155 for cycling and 120 to 130 for arm cranking. During this period, four to five brief (3 to 4 s) all-out sprints are interspersed, to give the child a feeling of what a sprint on the bike feels like. The braking force during these sprints is identical to, or close to, that used for the actual test. For patients with a motor disability, obesity, or severe malnutrition, the sprints are also used to determine the optimal force for the test itself, as described later in this section. The tester should emphasize to the child, as part of the initial instructions, that pedaling should be done at maximal speed right from the beginning and throughout the test. The tester should further tell the child that this is a very hard task but that when the child feels tired, "there are only a few seconds left" until the end of the test.

At the command "start," the child starts pedaling at maximal speed against zero force. Once the initial inertia of the bike has been overcome (within 2 to 3 s), the full force is applied and the counting starts. At the end of the 30-s period, the command "stop" is given and the child is then instructed to keep pedaling slowly, against a very low force, for a 2- to 3-min cool-down period. Three indexes are calculated, as shown in Figure 1. Peak power (PP) is the highest power during any 3-s interval (or any time interval at which power is calculated). In the example shown in Figure 1, PP was achieved at the first 3-s interval. Mean power (MP) is the average power over the 30-s period, and percent fatigue is the difference between the peak power and the lowest power (which, in Figure 1, occurred during the last 3-s interval), divided by the peak power and multiplied by 100. One can also calculate the total mechanical work over the 30 s. PP reflects muscle explosiveness, and MP (or total work) reflects muscle endurance. Thus, both PP and MP can be considered components of the child's fitness. Both PP and percent fatigue are correlated with the preponderance of fast-twitch muscle fibers (8). This may have clinical relevance because some pathologic processes affect the fast-twitch fibers preferentially, as shown, for example, in muscles that are spastic due to an upper neuron disease (12, 18). Surprisingly, neither high nor low percent fatigue correlate with any independent measure of fitness (6).

The optimal braking force (i.e., the force that would yield the highest mean power) depends on the child's size and on whether this is an arm or a leg test. It also depends on the circumference of the flywheel on which the force is applied. Tables 1 and 2 include a list of optimal braking forces for healthy children of various body weights who perform an arm or a leg test, respectively. Values are given for a Monark and for a Fleisch ergometer. These were generated experimentally (17), but extrapolation and interpolation were needed to include a wide range of body weights. Performance in the WAnT depends on the fat-free mass of the child (11), so it is more logical that optimal forces should be determined according to the fat-free, rather than the total, body mass. This, however, may not be practical for laboratories, which do not have the ability to assess fat-free mass accurately. In a patient with abnormal body composition (e.g., obesity, anorexia) or with a motor disability, there is an abnormal ratio between muscle mass and total body mass. The optimal braking forces as listed in Tables 1 and 2 are not applicable for such patients. Instead, one must customize the force for each child. This is done based on the sprints during the warm-up period. One keeps increasing the braking force from one sprint to the next until it becomes apparent that the

Table 1   Optimal Braking Force for the Wingate Anaerobic Leg Test

Body weight (kg)	Monark (kp)		Fleisch (weights)	
	Girls	Boys	Girls	Boys
20-24.9	1.3-1.7	1.4-1.8	13-17	14-18
25-29.9	1.7-2.0	1.8-2.0	17-20	18-20
30-34.9	2.0-2.3	2.1-2.5	20-23	21-25
35-39.9	2.3-2.7	2.5-2.7	23-27	25-27
40-44.9	2.7-3.0	2.8-3.2	27-30	28-32
45-49.9	3.0-3.3	3.2-3.5	30-33	32-35
50-54.9	3.3-3.7	3.5-3.9	33-37	35-39
55-59.9	3.7-4.0	3.9-4.2	37-40	39-42
60-64.9	4.0-4.3	4.2-4.6	40-43	42-46
65-69.9	4.3-4.7	4.6-4.9	43-47	46-49

Table 2   Optimal Braking Force for the Wingate Anaerobic Arm Test

Body weight (kg)	Monark (kp)		Fleisch (weights)	
	Girls	Boys	Girls	Boys
20-24.9	0.8-1.0	0.8-1.1	8-10	8-11
25-29.9	1.0-1.2	1.1-1.3	10-12	11-13
30-34.9	1.2-1.4	1.3-1.5	12-14	13-15
35-39.9	1.4-1.6	1.5-1.6	14-16	15-16
40-44.9	1.6-1.8	1.7-1.9	16-18	17-19
45-49.9	1.8-2.0	1.9-2.1	18-20	19-21
50-54.9	2.0-2.2	2.1-2.3	20-22	21-23
55-59.9	2.2-2.4	2.3-2.5	22-24	23-25
60-64.9	2.4-2.6	2.5-2.8	24-26	25-28
65-69.9	2.6-2.8	2.8-3.0	26-28	28-30

child can no longer sprint. Further research is needed to obtain a more generic approach to optimization for such patients.

An alternative method for identifying the optimal braking force has been offered by Van Praagh et al. (54). In a separate session, the child performs several all-out sprints on a cycle ergometer, each lasting 5 to 6 s. The force is increased from one sprint to the next. A velocity-to-force regression line is then drawn and extrapolated to zero velocity. At this velocity, the force can be considered maximal. The optimal force for the subsequent WAnT is 50% of the above maximal force.

Characteristics of the WAnT

Considerable research has evaluated the feasibility, reliability, validity, and sensitivity of the WAnT. For a review, see Bar-Or (6).

Feasibility. The WAnT has been found feasible for healthy children as young as 5 years old and of a variety of mental ages. In our clinical experience, children with mental retardation who cannot perform a maximal aerobic cycling test (because of inability to keep the required cadence or to persevere for several minutes) can successfully perform the 30-s WAnT. In a recent study by Tirosh et al. (53), 66 patients ages 6 to 20 with a variety of advanced neuromuscular diseases attempted the WAnT arm test. Sixty-two (94%) completed it successfully once. Fifty-eight (88%) completed it twice. In contrast, the leg WAnT was completed once by 61% and twice by 58%. The leg test was particularly hard for patients with Duchenne muscular dystrophy (15% success) because of the loss of function of their proximal lower limb muscles. A similarly high rate of completion was obtained in another study in our laboratory (unpublished) among children and adolescents with cerebral palsy. Children seem to recover from the WAnT faster than adults (28). Thus, if a test has to be performed twice on the same day, healthy children can repeat it, with equal results, within 10 to 15 min. We have no data as to how long a child with a motor disability needs to wait if a test is to be repeated.

Reliability. As the data in Table 3 indicate, the test is highly reliable. Test-retest reliability coefficients in healthy adults and children are usually above

Table 3   Test-Retest Reliability Coefficients of Peak Power (PP) and Mean Power (MP) in Children and Adolescents

Subjects	r	Comments	Reference
Healthy children & adolescents	.95-.97	Various studies	Bar-Or et al. (7)
12-year-old girls & boys	.89-.93	3 climates, 2 weeks apart	Dotan & Bar-Or (17)
6 to 20 years old with a neuromuscular disease	.94-.98	Arm test, 1-2 weeks apart	Tirosh et al. (53)
6 to 20 years old with a neuromuscular disease	.96	Leg test, 1-2 weeks apart	Tirosh et al. (53)

Data are from studies reported in the literature.

Note. From ''The Wingate Anaerobic Test: An Update on Methodology, Reliability and Validity'' by O. Bar-Or, *Sports Med.* 4:386, 1987. Copyright 1987 by Adis International. Adapted by permission.

.95 (7, 19, 39). When repeat testing of 10- to 12-year-old girls and boys was done 2 weeks apart and in three different climates, r values ranged from .89 to .93 (16). In a recent study of 6- to 20-year-old patients with spastic cerebral palsy ($n = 25$), athetotic cerebral palsy ($n = 9$), Duchenne muscular dystrophy ($n = 9$), and other neuromuscular disorders ($n = 15$), test-retest (1 to 2 weeks apart) correlations of the arm test were .95 to .99 for peak power and .92 to .99 for mean power. Thirty-eight of these patients also performed the leg test. Test-retest correlations for those with spastic cerebral palsy and other (non-Duchenne) neuromuscular diseases ranged from .95 to .98. They were lower ($.70 \leq r \leq .82$) for those with athetosis.

Validity.   In the absence of a single "gold standard" for measuring peak power and local muscle endurance, the WAnT was compared in a series of studies against performance items or physiologic variables that are considered to reflect anaerobic muscle characteristics. Performance items such as sprinting, jumping, and speed skating were measured in children (see Table 4). In other studies, mostly with adults, performance indexes in the WAnT were correlated with physiologic characteristics such as maximal O_2 debt, blood lactate, and preponderance of fast-twitch muscle fibers. Some of these correlations are listed in Table 5. Altogether, 40% to 65% of the variance in PP and MP can be explained by these anaerobic variables. Additional validation of the anaerobic nature of the WAnT can be deduced from the extremely high levels of muscle lactate (more than 73.9 mmol/kg in young adult males and 60.5 mmol/kg in young adult females—values obviously much higher than

Table 4   Correlation Between Power Indexes in the Wingate Anaerobic Test (WAnT) and Performance in Anaerobic Tasks in Children and Adolescents

WAnT index	Performance task	r	Reference
PP[a]	40-m run speed	.84	Bar-Or & Inbar (9)
PP	4 × 100-yard skate	.83	Rhodes et al. (47)
PP/kg	50-yard time	−.69	Tharp et al. (52)
PP	Vertical jump	.70	Tharp et al. (52)
MP[b]	25-m swim time	−.90	Inbar & Bar-Or (30)
MP (arm)	25-m swim time	−.92	Inbar & Bar-Or (30)
MP	300-m run time	−.88	Inbar & Bar-Or (30)
MP	4 × 100-yard skate	.71	Rhodes et al. (47)
MP/kg	50-yard time	.69	Tharp et al. (52)
MP	Vertical jump	.74	Tharp et al. (52)

[a]PP = peak mechanical power. [b]MP = mean mechanical power.

Note. From "The Wingate Anaerobic Test: An Update on Methodology, Reliability and Validity" by O. Bar-Or, *Sports Med.* 4:388, 1987. Copyright 1987 by Adis International. Adapted by permission.

Table 5   Correlation Between Power Indexes in the Wingate Anaerobic Test (WAnT) and Physiological Indexes of Anaerobic Metabolism

WAnT index	Physiologic variable	r	Reference
PP[a]	PP Thorstenson test	.61	Inbar et al. (32)
MP[b]	MP Thorstenson test	.78	Inbar et al. (32)
MP	Maximal O_2 debt	.86	Bar-Or et al. (7)
PP/LBM[c]	% FT[d] area	.60	Bar-Or et al. (8)
% fatigue	FT area/ST area	.75	Bar-Or et al. (8)
PP	FT area	.84	Kaczkowski et al. (39)
MP	FT area	.83	Kaczkowski et al. (39)
Rev[e]/30 s	Blood lactate post-WAnT	.60	Jacobs (33)

[a]PP = peak mechanical power. [b]MP = mean mechanical power. [c]LBM = lean body mass. [d]FT = fast-twitch fiber type. [e]Rev = pedal revolutions.

Note. From "The Wingate Anaerobic Test: An Update on Methodology, Reliability and Validity" by O. Bar-Or, *Sports Med.* 4:390, 1987. Copyright 1987 by Adis International. Adapted by permission.

in the blood) found at the end of the 30-s test (34, 35). For ethical reasons, validation studies that require invasive techniques have not been done with children.

Sensitivity.   For a test to be clinically useful, its indexes should be sensitive to reflect changes due to training and rehabilitation programs on the one hand and due to deterioration in muscle function on the other. A training study with 11- to 12-year-old boys, which included 8 weeks of sprint running or sprint cycling, induced significant increases of 3% to 5% in PP and MP. A control group had no changes in these indices (26). An increase of 8% to 10% in PP and MP was elicited in 12- to 13-year-old girls and boys who were given additional physical education classes during an 8-month period (25). In young adults, increases of up to 15% were obtained as a result of an 8-week sprint cycling or arm cranking program. These increases were specific to the muscle group (arms or legs) that was trained (31).

I am not aware of studies on training-induced changes of peak muscle power or muscle endurance in pediatric populations with a neuromuscular disease. Nor have studies documented a reduction in these indexes as a result of the progression of a disease process. Data are available, however, for individual case studies that have not been published. Figure 2 represents serial testing of a boy with Duchenne muscular dystrophy. He was first seen in our clinic at age 7.5 years, when he was given a mild muscle-strengthening program for his upper and lower limbs. At that stage he was still ambulatory. He maintained the muscle function of the limbs for several months. At age 8.2 he underwent surgery (heel cord release), which was accompanied by 3

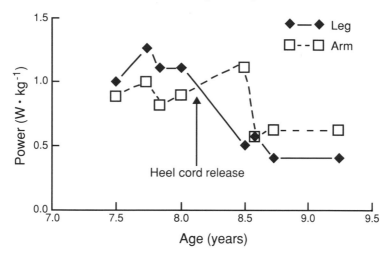

Figure 2:   Changes over 20 months in peak mechanical power of the arms and legs in a boy with Duchenne muscular dystrophy, measured with the Wingate Anaerobic Test. The arrow denotes time of surgery for a bilateral release of the Achilles tendon. Data are from the author's laboratory.

to 4 weeks of bed rest. Following that period he could no longer walk and had to use a wheelchair. When tested at age 8.5, the peak power of his lower limbs had declined by nearly 60% from its presurgery level. The respective upper limbs power followed suit one month later.

Testing of a Single Limb

Occasionally it may be necessary to test a single limb, or to compare the performance of one limb with the contralateral one. This was the case with a 9.7-year-old boy with sacral lipomeningocele and sacral tethering, who was referred to our clinic. Clinical criteria showed the neurological deficit was mostly apparent on the left side, as evidenced by a smaller calf circumference, cavus foot, toe clawing, and foot slapping on the left. To determine whether there was any difference between the two limbs in the development over time of their muscle power, we performed unilateral WAnT periodically over a 14-month span. When muscle power was measured in absolute terms (Watts), there was an increase over time in both legs. However, when calculated per kilogram of body weight (see Figure 3), the power in the left leg seemed to lag behind that of the right leg, suggesting a progressive increase in the deficit.

Growth-Hormone Deficiency Test

Growth-hormone (GH) deficiency can be an isolated, often idiopathic, condition or part of a general hypopituitarism. Its main manifestation is an

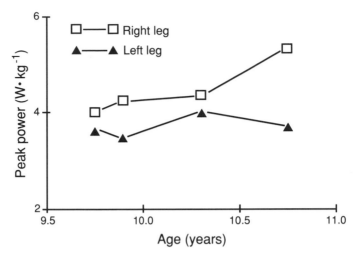

Figure 3:   Changes over 13 months in peak mechanical power of the right leg and the left leg in a boy with sacral lipomeningocele, measured with the unilateral Wingate Anaerobic Test. Data are from the author's laboratory.

exceptionally short stature and a low height velocity. The diagnosis of GH deficiency is important because this is one of the few treatable causes of short stature (it can be treated with injections of GH). With the advent of synthetic GH, diagnosing GH deficiency has been gaining particular interest.

During most waking hours, the concentration of GH in the serum, even in a child with normal pituitary function, is low (1 to 7 ng/ml), particularly in prepubescents (14), so it is impractical to identify GH deficiency through random blood tests. The common approach is to provoke the secretion of GH and monitor its serum levels. Such a provocation can be done by pharmaco-logic agents (e.g., injection of insulin to induce hypoglycemia or oral adminis-tration of clonidine) or by physiologic means. The latter include overnight sleeping or physical exercise. The physiologic stimuli and the insulin-induced hypoglycemia activate the hypothalamic-pituitary-adrenal axis and induce secretion of adrenocorticotropic hormone (ACTH) and cortisol which, in turn, facilitate release of GH. Clonidine seems to enhance the secretion of growth hormones from the hypothalamus (23).

That exercise can induce a rise in GH level was first shown in 1963 (48). Exercise provocation tests have been used in many laboratories since the 1970s, usually in conjunction with pharmacologic provocations. A positive test is commonly accepted as one in which serum GH does not reach 8 ng/ml (in some laboratories, 6 ng/ml) during or after the provocation. In some medical centers, an exercise test is used for screening (15, 37, 45): If it triggers a rise in GH above 8 ng/ml, there is no need for additional tests. But if the test is positive, one or two pharmacologic tests are subsequently performed to confirm the diagnosis.

The Exercise Test

Various protocols have been described in the literature for the GH-deficiency test. They vary in ergometers, exercise duration, and intensity. There has been no systematic comparison to identify an optimal protocol, but either a cycle ergometer or a treadmill is usually acceptable. One exception is for preschoolers, or older children with very small stature. Such children may not be able to sustain a cycling task and should be tested on the treadmill. As shown by Nicoll et al. (43), a treadmill can be used for a GH-provocation test with children as young as 3 years. The test should last 10 to 15 min at an intensity of 70% to 80% of the patient's maximal aerobic power. Blood should be drawn before the provocation and at least once after it. The second blood sample should be taken at approximately 20 min after the start of exercise. Some authors (37) have suggested that there is no need to obtain blood sample before exercise and that a single postexercise sample is sufficient for screening. I do not recommend this approach because some children who have a high GH level at rest have a paradoxical decrease in its concentration following exercise. In such a case, a single postexercise sample would elicit a false-positive result.

To minimize the likelihood of false-positive results (due to either an insufficient provocation or too few blood samples), our clinic subjects the child to two exercise tasks, with a 10-min rest in between. The first task is a progressively increasing cycling protocol (loads increasing every 2 min) until the child reaches maximal aerobic power, which is the highest mechanical power sustained by the child for 2 min (for details, see Reference 3, p. 320). The second task lasts 10 min, at 75% to 80% of maximal power. Six blood samples, from an indwelling venous catheter, are taken as follows: before the maximal task, immediately at its end, 10 min later (just before the submaximal task), at the end of the submaximal task, 10 min later, and after a further 20 min. Figure 4 depicts the response to this protocol in 2 boys of short stature. One had a normal rise in his serum GH level, and the other had an insufficient rise, which confirmed a positive GH diagnosis, based on a pharmacologic stimulus. For an alternative protocol, based on a single 15-min submaximal cycling test, see Seip et al. (49). It has been suggested (36, 51) that the infusion of propranolol during exercise can increase the magnitude of the provocation, further reducing the likelihood of a false-positive response. The rationale is that beta-adrenoreceptors may play an inhibitory role on the secretion of ACTH and GH (36). I am not aware, however, of laboratories that use this approach in a clinical context.

Characteristics of the Test

In evaluating a diagnostic test, one should determine the extent of false-positive and false-negative results that it yields, as well as its sensitivity and

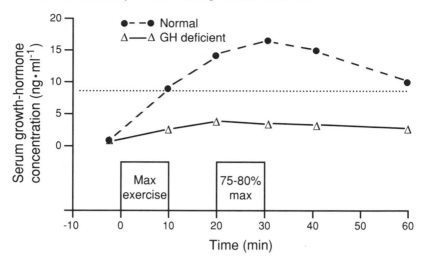

Figure 4: Serum growth hormone during an exercise provocation test in 2 children with growth retardation. The broken line depicts a typical normal response. The full line suggests growth-hormone deficiency. The horizontal dotted line at 8 ng/ml represents the minimal level for a normal response. Data are from the author's laboratory.

specificity. In a literature survey (3), results were analyzed from studies published until 1982 on 601 children with short stature. All had undergone an exercise provocation test and pharmacologic provocation. The latter served as the gold standard. As seen in Table 6, the exercise provocation yielded 15.6% false positives and 10.5% false negatives. Its sensitivity was 89.5% and the specificity was 84.4%. Such a high sensitivity suggests that, indeed, exercise provocation is a good screening test. Because the stimuli performed in these studies were not always optimal, one can assume that, with improved protocols, the actual specificity and sensitivity would be even higher.

Several environmental and individual factors may enhance or attenuate the GH response to exercise. An increase in environmental temperature, when

Table 6   Comparison of Diagnostic Results of Growth-Hormone Deficiency, as Obtained by an Exercise Provocation Test and a Pharmacologic Test

		Growth-hormone deficiency	
		Present	Absent
		57	544
Exercise test	Positive	51	85
	Negative	6	459

Note. The pharmacologic test served as a ''gold standard.'' Data were collected from the literature on 601 short-statured children (3).

superimposed on the exercise provocation, will enhance the rise in GH (21, 44). In contrast, lowering of ambient temperature may result in attenuation of the response (13). Therefore, the temperature in a testing laboratory should be kept constant and not lower than 23 °C. Amirav et al. (2) have recently shown that children with asthma have an enhanced rise in GH, compared with healthy children. This pattern occurred even when the patients did not develop bronchoconstriction following the exercise provocation. Likewise, children with insulin-dependent diabetes mellitus may have an enhanced GH response to exercise (22, 27). In contrast, the response in obese children is lower than in the nonobese (22, 56).

Blood Glucose Profile During Prolonged Exercise

Patients with insulin-dependent diabetes mellitus often say they feel weakness, muscle soreness, hunger, or tremor during or after prolonged exercise (3). When asked to interpret these symptoms, some patients think that the symptoms represent hypoglycemia, whereas others do not associate them with hypoglycemia. For therapeutic and educational reasons, it is sometimes important to document whether indeed a child or adolescent undergoes hypoglycemia as a result of a prolonged physical activity.

The Protocol

A test has been developed in my laboratory, in which blood glucose is monitored periodically while the patient performs prolonged, intermittent exercise. The protocol was designed to simulate a real-life situation yet be carried out in the laboratory. For nonathletes, there are six bouts, 10 min each, interspersed by 5-min rest periods. For an athlete, the number of bouts may be higher, depending on the duration of her or his typical training session or competition (e.g., a 5-set tennis match is equivalent to as many as ten bouts). This is determined in consultation with the athlete. To simulate real-life conditions, the exercise intensity is determined by the athlete. For nonathletes, an intensity is chosen to yield a heart rate of 140 to 145 beat/min. The ergometer for the nonathletes is a cycle. An athlete can choose either a cycle or a treadmill (or alternate between the two). Blood glucose is sampled through an indwelling venous catheter before the test, at the end of each exercise bout, and periodically following the last bout. This blood is sent to the laboratory for analysis. In addition, an on-the-spot analysis is made with a glucometer, to help the supervising physician decide whether a test should be terminated prematurely for the patient's safety. When each blood sample is taken, the patient is asked to guess the level of blood glucose. Heart rate is monitored periodically. Figure 5 depicts the test results for a 16-year-old boy with insulin-dependent diabetes mellitus.

The patient is instructed to inject the usual dosage of insulin at the normal time and site and to eat a typical meal at the regular time before coming to the laboratory. A detailed record is kept of the patient's food intake during the 3 days prior to the test. Furthermore, the patient brings a beverage of her or his choice to drink during the test, and the patient determines how much he or she drinks, and how often. All of this information is monitored and recorded. Body weight is determined before and after the test, to assess changes in hydration. The patient is encouraged periodically to report any symptoms that may develop.

Once the results are obtained, the patient and the parent are invited to discuss the findings and their implications, including needed modifications in diet prior to prolonged activities, composition and quantity of beverage consumed during an activity, dose of insulin, and injection site. Such an educational session has proved beneficial to most patients and their parents. It has been of particular benefit to young elite athletes who seek to fine-tune their response to exercise.

Characteristics of the Test

Because this test is new, little information is available about its utility. A test-retest reliability and reproducibility is currently being determined in my laboratory. Items being evaluated include the drop in blood glucose concentration, the concentration reached at the end of the last bout (and 30-min

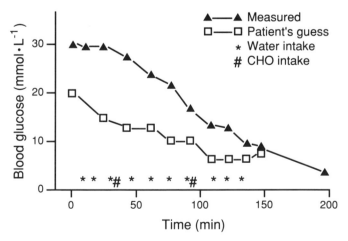

Figure 5: Changes in blood glucose concentration during an intermittent 150-min exercise and 50-min recovery in an adolescent boy with insulin-dependent diabetes mellitus (triangles). The squares depict the patient's perceived concentration of blood glucose. Data are from the author's laboratory.

postexercise), and the level of blood glucose at which the patient reports hypoglycemic symptoms.

Physiologic Cost of Locomotion

The metabolic cost of performing a given activity is an important determinant of a child's ability to sustain the activity. This is particularly so in children with motor disabilities (e.g., 4, 5). One may assume that it is the metabolic reserve (the difference between a child's maximal O_2 uptake and the O_2 requirements for a given task) that limits the child's ability to sustain exercise. Conditions in which energy cost is abnormally high include spastic (1, 41) and athetotic (41) cerebral palsy, muscular dystrophy, muscular atrophy, advanced arthritis, use of a prosthesis (e.g., in leg amputees), advanced kyphoscoliosis (40), and marked obesity. In kyphoscoliosis and advanced obesity, the high O_2 cost is due not only to a wasteful gait style but also to a high O_2 cost of breathing (10, 55).

One rationale for measuring the O_2 cost of locomotion in the pediatric exercise laboratory is to document the degree of physiologic wastefulness in a patient's gait. Unfortunately, there are no valid norms for the energy cost of locomotion in healthy children, but some reference values can be obtained in reports, among others, by MacDougall et al. (42) and Skinner et al. (50).

Another rationale is to monitor the response to treatment. It is important, for example, to note whether a surgical correction (e.g., release of Achilles tendon in muscular dystrophy or release of adductors in spastic cerebral palsy) has also reduced the metabolic (and cardiorespiratory) cost of locomotion. Treatments to which this test is relevant include strengthening of a muscle group, an increase in the range of motion, and the use of an orthosis or other assistive device. Figure 6 depicts the metabolic, ventilatory, and cardiovascular cost of walking with and without shoe inserts. The patient studied in our laboratory was an 11.3-year-old boy with spina bifida occulta, who complained of ankle and heel cramps while walking and had valgus heels (flatfeet). Shoe inserts were prescribed to support the longitudinal arch of both feet. To assess the physiologic effectiveness of this treatment, the boy performed treadmill walks at three speeds, with and without the inserts. As shown in Figure 6, the inserts seem to have provided a decrease of 10% to 15% in the physiologic cost, especially during the higher walking speeds. This coincided with alleviation of the child's symptoms.

The Protocol

No single protocol can be used for all patients. The protocol used depends on the speeds at which the child can walk or run comfortably (preferably on a

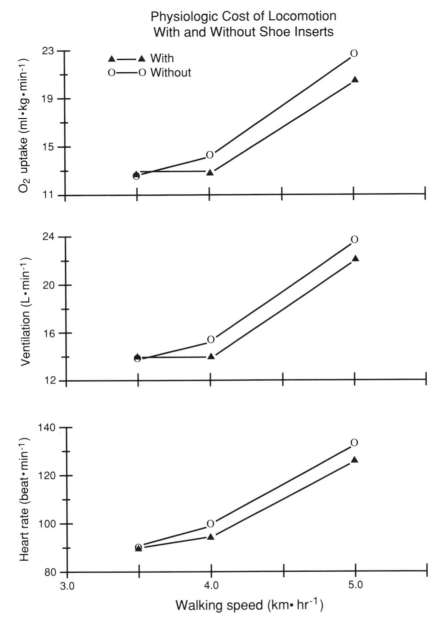

Figure 6:   Physiologic cost of locomotion, with and without bilateral shoe inserts, in a 13-year-old boy with spina bifida occulta, valgus heel, and leg cramps. Data are from the author's laboratory.

treadmill but, with proper pacing and equipment for collecting expired gas, the child can be tested while walking or running overground) and the specific clinical question at hand. The following are principles to be considered in conducting the test:

- The child should be thoroughly habituated to the testing situation, so he or she can achieve proficiency in treadmill walking or running and feel comfortable with equipment such as the nose clip, mouthpiece, and electrodes. It is advisable to conduct a separate habituation session, the data from which can be discarded. Also, if the objective is to evaluate an assistive device (e.g., ankle-foot orthosis), allow the child to use this device for several days or weeks prior to conducting the test, until he or she has become accustomed to it.
- Include several walking or running trials, or both, each at a different speed. As shown in Figure 6, a high physiologic cost of an activity may be apparent at some speeds but not at others.
- Each trial should last long enough (preferably 4 min or more) so that the child will reach steady state.
- Each trial should not last too long (e.g., more than 6 min), in order to prevent fatigue. However, when the question at hand is what happens to the cost of locomotion as fatigue develops, the trials should last longer.
- To prevent fatigue, allow sufficient time for rest between trials.
- If the objective is to assess an assistive device during a single session, reverse the sequence of trials at different speeds. For example, if at the first speed the child is first tested with the device and then without it, the order should be reversed for the second speed.

Conclusion

Exercise testing can provide valuable clinical information beyond that of cardiovascular and pulmonary function. Many illnesses that do not involve aerobic mechanisms are evaluated through tests of muscle power and endurance, submaximal exercise economy, and anaerobic capacity. Testing is also useful in the evaluation of metabolic and endocrinologic response to exercise. Further research is needed to standardize these tests and assess their validity, specificity, and sensitivity.

References

1. Adler, N.S., and E.E. Bleck. Correlations of balance, motion and efficiency of gait in cerebral palsy [Abstract]. *Dev. Med. Child Neurol.* 28(Suppl. 53):3, 1986.

2. Amirav, I., R.J. Dowdeswell, M. Plit, V.R. Panz, B.I. Joffe, and H.C. Seftel. Growth hormone response to exercise in asthmatic and normal children. *Eur. J. Pediatr.* 149:443-446, 1990.

3. Bar-Or, O. *Pediatric Sports Medicine for the Practitioner: From Physiologic Principles to Clinical Applications.* New York: Springer-Verlag, 1983.

4. Bar-Or, O. The oxygen cost of children's movement in health and disease. In: *Exercise, Nutrition and Performance*, P. Russo and L.G. Gass (Eds.). Sydney, Australia: Sport Sciences and Research Center, Cumberland College of Health Sciences, 1985, pp. 97-104.

5. Bar-Or, O. Pathophysiologic factors which limit the exercise capacity of the sick child. *Med. Sci. Sports Exerc.* 18:269-276, 1986.

6. Bar-Or, O. The Wingate Anaerobic Test: An update on methodology, reliability and validity. *Sports Med.* 4:381-394, 1987.

7. Bar-Or, O., R. Dotan, and O. Inbar. A 30-second all-out ergometric test: Its reliability and validity for anaerobic capacity. *Isr. J. Med. Sci.* 13:326, 1977.

8. Bar-Or, O., R. Dotan, O. Inbar, A. Rotshtein, J. Karlsson, and P. Tesch. Anaerobic capacity and muscle fiber type distribution in man. *Int. J. Sports Med.* 1:89-92, 1980.

9. Bar-Or, O., and O. Inbar. Relationships among anaerobic capacity, sprint and middle distance running of school children. In: *Physical Fitness Assessment*, R.J. Shephard and H. Lavallee (Eds.). Springfield, IL: Charles C Thomas, 1978, pp. 142-147.

10. Bergofsky, E.H., G.M. Turino, and A.P. Fishman. Cardiorespiratory failure in kyphoscoliosis. *Medicine* 38:263-317, 1959.

11. Blimkie, C.J.R., P. Roche, J.T. Hay, and O. Bar-Or. Anaerobic power of arms in teenage boys and girls: Relationship to lean tissue. *Eur. J. Appl. Physiol.* 57:677-683, 1988.

12. Brooke, M.H., and W.K. Engel. The histographic analysis of human muscle biopsies with regard to fiber types: II. Diseases of the upper and lower motor neuron. *Neurology* 19:378-393, 1969.

13. Buckler, J.H.M. The relationship between changes in plasma growth hormone levels and body temperature occurring with exercise in man. *Biomedicine* 19:193-197, 1973.

14. Costin, G., and F. Ratner-Kaufman. Growth hormone secretory patterns in children with short stature. *J. Pediatr.* 11:362-368, 1987.

15. De San Lazao, C., J.M. Parkin, and S.J. Turner. Treadmill exercise test in short children. *Arch. Dis. Child.* 59:1179-1182, 1984.

16. Dotan, R., and O. Bar-Or. Climatic heat stress and performance in the Wingate Anaerobic Test. *Eur. J. Appl. Physiol.* 44:237-243, 1980.

17. Dotan, R., and O. Bar-Or. Load optimization for the Wingate Anaerobic Test. *Eur. J. Appl. Physiol.* 51:409-417, 1983.

18. Edstrom, L. Selective changes in the size of red and white muscle fibers with upper motor lesions and Parkinsonism. *J. Neurol. Sci.* 11:537-590, 1970.

19. Evans, J.A., and H.A. Quinney. Determination of resistance settings for anaerobic power testing. *Can. J. Appl. Sport Sci.* 6:53-56, 1981.
20. Fessel, W.J., J.A. Taylor, and E.S. Johnson. Evaluating the complaint of muscle weakness: Simple quantitative clinical tests. In: *First International Congress on Muscle Disease*, J.N. Walton, N. Canal, and G. Scarlato (Eds.). Amsterdam: Excerpta Medica, 1970, pp. 544-545.
21. Frewin, D.B., A.G. Frantz, and J.A. Downey. The effect of ambient temperature on the growth hormone and prolactin response to exercise. *Aus. J. Exp. Biol. Med. Sci.* 54:97-101, 1976.
22. Garlaschi, C., B. di Natatel, M.J. del Guerico, A. Caccamo, L. Gargantini, and G. Chiumello. Effect of physical exercise on secretion of growth hormone, glucagon, and cortisol in obese and diabetic children. *Diabetes* 24:758-761, 1975.
23. Gil-Ad, I., N. Leibowitch, Z. Josefsberg, M. Wasserman, and Z. Laron. Effect of oral clonidine, insulin-induced hypoglycemia and exercise on plasma GHRH levels in short-stature children. *Acta Endocrinol.* 122:89-95, 1990.
24. Godfrey, S. *Exercise Testing in Children: Applications in Health and Disease.* London: Saunders, 1974.
25. Grodjinovsky, A., and O. Bar-Or. Influence of added physical education hours upon anaerobic capacity, adiposity, and grip strength in 12-13-year-old children enrolled in a sports class. In: *Children and Sport*, J. Ilmarinen and I. Valimaki (Eds.). Berlin: Springer-Verlag, 1984, pp. 162-169.
26. Grodjinovsky, A., O. Bar-Or, R. Dotan, and O. Inbar. Training effect in children on the anaerobic performance as measured by the Wingate Anaerobic Test. In: *Children and Exercise IX*, K. Berg and B.O. Eriksson (Eds.). Baltimore: University Park Press, 1980, pp. 139-145.
27. Hansen, A.P. Abnormal serum growth hormone response to exercise in juvenile diabetics. *J. Clin. Invest.* 49:1467-1478, 1970.
28. Hebestreit, H., K. Mimura, and O. Bar-Or. Recovery of anaerobic muscle power after supramaximal short-term exercise: Comparing boys and men. *Pediatr. Exerc. Sci.* (in press).
29. Hosking, C.P., U.S. Bhat, V. Dubowitz, and H.T. Edwards. Measurements of muscle strength and performance in children with normal and diseased muscle. *Arch. Dis. Child.* 51:957-963, 1976.
30. Inbar, O., and O. Bar-Or. Relationship of anaerobic and aerobic arm and leg capacities to swimming performance of 8-12-year-old children. In: *Frontiers of Activity and Child Health*, R.J. Shephard and H. Lavallee (Eds.). Quebec, PQ: Pelican, 1977, pp. 283-292.
31. Inbar, O., and O. Bar-Or. Changes in arm and leg performance in laboratory and field tests, following physical training. In: *Proceedings: International Seminar on Art and Science in Coaching*, U. Simri (Ed.). Natanya, Israel: Wingate Institute, 1980, pp. 38-48.

32. Inbar, O., P. Kaiser, and P. Tesch. Relationships between leg muscle fiber type distribution and leg exercise performance. *Int. J. Sports Med.* 2:154-159, 1981.

33. Jacobs, I. The effects of thermal dehydration on performance of the Wingate test of anaerobic power. Windsor, ON: University of Windsor, 1979. M.S. thesis, pp. 1-76.

34. Jacobs, I., O. Bar-Or, J. Karlsson, R. Dotan, and P. Tesch. Changes in muscle metabolites in females with 30-s exhaustive exercise. *Med. Sci. Sports Exerc.* 14:457-460, 1982.

35. Jacobs, I., P.A. Tesch, O. Bar-Or, J. Karlsson, and R. Dotan. Lactate in human skeletal muscle after 10 and 30 s of supramaximal exercise. *J. Appl. Physiol.* 55:365-367, 1983.

36. Jezova, D., I. Vigas, I. Klimes, and J. Jurcovicova. Adenopituitary hormone response to exercise combined with propranolol infusion in man. *Endocrinol. Exp.* (Bratisl.) 17:91-97, 1983.

37. Johnsonbaugh, R.E., D.E.. Bybee, and L.P. Georges. Exercise tolerance test: Single-sample screening technique to rule out growth-hormone deficiency. *JAMA* 240:664-666, 1978.

38. Jones, N.L., and E.J.M. Campbell. *Clinical Exercise Testing.* Philadelphia: Saunders, 1982.

39. Kaczkowski, W., D.L. Montgomery, A.W. Taylor, and V. Klissouras. The relationship between muscle fiber composition and maximal anaerobic power and capacity. *J. Sports Med. Phys. Fitness* 22:407-413, 1982.

40. Lindh, M. Energy expenditure during walking in patients with scoliosis: The effect of surgical correction. *Spine* 3:122-134, 1978.

41. Lundberg, A. Oxygen consumption in relation to work load in students with cerebral palsy. *J. Appl. Physiol.* 40:873-875, 1976.

42. MacDougall, J.D., P.D. Roche, O. Bar-Or, and J.R. Moroz. Maximal aerobic capacity of Canadian school children: Prediction based on age-related oxygen cost of running. *Int. J. Sports Med.* 4:194-198, 1983.

43. Nicoll, A.G., P.J. Smail, and C.C. Forsyth. Exercise test for growth hormone deficiency. *Arch. Dis. Child.* 59:1177-1190, 1984.

44. Okada, Y., T. Matsuoka, and Y. Kumahara. Human growth hormone secretion during exposure to hot air in normal adult male subjects. *J. Clin. Endocrinol. Metab.* 34:759-763, 1972.

45. Okada, Y., K. Watanabe, T. Takenchi, T. Onishi, K. Tanaka, M. Tsuji, S. Morimoto, and Y. Kumahara. Re-evaluation of exercise as a screening test for ruling out human growth hormone deficiency. *Endocrinol. Jpn.* 25:437-442, 1978.

46. Parker, D.F., L. Carriere, H. Hebestreit, and O. Bar-Or. Anaerobic endurance and peak muscle power in children with spastic cerebral palsy. *Am. J. Dis. Child.* (in press).

47. Rhodes, E.C., R.E. Mosher, and J.E. Potts. Anaerobic capacity of elite prepubertal ice hockey players. *Med. Sci. Sports Exerc.* 17:265, 1985.

48. Roth, J., S.M. Glick, R.S. Yalow, and S.A. Berson. Secretion of human growth hormone: Physiologic and experimental modification. *Metabolism* 12:577-579, 1963.

49. Seip, R.L., A. Weltman, D. Goodman, and A.D. Rogol. Clinical utility of cycle exercise for the physiologic assessment of growth hormone release in children. *Am. J. Dis. Child.* 144:998-1000, 1990.

50. Skinner, J.S., O. Bar-Or, V. Bergsteinova, C.W. Bell, D. Royer, and E.R. Buskirk. Comparison of continuous and intermittent test for determining maximal oxygen intake in children. *Acta Paediatr. Scand.* 217(Suppl.): 24-38, 1971.

51. Sutton, G.H., and L. Lazarus. Effect of adrenergic blocking agents on growth hormone response to physical exercise. *Horm. Metab. Res.* 6:428-429, 1974.

52. Tharp, G.D., R.K. Newhouse, L. Uffelman, W.G. Thorland, and G.O. Johnson. Comparison of sprint and run times with performance on the Wingate Anaerobic Test. *Res. Q. Exerc. Sport* 56:73-76, 1985.

53. Tirosch, E., O. Bar-Or, and P. Rosenbaum. New muscle power test in neuromuscular disease. *Am. J. Dis. Child.* 144:1083-1087, 1990.

54. Van Praagh, E., G. Falgairette, M. Bedu, N. Fellmann, and J. Codert. Laboratory and field test in 7-year-old boys. In: *Children and Exercise XIII*, S. Oseid and K.H. Carlsen (Eds.). Champaign, IL: Human Kinetics, 1989, pp. 11-17.

55. Whipp, B.J., and J.A. Davis. The ventilatory stress of exercise in obesity. *Am. Rev. Resp. Dis.* 129(Suppl):S90-S92, 1984.

56. Wilkinson, P.W., and J.M. Parkin. Growth-hormone response to exercise in obese children [letter]. *Lancet* 2:55, 1974.

Index